MW00928307

AFTER EDEN

AFTER EDEN

✦

A Love Story

Owen Stanley Surman, M.D.

iUniverse, Inc.
New York Lincoln Shanghai

AFTER EDEN
A Love Story

Copyright © 2005 by Owen S. Surman

All rights reserved. No part of this book may be used or reproduced by any means, graphic, electronic, or mechanical, including photocopying, recording, taping or by any information storage retrieval system without the written permission of the publisher except in the case of brief quotations embodied in critical articles and reviews.

iUniverse books may be ordered through booksellers or by contacting:

iUniverse
2021 Pine Lake Road, Suite 100
Lincoln, NE 68512
www.iuniverse.com
1-800-Authors (1-800-288-4677)

For the purpose of privacy and identity protection, characters in this book—other than family—are de-identified.

ISBN-13: 978-0-595-35917-2 (pbk)
ISBN-13: 978-0-595-80371-2 (ebk)
ISBN-10: 0-595-35917-5 (pbk)
ISBN-10: 0-595-80371-7 (ebk)

Printed in the United States of America

To Craig, Kate, and Edith.
And to Hugh McLennan who told me, "You can write."

Contents

ABOUT THE BOOK

Dr. Surman is Associate Professor of Psychiatry at Harvard Medical School. In the process of bringing this nonfiction novel to press, Owen has shared it with friends, colleagues, family, and members of the clergy. He extends special thanks to Cheryl Lopanik, whose editorial assistance has been of inestimable value. He acknowledges the tireless support of his wife, Amy Surman, of his mother, Edith Surman, and of close friends Asa Allen, Edward Mank, and Susie and Richard Pallan. Helen Rees graciously represented this book and editors at three university presses vetted it with encouraging enthusiasm. Three colleagues provided formal reviews. Their comments follow:

"This book touches the heart immediately as you read the story of love and loss—that most human of all human experiences. It is an important read for anyone who is struggling with these issues. There are insights that bring the head and heart together in coping with loss."
Jimmie Holland, M.D., Wayne Chapman Chair in Psychiatric Oncology at Memorial Sloan-Kettering Cancer Center

"This is an exquisitely challenging record of deepest mutual love between a husband and wife, the almost unimaginable foreclosing of the future by cancer and the wife's early death, a disturbingly open confession of the depths of personal and family disruption caused by her illness and death, and a testament to the power to mourn and to recover. Written by a remarkably brilliant, sensitive and gifted psychiatrist with unique insight and absolute self-revelatory candor, this book will almost certainly change the reader's life and expand his/her understanding of the real human responses resulting from life-threatening illness of a still young spouse. It is the most powerful description of spousal love and loss I have ever experienced. I will never be the same."
Deane Wolcott, M.D., Vice President, Clinical Systems, Aptium Oncology.

"As *After Eden* unfolds, the reader experiences an uncommon and moving story of love, loss, grief, and resolution. Dr. Surman's honest and touching account will be invaluable both for others who are facing the loss of a treasured family

member or friend and for healthcare providers and countless others caring for those experiencing loss."
Julie R. Ingelfinger, M.D., Professor of Pediatrics at Harvard Medical School

PROLOGUE

✦

QUESTIONS FOR THE SPHINX

o o o o o o o o o o o o o o o o o o o o o o o o o o o o o o o o o o o

What is the creature which walks sometimes on two legs,
sometimes on three, sometimes on four
and which…is at its weakest when it uses the most legs?

—*Oedipus*
Sophocles

Sundays are for making love…for sleeping in, "Meet the Press," and sometimes for religion. This Sunday—April 12, 1999—I am in Boston at the exhibit of Mary Cassatt's mother-daughter paintings. I rarely get to the Museum of Fine Arts—and never on a Sunday morning, but I have been making different choices since Lezlie died—restless choices. I am the creature that wants to know itself and moves with legs as it changes in number: first four, then two, then three…crawling, walking, leaning. In the beginning I lived in my mother. Later, I lived alone until there was a woman who became so much a part of my being that I owned a new identity with her. Now I am struggling to understand another metamorphosis that bereavement has imposed. It is the mystery of being and becoming…and becoming again. I want to know how and where this process will take me. Sometimes I have the illusion of a mystical force that guides me through the universe of possibilities. It is a journey that I make on every combination of legs, and at some indeterminate future time, I will make the passage on none.

I rent a portable audio cassette player and earphones for four dollars. With the delicate black foam ear cups in place, I join the crowd and look about hopefully for a familiar face. After thirty years of psychiatric practice in a large general hospital, I expect the welcoming smile of a patient or colleague, but none are present.

1

Being alone among strangers sharpens the senses. I fumble for the green button that will begin this guided tour, then gaze at portrait images that change like figures in a dream until they are the faces of my two children and their mother. It is like a memorial for the woman who was a part of me for twenty-eight years, and who is still a part of me after four years of death. Her love remains…boundless and eternal.

Lezlie was a pediatric nurse before she was a mother. Her graveside memorial bears a replica of the Boston Children's Hospital insignia—a nurse holding an ailing child to her bosom. That was Lezlie's full time job until she left nursing after she first gave birth. Having kids of her own can make it intolerable for a woman to face the suffering of others' children.

Cassatt's paintings are true to the bond of motherhood. Her meticulous repetition inspires me. She painted the same theme—mother/daughter love—in multiple bold perspectives, sometimes using the device of a mirror to allow at once for more than one view. It is the perseverance of her craft that I find so remarkable, the attention to detail, the doing…and doing again.

Cassatt's brilliant composition is a reminder of how much my life until now has been about family and how perfect that life has been. There are no signposts in Eden. It is only in the leaving of it that we know we were there.

After leaving the exhibit, I travel the long museum corridors and pass the adjoining galleries. Here is one with an alabaster sculpture: "Woman in a Crypt." I enter hesitantly—almost painfully. No one else is present. I approach the figure as if I were invading a funeral director's secret vault.

This is not the image of death that I know. Lezlie left no alabaster replica in her passing. At death, when the spirit of her had left her body—after I felt it leave her—there remained but a corporeal shell. My son Craig and I followed the shell as the mortuary workers, a short woman and a tall man, each in black attire, carried it in a closed sack to the waiting hearse. "That's not your mother," I told my son on November 5, 1994. "It's the house she used to live in."

My attention shifts to a nineteenth century romantic painting, "Questioning the Sphinx," on the wall to the right of the gallery entrance. I walk deliberately to the canvas as if about to step into its arid expanse. At the center of the painting that reverses the theme of a Greek myth, a lone man positions himself with one knee half bent and his right ear pressed expectantly to the mouth of a great stone creature that has the head of a woman, the body of a bird, and the hindquarter of a lion. The man's skin is dark with the exposure of a long journey. His eyes search hopefully as he waits with patience and with wonder, as if unaware that no stone ever speaks. I realize then that we can only strive for answers to the mystery of life—but the striving is firmly in our nature. It makes us who we are.

I have spent four years arranging my Lezlie memories like photographs in a family album, searching for the meaning of it all—of her coming into my life and going out of it again. I want to tell about the memories, to make sense of what has passed and what remains and what the future may hold.

1

SUBURBAN SWEEPSTAKES

Here is a picture of the four of us in March of 1994. There is Kate at the far left. (She is also the most politically liberal.) Kate is a month past her eighteenth birthday in this photo. You can see her gentle smile, blue eyes and shoulder length brown hair against her oval-shaped face. Her expression seems to say, "Well, here we are. This is the group!" She is tall—about five foot, eleven inches—and graceful. Her equestrian activities have spared her the round-shouldered slouch so common in young women of her height.

Craig is next to Kate. As you see, his right hand encircles his sister's shoulder. He is four years older and very loving. Craig is the family archivist. He has traced his mother's genealogy to the seventh century and mine through three generations from Eastern Europe. Craig has a sinewy build like his English Canadian grandfather, A. Bruce Humber, Lezlie's dad. We lost him to cancer two years before this picture was taken. Bruce swapped track shoes with Jesse Owens at the 1936 Berlin games and later helped a number of fine young athletes develop their running skills. "I hope you'll name him Bruce," he said when Craig was born, so we added the name and called him Craig Bruce. Lezlie's dad was the kindest man I ever met. Craig is like that. You can see it in his expression. Craig is the one in the family who rescues moths and sets them free on summer evenings. He is six foot in height and has big ears like me. Craig, too, will be a psychiatrist. I know he will be good at it. He is very perceptive and nurturing.

That is a good likeness of Lezlie standing between Craig and me. Her eyes are full of joy. There is the smile I fell in love with when we first met. I knew right away that her capacity for love was boundless. It is funny to say but I also loved that classic oval chin that the children later inherited. Lezlie is aged fifty-one here, plus a couple of months, but one of my patients will see this picture in my hospital office and ask if Lezlie is my daughter. I always think of her as the world's greatest mother. That was her fulltime job when she left nursing after giving birth to Craig. She taught at Children's Hospital while I trained in psychiatry at Harvard Medical School. We used her salary to pay the rent while my income supported our weekend skiing. She never did go back to nursing. When Craig and Kate were older, Lezlie taught knitting to earn some extra money. After that, she tried her hand at cosmetic sales and became a NuSkin representative. She had five customers and counted on me for a monthly order of hair restorer. Kate still insists that the Nutriol keeps my hair from thinning.

I'm at the far right, most conservative of the group and the only Republican, although I am liberal by Republican standards. Craig insists that my political affiliation is a symptom of ethnic rebellion. I am outgoing and friendly but you would never know it from my stiff expression in the picture. Actually, I am camera shy, although, among the four of us, I am probably the most open. One time Lezlie called me at the hospital to tell me we were overdrawn at the bank. I told her that one of my affluent patients owed us a fair amount of money.

"Did you call him?" she asked when we next spoke.

"Yes," I said. "I told him we're overdrawn. He lives nearby and brought a check right over."

"Why did you tell him that!" she said.

We were always very different in that way. I have no secrets. I also tend to strike up conversations in public places. If you encounter a friendly stranger who jokes amiably with you on an elevator, that's probably me. I take after my father, a wonderful salesman and a good-natured altruist. Dad is also gone now. I miss our nightly phone calls and political debates. He was an ardent Democrat and a generous businessman. Dad graduated from Bentley College during the Depression and started up a modest haberdashery in the currently depressed Roxbury section of Boston. He was a man of the community, active in the Roxbury Kiwanis and the Masons, and a board member of the Temple I attended in my youth. I learned more psychiatry from Dad than I did at Harvard Medical School.

You can see that I am tallest of our bunch—six foot two—and the only overweight person. "When you get older, your metabolism changes," Lezlie warned. "You used to gain weight, then lose. Now you just gain." I tend to work late and forage about the kitchen when I get home, but when this picture was taken, I could bench press 220 pounds, and in the summers I swam two miles around the lake. Lezlie would watch from the shore and work at her knitting. Sometimes on a summer morning we made love standing out of view in the water near the boat landing. I tended to fall over because I am not coordinated.

The blue eyes are my best feature, and that nubbin of a chin is my worst. You can see from this frontal view that the Nutriol is actually preventing hair loss. To be honest with you, my head is a bit bald at the back.

Photographs migrate—like Canadian geese. For a long time, this one found its home on our old avocado-colored Frigidaire. Lezlie and I focused on the children but did a poor job of keeping up with the appliances. We covered the worn places with memos, receipts and pictures. In this picture, she and I were with the children by the side of our house. In the background you see a line of overgrown yews and behind them a stand of scotch pines that separate our property from the main road. The previous owners had planted fifty seedlings and I added three dozen more in the mid 1970s when we moved from Pearl Harbor after I completed three years of active duty as a Lieutenant Commander in the Navy Medical Reserve. I was born in 1943, in case you too think that Lezlie looks like my daughter in this picture! I liked to tease her that she got to try out all the new ages first.

You cannot see the house here. It is a simple eight-room barn red Garrison Colonial on an acre of land—mostly lawn. This picture is set on a flat rectangular expanse of green, a good place to play ball when the children were young. We called it the "North Forty." Craig was three when we moved to Sherborn. I well recall his look of awe when he confidently carried his sand pail out into his first New England snowfall. Kate was born a month after I began work as a staff psychiatrist at Boston Hospital. I often think of her running in the North Forty when she was six. She never did learn how to play catch. Every time I threw the ball to her she ran away with it. I was sure that she learned that from our unruly golden retriever. When Craig was older, he tried valiantly to snag the high flies I threw him. He was never any better at catching a ball than Kate was at bringing it back. Like me, the children proved better athletes in the water. Grandpa Bruce's track and field genes obviously passed them by.

After leaving its home on the Frigidaire, the picture found its way to the side of a filing cabinet in my clinic office. I suspended it with scotch tape next to a printout of Desiderata. I was never much at blank screen psychiatry and wanted my patients to know that I was a real person with a beautiful wife and two kids that I was proud of. It was a happy time. Craig received his acceptance to the University of Massachusetts School of Medicine, and Kate was beginning to hear from colleges. In March, the pressure of college applications was behind us. Kate had a place at either Vassar or Bates and was about to hear favorably from Haverford.

Our family life in Sherborn was idyllic. I was a board member at the Unitarian Church and Lezlie taught Sunday school. Craig was an Eagle Scout and Kate was president of the Wild and Woolly Shepherd's Four H Club. She had her own horse, Funny Girl, part thoroughbred and part Welsh pony. They were best friends as only a girl and a horse can be. It alarmed me only slightly when I once overheard their conspiratorial discourse. "Let's trample Daddy," Kate said.

We were not rich, just lucky. As a Navy psychiatrist in Hawaii, I took our five thousand dollars in savings and bought a condominium in Waikiki. When we shipped back to Boston, the condominium became an entry level house. The house appreciated fivefold and we drew out the equity to pay for independent schools and colleges. Our lives were child-centered as were the lives of close friends and neighbors.

No matter how busy we were, Lezlie and I talked for two hours every evening, reviewing the day's experiences. We talked about the kids, the extended family, the neighborhood, and events in my practice. On weekends, I carted my academic work about as we attended to household chores and family events: the swim meets, the downhill ski races, the soccer, the baseball, the museum trips, the 4-H fairs, the Christmas wreath sales for Troop 1. It was a joy and in a subtle way a kind of suburban competition—like a sweepstakes. There was a loving sameness to our lives that neither Lezlie nor I expected to change.

That same March, I photographed a cardinal that built her nest in an open area that was clearly visible to us from a second story bathroom window on the north side of the house. Cardinals are beautiful for their color and beautiful in a spiritual sense because they mate for life.

Mornings before leaving for work, I peered through the portrait lens of my old 35mm Minolta—a relic of the Navy years—and watched her retrieve food for the newly-hatched chicks. I did not save the photos because it ended badly. One night we heard a brief and malignant commotion. In the morning, the nest was empty and a trace of Mrs. Cardinal's plumage was all that remained.

I never shared that story with anyone, but I am a mystic by nature, and the incident made me feel that something was not right in our lives.

2

WEAVERS BLEND

o o o o o o o o o o o o o o o o o o o o o o o o o o o o o o o o o

Joy and Woe are woven fine,
Clothing for the soul divine...

—*William Blake*

It started in April of 1994.

"I'm feeling bloated," Lezlie said. We were dressing together. Lezlie had a certain modesty and deftly covered her breasts before turning her side to me as she slipped into a skirt and blouse. Her waistline looked different. The strong inward curve of her lower back normally gave her belly a subtle protuberance. Now something in her profile looked misshapen.

"Let's have a look at your tummy," I said. I thought how I used to examine her when she studied nursing and I was a medical student in Montreal. Those were our new-love years. Lezlie hesitated for a moment—it was only a slight hesitation—then positioned herself on the bed. It was the same bed that we had purchased when we first came to Boston.

Self-consciously I percussed her belly with the technique doctors learned from old-time brewers tapping at their barrels to find a fluid level. Physical examination has always seemed absurd to me.

The percussion note was dull. "Lie on your side," I said. "This way...." The dull sound shifted to the side of her that was not pressed against the bed. *Shifting dullness. That's ridiculous. You're finding things that aren't there.* There was fluid in her abdomen—ascites.

"Hmmm, that's strange, "I said. "Why would you have fluid in your abdomen?" There was an empty feeling in my chest as if I had discovered something horrible and wanted desperately to unfind it.

"What does it mean?" she asked.

I was silent for a time and sorted through my thoughts like tangled string. When there is no immediate answer between lovers, it is answer enough.

"I'm not sure...a lot of things...maybe some kind of inflammation." *Some kind of inflammation? It's cancer, damn it...You might as well yell it through a megaphone.*

She looked frightened. Secrets were not a part of how we were together.

"I suppose...at the worst...it could be some kind of lymphatic tumor...maybe even a cancer. I'm not saying that's what it is...I could just be imagining it...but if that's what it is, you can treat it." I thought about a colleague who had been diagnosed with Stage Four Hodgkins disease more than five years before. It was terrible, but the radiation and chemotherapy took care of it. I remembered his fear that we talked about in my office. I taught him to do self-hypnosis. It didn't seem to do much good, but that didn't matter because they cured it. Nothing matters when you cure a cancer—but when you don't cure it, it's lousy.

Lezlie waited most of the week before calling her gynecologist. She was too scared. The delay troubled me but I said little about it. As a psychiatrist I annoy my patients by energetically repeating the same advice—then I blame it on my Eastern European Jewish ancestry. Lezlie had never put up with that nor had she tolerated my obsessive queries. "I say it once," she would say.

On Sunday, April 17, 1994, the day before her first appointment with Alex Godley, I struggled out of bed against a feeling of invisible weight pressing against me like a bad case of flu. I was aware of a pulsing sensation in my face. Lezlie was already downstairs making coffee. I was glad not to see her and tried to wash my face into a brighter perspective.

"Let's go for a walk," I suggested. I wanted to be busy with her. It was a Lezlie kind of strategy, like the time after the big blizzard of 1978 when she kept all of us active during days of school cancellation and lost work.

"Sure," she said.

Our house faced a quiet child-populated street that ended in a cul-de-sac bordering on woodlands and a network of horse trails. "Just in case," I muttered while sliding a canister of Mace into my jeans front pocket. There is no leash law in Sherborn and two unruly German shepherd dogs routinely terrorized passersby. One of the delinquent canines had recently nipped menacingly at Lezlie's heels while she retreated to a neighbor's porch. I was angry about the incident but she asked me not to intervene. The owner was a single man with a large family. "He has a hundred and twelve children," she liked to say.

"You don't need that," she now admonished, nodding toward the Mace. "Put it away."

I shrugged absently and found another pocket for the licensed weapon. A long-time patient routinely brought me an unsolicited supply. "You never know when I might need you," he would say. He was an out-of-work middle-aged man with the expression of a boy trading baseball cards. Lezlie knew about him as she did about many patients whose stories she shared thoughtfully and with dependable confidentiality.

We walked silently, ponderously, to the top of our street. Shadow, our timid black lab tugged at her leash beside us. "Shadow the Friendly Dog," as I liked to call her, seemed to understand about fifty words in English and one, *sientite,* in Spanish. Leash training was another matter.

Suddenly, one of the shepherds burst growling from our neighbor's unfenced yard and nipped aggressively at Shadow's retreating hindquarter. We struggled to separate the dogs. Shadow squealed.

"Owen!" Lezlie shouted as the neighbor retrieved her beast, "Get your Mace!"

We reached the trails, and Shadow recovered from her fright. There was no sign of physical injury. Freed from the leash, she sniffed frantically for the local woodland news. The deer tracks piqued her interest. Lezlie and I walked along the trail. I felt weighed down by sadness as if we were doing this together for the last time.

We sat down beside the well-marked path and leaned side by side against the trunk of a large maple tree brought down by the winter's storms. I could see the bulge in her abdomen. It was bigger than it had been only a few days earlier. I felt it again carefully. She did not object. We had always been playful together—but not this time. We sat together in silence and I felt her warmth against me. She seemed weary.

For me it was a tragic moment as much as I tried to mute its intensity. I felt the pain as if testing a hot burner. I remember the odd mixture of horror and rationalization. As we sat against the log, I thought to myself that my life with Lezlie would soon be over, but the thought, gripping though it was, yielded intermittently to self assurance, to a preferred conviction that I was overreacting, that the swelling making Lezlie appear pregnant was an explainable phenomenon that would soon be set right. She could have a curable cancer, a lymphoma like Hodgkin's disease. I knew, however, that this was bad…very bad. I knew and yet I dismissed the thought. Then the process of recognition and denial recycled…like a nightmare.

We walked back to the house in the silence that comes when there is too much that needs saying. Our minds have a built-in editing process that frames experience to make the tough times manageable. From that time in the woods together,

Lezlie took refuge in denial as though it were a form of psychological Mace that one could spray at the intolerable. I understood, better from instinct than education, that she needed that haven.

After a light dinner, we sat together in our family room. The walls are paneled with a cherry-stained pine. One of my patients, a primitive artist, had sold us an antique fireplace screen on which he had painted a country scene. The room was full of warmth. Lezlie knitted in the winged back easy chair that she and the children had given me at Christmas one year. I perfunctorily completed some office work and tried unsuccessfully to read my journals. I could not focus. My mind was filled with thoughts of Lezlie and how we first met at McGill University in the cold Montreal autumn of 1965.

Lezlie was completing her bachelor's degree in nursing and I was a second year medical student. I lived on the third floor of an Aylmer Street apartment building less than a block from Molson Stadium. It was a quaint area of three-story brick structures fused side to side as if by architectural error.

Four roommates from British Columbia shared a flat on the first floor. Lezlie and Sandra Ross were the two unengaged first floor tenants and best friends from childhood. While watching television in their apartment one evening, my extended left foot found Lezlie's right and nestled beside it. "We're holding feet," I told her.

Lezlie's was a vital and generous spirit. She had an ingenuous blend of unadorned Anglo-Saxon beauty and a 1950s kind of wholesomeness. Her smile lit up my world. Sandra was a loyal friend with boundless warmth and an endearingly desultory nature. We all agreed in the years that followed that neither of us would have accomplished a thing had Sandra and I become a pair. We were both such daydreamers. "Oh, deeeeer," Sandra would muse in her frequent moments of comfortable indecision. "Now, let's seeeee...."

My first date with Lezlie was going to an art movie house called Cinema Verdi. The show, "And Quiet Flows the Don, Part III," played in Russian with English subtitles. It didn't matter that we had missed parts I and II. We were twenty-two, and everything we shared became an adventure: the movies, the precooked barbecue chicken dinners, the parties, the lovemaking, the walks on fresh snow that crunched underfoot like peanut brittle in the frigid Montreal winter.

I was certainly different from anyone Lezlie had encountered in Victoria society. For one thing, she had never met a Jewish person until she moved east. The young men in her coterie were pre-Olympic athletes, naval cadets, and sons of affluent Victorians. None were intellectuals or future academics. She loved to listen to my short stories and poetry reading—much of it gloriously romantic—and we listened endlessly to the theme song from the French film *Un Homme et Une Femme* ("A Man and A Woman") while sipping Dry Sac or Harvey's Bristol Creme Sherry in the post-adolescent ambiance of my living room. An old cow skull that I retrieved from the Laurentians served as the fireplace ornament. Lezlie added her own decorative touch with a full-length poster of her father as a political candidate for the Liberal Party. I kept it in the closet.

Our courtship was similarly unique. I was not only an attentive lover, but also an inquisitive medical student eager to master an understanding of female anatomy. It was a practical and funny way to learn the art of physical examination and at times a bit silly.

"I think there's something wrong with your liver," I told her once with mixed apprehension and that odd excitement of discovery peculiar to medical students.

It was a short walk up University Street to the Emergency Room of the Royal Victoria Hospital that stood at the base of the Mount Royal woods like a stone empress. Lezlie was medically fine. It was her unconditional loving trust that was unusual. We were becoming a part of one another in a rare and special way. I was just suffering from the "sophomore syndrome." Second-year students think they have all the new diseases they learn about. I generously assigned them to Lezlie!

The worst of it occurred during my surgical subspecialty rotation in Ear, Nose, and Throat. We made love in the bedroom of my Aylmer Street apartment and lay together for a while before I decided to examine her jaw.

"This is your tempero-mandibular joint," I said, with the self-importance of someone who has acquired a valued new skill. "It's a little lax."

Lezlie moved her lower jaw forward and back then opened wide as I probed at the base of her left ear. I could feel her mandible slip out of position.

"Gee," I said, "That's weird." I tried to guide the bone back to its rightful place.

Lezlie raised her right hand and pointed to the area as if scolding it with her index finger. She made no sound. There was no pain. Her mouth just stuck open like a door with a broom handle lodged above a hinge.

Back we went to The Vic. Lezlie kept her poise, but I was disconsolate. Trailing a step behind her, I longed for obscurity. At the Emergency Room I did the best I could to explain things to the ENT resident who would no doubt suspect me of domestic violence. With an amused look, the real doctor deftly popped my girlfriend's TM joint into place. What a relief!

I cherished Lezlie, but waited through half of my internship to propose. It was hard to say "I love you," even though the two of us had fused like the apartment buildings on Aylmer Street. She became a part of everything—even knew about my secret war against the ants that I bombed with pennies while lingering in the bathroom of my hospital residence.

"Ask me and tell me why," she said, when I finally talked about marriage and a future together.

I felt as ridiculous as I had when I accidentally dislocated her jaw.

We married on July 19,1969, as American astronauts touched down for the first time on the moon's surface. I began residency training at Massachusetts General Hospital, and Lezlie took a job as nursing instructor at Boston Children's Hospital.

Now, on April 17, I looked across the family room at my wife's swollen belly, as if my mind were endeavoring to edit out an unwanted perception, then checking to see if it were gone. Lezlie was weary and gray. Her facial muscles were lax and her jaw drooped like a frost-laden bough. How unreal this all seemed. Could she have become so ill without a warning? I searched my memory for something that might have told me that she was getting into trouble. What had I missed? I thought back to one strange event one Saturday morning in February.

I had been dressing leisurely and replaying the week's happenings in my mind when suddenly she screamed. I raced downstairs, as if in a nightmare. Lezlie was in the kitchen. She clutched at her left forearm and stared at her scalded hand. The red kettle steamed silently on the Formica counter in a pool of boiled water that dripped insistently onto the tile floor.

"Get some cold water in a basin!" she said. Her face was gray and suddenly aged. Horrified, I looked about dumbly for an explanation. "Hurry!" Lezlie said. "I poured it into my hand instead of the cup."

I helped her to the family room couch and immersed her hand in a basin of iced water. No blisters had formed. With timely first aid, it would remain a first degree burn.

What's wrong with her? I wondered. It was such an odd thing for her to do. It seemed in that moment as if her youth had run out—like the kettle water. My thoughts turned catastrophic. Selfishly wondering if this were a prelude to Alzheimer's disease, I envisioned the privacy of our home overrun with geriatric nurses. Lezlie was the caretaker of our family. Were our roles about to reverse? The children would depart for adulthood and I would be left with a life partner who barely recalled my name!

I felt foolish and disloyal. My sense of time slowed. It was as if the world was engulfed in Jello and I was struggling through it. I got more ice and pulled up close in an old Lincoln rocker that we had found in New Hampshire during a fall foliage trip. Lezlie loved old chairs and intended to repair several that she stored in the basement.

I discussed that incident with Bob Best, a cancer specialist at Boston Hospital. I sometimes join him for the morning commute. Dr. Best is a skillful cancer doctor who taught me that an oncologist must take the patient close to death, then back. Bob said nothing about Lezlie's scald. There was nothing to say except that it was a bizarre sort of injury.

Our conversation that morning shifted to a mutual patient whose family had presented a psychiatric challenge when chemotherapy for her highly invasive cancer caused life-threatening complications.

"They're out of control," Bob had said when I responded to his emergency page. "Her brother began pushing me. I had to call Security!" Fortunately the family settled down and our patient recovered from the ill effects of the chemotherapy.

"I saw her last week," I said now as we continued our drive past the morning caravan of golfers at the Weston public golf course. "I told her, 'last time I saw you, you were practically dead.' She was in the cafeteria ordering an ice cream cone. I couldn't believe it."

"What did she say?"

"Nothing much. She just smiled. I told her how lucky she is to have you for a doctor. I believe that...If I ever get cancer, I'll come knock on your door."

Bob turned his head momentarily and raised his eyebrows.

"Don't get it," he said.

3

A DOCTOR'S WIFE

o o o o o o o o o o o o o o o o o o o o o o o o o o o o o o o o
"No man visits the same river twice."

—Heraclitus

Medical people are superstitious about caring for each other. There is a doctors' version of Murphy's Law: treat another doctor's family member and everything that can go wrong will. I thought about that on April 18 as we prepared for the visit with Dr. Godley.

I helped Lezlie into the car. It was a relief that Craig was in Ohio and that Kate, away on her spring break, would be spared the sight of her mother's swollen belly. A neighbor gathered leaves and dead branches on his adjoining property. Life was doing what it always did on Stoney Brook Road—but it was not the same for us. The simple task of backing the car up our inclined country driveway took on a new and ominous meaning.

Lezlie had fallen in love with the house and its sunny exposure when we returned to the Boston area from my tour of active duty two decades earlier. "I plan to go out feet first," she had said.

We arrived at Boston Hospital and stopped at my clinic to leave our coats. I felt oddly out of place in my altered role. I was not at the hospital as a doctor that Monday, but as a doctor-husband. I was on the wrong side of illness. There are many ways to learn and the worst of them is to learn through tragedy. Most doctors are compassionate but there is a stopping point—like a border crossing—that separates the healer from the victim. It is a border that sometimes is destroyed in the natural disaster of disease. When that happens, it is never again the same. It could not be the same for me because those I would later treat would be too much like myself.

I was surprised at my self-consciousness about Lezlie's condition, and by a fleeting desire that the clinic staff not recognize her. What should I wish for? When others see, our senses, too, are heightened. When others pretend not to see, the implications are worse.

There was no doubt then that the dearest person in my universe had cancer. The question was: what kind of cancer? I knew those cancers that patients, friends, and colleagues had overcome with treatment—however brutal.

I also knew the death row cancers, like the pancreatic cancer that killed our friend Sandra. She telephoned us in Boston in the summer of 1985. "Lezlie, I have something to tell you that's terrible," she said. "I'm dying...I've decided against chemotherapy...Will you come? It would mean a lot if I could see you and Owen."

We flew to British Columbia and visited her daily at Victoria General Hospital. Near the end Sandra hoped for a life to follow the one she would imminently lose. "I don't know what you'll find there," I told her. "But if there are any rooms, please save one with closet space for us."

The curable malignancies can be commuted or removed, but they leave a scar that is both surgical and psychological. There is a lasting measure of vulnerability—a biological parole. It was like that for us after Lezlie's first encounter with cancer.

It was in the winter of 1985, six months after Sandra's death. "I don't like the way this looks," Lezlie had said one morning, then showed me a mole ten inches up from her left knee on the outer thigh.

"It looks fine to me," I said. "Why don't you have Bob Gentilly look at it?" Dr. Gentilly was her primary care doctor at Boston Hospital. Bob agreed that it was benign but set up a dermatology referral to be certain. The referral seemed unnecessary. I checked the nevus frequently and saw no change in its appearance—until the day prior to Lezlie's scheduled visit with the skin specialist.

"I can't believe this!" I said to her. "Look at this thing. It's turned jet black. How in the world did you know?" What had looked benign was now obviously malignant. A biopsy confirmed the diagnosis of melanoma, a potentially lethal skin cancer that is 95% curable when detected early. It was a "thin melanoma" with a good prognosis. It would be easy to remove the lesion, but a wide incision would provide a margin of safety. Lezlie and I agreed that she would see senior surgeon Amos Archer, who routinely sent me patients for psychiatric care.

"He's very aggressive," I told her. "There won't be anything subtle about Amos' approach, but it will be the best insurance we can get that this thing is taken care of."

"He can cut off my leg if that's what it takes," Lezlie said.

"I think he'll want to do a wide excision," I said. "They don't cut off legs for this, Lezlie."

"I'm just saying that I want to live."

She trusted Amos. She knew him from hospital functions including his summer barbecues for close colleagues and their families. "First you see him at a barbecue…then he's going to operate on your leg," she said.

I remember that on the morning of Lezlie's 1985 melanoma operation, I awakened from a vivid nightmare and immediately recorded it. I was in the middle of a civil war in Beirut trying desperately to get to a woman who was being transfused for a stab wound.

As Lezlie dressed, I gazed at the magnificent shape of her legs. "They are your best part," I often told her when we first became lovers and learned to tease each other with affection. I knew the meaning of the dream and the six-inch surgical 'stab wound' she was about to endure and that would mar her beauty.

Dr. Archer excised the skin cancer under local anesthesia. He talked with her about her friend Sandra's recent death from pancreatic cancer. "Sometimes your immune system can be depressed after the death of someone that was very close to you," Amos told her.

I was amazed when Lezlie told me about the conversation that evening. Here was my friend Dr. Archer talking to my wife in the operating room and discussing the effect of psychology on her immune system. Incredible.

Even more incredible was the extent of our denial now. We left the Clinic and walked through the adjoining corridors to Alex Godley's department. The ascitic fluid insistently expanding in her abdomen imparted an incongruous appearance of third trimester pregnancy. She looked so old…Did she know that? I felt old—as if I had this cancer with her.

Alex greeted us like an old friend. He looked sad for both of us and sad because he felt a sense of responsibility for how things were turning out. In the previous year, Alex had followed Lezlie medically for a benign ovarian cyst. In January, 1994, he repeated an ultrasound examination. Repetition of the tests troubled me. Was there a risk of malignancy? As I sat beside Lezlie that day in the radiology department, I whispered in her ear. "Take them out," I said, as if a woman's ovaries could be extracted like wisdom teeth. "Can we talk about that?"

There was no clear medical indication for a hysterectomy or for removal of her ovaries, but it was not the first time that I had questioned it. For years she had recurrent difficulty with uterine fibroids, which she preferred to treat without surgery. "Besides," she confided, "I don't want to lie there naked on an operating table."

Now, Dr. Godley moved quickly. After seeing Lezlie on April 18, he ordered an abdominal CT scan and an abdominal tap—a paracentesis—to withdraw the ascitic fluid and obtain a sample for analysis. He also arranged for a visiting surgeon, Dr. Millard Watkins, to see her the next day.

It eased my mind to see Alex but there was still no answer.

We would have to wait.

4

THE JANUS MIRROR

o o o o o o o o o o o o o o o o o o o o o o o o o o o o o o o o

The world breaks everyone and afterward many are strong
at the broken places—but those that will not break, it kills.
It kills the very good and the very gentle and the very brave—impar-
tially.

—*A Farewell to Arms*
Ernest Hemingway

We waited. We didn't talk about it. There was nothing to say except that I loved her very much. I was relieved that Alex had seen her; that somebody who knew what to do was taking such a personal interest in her welfare. I was relieved as well that the fluid in her abdomen would be drained the next day. I wished that I did not know how easily it could re-accumulate. In a time like this the mind races back and forth between the reality of tragedy and the disbelief. *How could this be happening?...It wasn't happening....It was.... It would be all right—just a scare.... It would be terrible.*

Lezlie did not say what she was feeling. She did not need to tell me how much she was afraid. I could see it in the flatness of her gaze. I could not recall another time like that. She was always such a forthright 'let's get to it' person. Once in Hawaii while walking Craig in his stroller, she was accosted by a mental patient in a quiet side street behind our Waipuna condominium complex.

"I'll take that," he said. He had appeared without warning and grabbed for the pram with Craig in it.

"Oh no, you won't!" she told him. Lezlie gripped Craig's stroller and raced across the street. There was a little cluster of housing where a community of Samoans lent local color to Waikiki's "Dress Circle." She stayed there with them in silence until the danger was past.

20

As she related the story, I thought about the big brown-skinned people and the surprise they must have experienced. I admired her courage and ability to take quick and effective action.

It was different now…to see her fear.

Waiting is for many kinds of feeling: for fear…hope…detachment.

Waiting is for mirror gazing. Imagine looking into a glass that reflects two views in time. Like Janus, the two-headed god, you can see in two opposite directions at once. Look into the mirror from the right and you see the future. Look into the mirror from the left and you visit the past. My teachers have been my mirror to the future. My patients are my mirror to the past.

One of my patients, Steven D'Amico, provides such a mirror. His wife, Jackie, died a year ago of ovarian cancer. I have been counseling him with a level of understanding that I wish I did not possess.

"I don't think I'll ever get used to it," he told me recently. When his sons took over management of the family construction company, Steve and Jackie at last had some time together. They planned to travel, beginning with an opera tour to Italy. Then Jackie became ill. Now Steve is alone in the house.

"It's so full of her," he says, "that I'm…well…kind of reluctant to leave. The memories are just as much rewarding as they can be painful…I used to come into the house and say, 'Anybody Home?' and she'd say, 'Oh boy!' or 'Hot damn!'

"There aren't a lot of marriages like we had. I guess I'm kind of lucky. They say that only one percent of marriages are really close like that. One percent are great and one percent are horrible. About 25% of them are good marriages, 25% bad, and the rest in the middle…."

Steve is a big man with a sinewy build and a rough dark complexion. He loves to tell jokes and never leaves a session before sharing a "groaner." His primary care doctor, Alex Feldson, referred him initially for depression that responded well to the medication I prescribed. Steve continued to see me on a regular basis, but was unwilling to cut back on his alcohol intake. Three years ago, he bled heavily from a stomach ulcer. When I visited him, he said, "I just want to know when I can have my next martini."

"Any time you want to," I said. "Just call the blood bank and schedule a transfusion before you drink it." Steve says he still drinks a martini a day. In medical school we were taught to take an alcohol history, then multiply the patient's reported number of daily drinks by four.

When Jackie first showed signs of her illness, she and Steve talked openly about the possibility of cancer. She was a stoic woman. Steve said she did not expect to live much longer. He wanted me to meet her and arranged for a short session just prior to her first diagnostic visit with Dr. Feldson.

I had never met her before. She was a gentle woman with graying hair and a warm smile. As she slipped off her coat and shook my hand, I saw at once that her abdomen was grossly distended—just like Lezlie's was in the "cruelest month" of 1994.

When they left my office, Jackie disappeared around a bend in the corridor that leads through the clinic maze to my waiting room. Steve lingered momentarily before rejoining her. It is hard to describe Steve's appearance. It was the look of grief at its very beginning. His expression was at war with itself—that conflict of prescience and denial that is the emotional railbed to catastrophe. I think it is the way people might have appeared while boarding boxcars on the trains to Dachau and Auschwitz.

My eyes met Steve's momentarily as if in confirmation of his unspoken message. Then I clutched his shoulders and hugged him. When he left the office I secured the door and cried.

When I saw Steve D'Amico last year with his wife, I saw myself as I appeared on April 19, 1994. That Tuesday, Lezlie and I drove separately to Boston Hospital. I did not want her to go alone; but, in a tacit way, the two of us were adapting to a new turn in our lives. There would be a lot of trips to Boston Hospital in the months ahead.

Tuesday afternoons are the time for transplant team "family meetings." Alice Witherspoon is the surgeon in charge of the kidney transplant program. She is a superb surgeon with uncommon respect for the psychological needs of her patients.

Alice schedules the meetings so that our team can meet prospective transplant recipients and their families. It is a good way to provide teaching and informed consent—to prepare people for the psychological "roller coaster" of transplantation. The meeting was delayed for several minutes while we waited for the kidney specialist who was to present the prospective transplant recipients.

"What's wrong?" Alice Witherspoon asked.

I was surprised at how quickly she sensed that something was wrong—as if she could see a change in emotion that I had yet to feel.

"It's Lezlie," I said. "I think she has some kind of cancer."

I told Alice about Lezlie's swollen belly, about the tests Dr. Godley had performed, about the meeting with Dr. Watkins scheduled for five o'clock that same day.

Her look of concern alerted me that, like the prospective kidney recipients we would be seeing, I, too, was entering that other world of surgical patients and their families. As a transplantation psychiatrist, I had spent two decades in a world that was familiar and comfortable for me, but full of unknowns for those who hoped to gain freedom from hemodialysis and to improve the quality of their lives. Now, very suddenly—unexpectedly—I was like them. I wanted answers, but only good answers. I needed the skillful help of a surgeon who could make things right, but I was in dread of the dependence that nature had imposed.

Alice seemed ill-at-ease when I mentioned Watkins. He was a world famous cancer surgeon who had recently come to Boston Hospital from Toronto. He was the kind of doctor whose ego requires him to be right and who craves acknowledgement. He was not a team player. His accomplishments included a long list of research publication—more than 250 original papers—in which he was almost invariably named as first author.

"Do you think Lezlie should see Amos?" I asked hesitantly. I felt for a moment as if I had done something wrong in bringing Lezlie first to Alex Godley. Maybe Lezlie and I should have started with Bob Gentilly, her primary care doctor, or with Amos Archer who had operated on the melanoma seven years earlier. "It's just that Alex wanted us to see…"

Alice ignored the question and logged into the transplant unit computer terminal. "Do you mind my having a look at things?" she asked.

"No," I said. I was startled, like a deer caught in car headlights on a country road, but there were no safe woods for escape. I would have to stand there waiting to be hit by the bad news. My wait was over.

"Just tell me to 'butt out' and I will," Alice said. *For a moment I wanted to stop her. What are the ethics? I **am** Lezlie's health proxy…but she is not in a coma somewhere. How will she feel about my doing this? Will I tell her? Maybe yes…maybe no. I'll have to think about it more. I need some time. Tell Alice to wait…The hell with ethics! Do I want to know? That's the main thing. I can feel it in my gut. I don't want to know…I must know!*

Alice typed out Lezlie's name and birth date. The machine displayed the PCIS logo. Alice scrolled through the database.

I peered over Alice's shoulder at the monitor. *The chemistries are normal…*

No…one of her liver enzymes is elevated…It can't be…Look again…It is elevated. What could be wrong with her liver?…This is a nightmare!

I watched Alice's face as she read the CT report then stole a glance at the screen, filled with rising sentences like movie credits. I could make out some of the words: There was "extensive omental caking," the report said, "and multiple tiny lesions on the liver." *Why are there spots on her liver?...She has cancer...but she just got it...It can't be in her liver that fast...How can it be in her liver?...I can't believe this!...It must be growing like crazy...It's not just cancer—it's a bad cancer...She's going to die...Lezlie is going to die...No, it's a mistake...It's not a mistake...I wish it were a mistake, but it's not...She is going to die!*

Good God! It's all over.

I could feel the blood drain from my face beneath the skin. It felt cold and wet. I stepped away from the computer and poured myself a cup of coffee in the chart room behind the nurses' station.

My wife's belly was full of cancer!

Alice telephoned the lab. "Let's see what cell type it is," she said.

Could she find that out, too? Of course, the results will be in from the paracentesis. "It's ovarian cell," Alice's voice said. "Lezlie is in the right place...Go be with her. She'll fight."

5

INFORMED CONSENT

o o o o o o o o o o o o o o o o o o o o o o o o o o o o o o o o o
Dr. Coutras had delivered sentences on of death on many men, and he could never overcome the horror with which it filled him. He felt always the furious hatred that must seize a man condemned when he compared himself with the doctor, sane and healthy, who had the inestimable privilege of life.

—*The Moon and Sixpence*
W. Somerset Maugham

Lezlie was sitting solemnly in Millard Watkins' office when I arrived at five minutes after five. He had just begun to talk with her across a large desk that looked like a fortress. He was beginning to tell Lezlie the same information that I had just learned. *He might as well be sitting in the next room,* I thought. *She's not going to like him.*

Millard was a tall heavyset man with thick red hair that fell boyishly across the center of his forehead. I thought he was in his mid to late thirties—impeccably groomed and very hearty in appearance. On the wall was a picture of him at a polo match. He posed beside a second man in equestrian attire who looked like Prince Charles. I thought it was Prince Charles and decided not to ask. I wondered what Lezlie was thinking. Was this the way they looked at the Royal Victoria Yacht Club?

I was grateful to know what was coming next, because I could help cushion the blow and do my best to help her gain rapport with the surgeon who sat erect across the wide expanse of desk…and who would soon attempt to cut out her cancer.

His voice was surprisingly gentle but sterile, as if he had pruned his emotions like a hedge. He did not mention the details of the CT scan. Lezlie would not hear that her omentum, the thick apron of tissue that sits astride the abdominal contents, was matted with cancer. The thought of it sickened me.

"It seems there are some abnormal cells in the fluid we took from your abdomen this morning," he said.

"What kind of cells?" Lezlie wanted to know. Her expression was stern.

Watkins paused. He was obviously uncomfortable as if he had been in this situation before and dreaded it. Still, he needed to tell her straight; it wouldn't do to equivocate.

"Is it cancer?" I asked.

Lezlie turned to look at me, then stared across the desk at Watkins.

"Yes," he said. "It is ovarian cancer."

He knew that I was trying to make this less terrible. I could not tell if he was grateful for that or resentful of my interruption. I guessed that he was both.

"Where do I have it?"

"It is confined to the abdomen, so it's a Stage 3 cancer."

I had learned that Stage 1 ovarian cancer was best. Stage 4 meant the spread was beyond the abdomen. Stage 3 sounded like the place where they make horror movies in a film studio.

Dr. Watkins explained what would come next. I thought of him then as Dr. Watkins…not just Watkins. I needed him to be more than just Watkins.

It's okay how you're telling her, I thought.

The ovarian cancer was not localized. He would therefore perform what was called a "debulking" procedure.

I had not heard the term before and didn't like the sound of it. I pictured great mounds of cancer like cumulus clouds. It did not mean that. There were no clouds. It meant that Millard would perform a hysterectomy and that he would explore her abdomen and remove the cancer wherever he could see it. He would biopsy the lymph nodes in Lezlie's pelvis. That would complete the staging process. If there was any cancer in the lymph nodes, it would be Stage 3-b.

After she recovered, he would begin a standard chemotherapy protocol. The two drugs that he used were Cisplatinum and Taxol. I didn't like the sound of Cisplatinum because I knew it could be very toxic. Taxol was a new drug that I had learned about in my work on the hospital's ethics committee for human research. Taxol came from the yew trees common to British Columbia. That was good. *We now have a Canadian surgeon and a cure from Lezlie's home province.* Friends with acreage in the Victoria Highlands had a lot of yew trees.

Then there was the matter of Lezlie's bowels. Sometimes they too were involved with ovarian cancer. Dr. Watkins might need to remove a portion of her large intestine. It was unlikely, he said, but she might need to wear a colostomy bag if a lot of intestine were affected.

"Dr. Archer operated on my melanoma," Lezlie said. "If you have to remove a part of my bowel, can he do that?"

I added that I would like my close colleagues to be included in her care.

"Many minds...one set of hands," he said. He looked at Lezlie in a way that was benign, patriarchal, and annoying. His expression seemed to say, "Just leave everything to me and it will all work out for the best."

I did not want to leave everything to him—nor did Lezlie. There was no question that Dr. Watkins could see that. I liked to think that I would see it if the roles were reversed. I would think the patient was mixing me up with the disease. I would diffuse the situation by immediately extending an offer for consultation. I might not like to do it that way, but that is the way I would do it...It was not the way Dr. Watkins did it.

"We find that when general surgeons are involved, people end up with colostomies." He fondled a book as he spoke and lifted it from the desktop like a prized cat. It was his own book...University of Toronto Press...copyright 1993...*Surgical Care of Ovarian Cancer*. Millard R. Watkins, Ph.D., M.D.

I watched my wife's silent terror.

I felt helpless...then angry. The anger seemed to start in my belly and surge upwards like an anti-gravity avalanche. I said nothing and struggled with my facial muscles to maintain composure.

What a jerk, I thought. *He's going to make it hard for Lezlie to trust him. "Many minds...one set of hands." Did he have to say that? Amos Archer is one of the best abdominal surgeons in the country...Don't lose it, Owen. You know how angry you can get...it will make things a lot worse. He doesn't mean to offend us. It's just the way he is...and we need him. She has an 80% chance of dying. My God...It's so incredible that she's this ill—so totally out of the blue! This can't be happening.*

Watkins had established his need for authority. In the process, he had brushed off Lezlie's request to involve a world-class surgeon who had treated her in the past and was also a friend. For a moment I wished she had another cancer—even if it was as bad—and a cancer that fell in Amos Archer's area of specialization...a cancer he could operate on.

But what if it were to go badly...what if she isn't going to recover...and Amos were her surgeon and he refused to back off? Like Millard Watkins, Amos managed every aspect of his patients' medical care, and he had a reputation for persevering when others thought things irretrievable.

The patients Amos asks me to see do not have terminal cancer. But what if she did have that and he still wouldn't quit? Of course Amos would do everything to help her be comfortable if that's what it came to. It would be better with another kind of cancer. But it isn't another kind...it is this kind...and it is this surgeon...and we need his skills.

I could not avoid comparing the two surgeons. Like Millard Watkins, Dr. Archer's was the final voice in the care of his patients. In one case that we shared, for example, every member of his team thought it futile to perform kidney dialysis on a patient whose illness looked irreversibly fatal. "You are pulling this cart on your own," I had told him.

"That's fine with me," Amos had said. Amos was all about saving lives, and did not believe that it was time to stop. That patient recovered. Some patients did not recover, but Amos was right more than he was wrong, and he was more often right than his colleagues. How keen was Dr. Watkins' judgment? I did not know the answer. That in itself was terrifying. I did know, however, that Amos Archer surrounded himself with experts that he trusted from other medical disciplines. He might choose to disagree with them and often did...but he listened. That was a considerable difference.

Watkins needed to be admired; that was the fuel that appeared to drive him. Amos, in contrast, was less interested in being right than in being effective...and he invariably changed course when faced with a convincing argument.

I felt isolated, vulnerable. I knew medicine, but could see that my opinions would not count with Watkins...nor would anyone else's opinion, however well reasoned.

"Many minds...one set of hands." The phrase repeated itself in my thinking like an intrusive melody. I struggled with it while reminding myself that Millard Watkins was constantly dealing with poor prognosis disease.

Would you be any better at this than he is? Remember, most of his patients die...And your wife is one of them.

I know that Lezlie and I did not really stagger from the office, but it felt like staggering.

"I hate him!" she said. "Who cares if I have to wear a bag? I don't want cancer!"

6

THE OTHER SIDE OF YESTERDAY

o o o o o o o o o o o o o o o o o o o o o o o o o o o o o o o o
What of a much of a witch of a wind
Gives the truth to summer lies?

—e e cummings

Millard Watkins scheduled the operation for the following Monday, April 25.

"Please don't tell me that!" my father said when we informed my parents. Poor Dad. He had been fighting his own cancer war for a decade. His was a transitional cell carcinoma of the bladder. It was agonizing for him, and April 25 was his birthday. He would be eighty-five. It was an age that Lezlie would never live to see. She would not even come close.

"Don't tell me that!" He said it often in the week prior to her surgery. Dad was a revisionist. When troubled by an event that distressed him, like Lezlie's cancer, he did everything possible to change the story. When he said, "Don't tell me that," I believe that he meant it. Who could blame him for wanting to dictate the news? To lose a precious daughter-in-law would be too tragic. He had seen enough tragedy. As eldest son in a family of four, it was Dad's job to prevent the mishaps. Among Dad's responsibilities in the Depression years was supervision of his asthmatic brother Frankie, the handsome one, who later died with lethal addiction.

Unlike Dad, my mother Edith was always a realist…and she always asserted her point of view. Dad jokingly referred to her as "Mother Superior." Mother was obsessive compulsive. When I became a psychiatrist, I gave her a book about the disorder. *Getting Control* was a quick read that one of my former students wrote for the popular market. Lezlie and I and the children watched as Edith turned the pages. "I don't do that," she said. "No, I don't do that either."

To my knowledge it was the only truth my mother ever denied.

Mother's response to Lezlie's illness was simply this: it broke her heart. In time I would resent her tears because they challenged my defenses. For my parents, illness and death were a familiar part of the social landscape. They had come to terms with their own impermanence. It was a part of Nature's law. Lezlie's condition made no sense to them because she and I were still "the kids." In truth, my mother and dad knew more about death than I did, despite my years of helping people face catastrophic illness.

I was always very close to my patients but never as close as I have been since Lezlie's war with ovarian cancer. I was always on the other side of the mirror. It was other people who were ultimately vulnerable. When I gazed into the glass, the face of tragedy was never there. Of course, we had illness to contend with in our immediate family, but everything was manageable. If there were a health problem, I could get a doctor—the best doctor.

Vulnerability of the self is a truth my parents knew better. At a later date—in the summer of 1996—when Dad was eighty-seven and dying of acute leukemia, I would ask him, "What can you say now about your life? How do you see it?"

"I lived. I died," he would say. With that simple elegance he summed up Nature's great dichotomy. We live. We die.

Life creates and destroys, cuts and heals, digests and rebuilds. It is an extraordinary balance of growth and decay ever evolving to a mysterious goal. We each share in that creation and in that oblivion. None of us is exempt.

In April, 1994, nature was in its destructive phase, the part that some people refer to as "God's will." It is another way of surrendering to life's plan. I didn't like the plan that April and I didn't want to surrender. I would do whatever anyone could do to help Lezlie become whole again. It was a mission…Sometimes it was a desperate mission.

It is not right to say that she was not whole then, because her loving determination never failed, and that is the most important part of being…Possibly it is the only important part.

The first task we faced together was how to tell the children. Kate returned from spring break. She came home to the golden yellow splash of forsythia, the daffodils in bloom, the crocuses. She came home to cancer.

"Mom has a tumor," I said. "It is a kind of cancer—called ovarian carcinoma."

"What is carcinoma?"

"Cancer. It means the tumor is malignant."

"Oh."

"Well, there are different kinds of cancer. This is not a good kind. It is hard to detect because of where ovaries are. You know where they are, deep in the abdominal cavity."

"Yes."

"The good part is that Lezlie's cancer should respond well to chemotherapy. It's the opposite of what you'd think. The cancer grew fast, but fast-growing cells are easiest to destroy with chemotherapy or radiation. Dr. Watkins...he's a world expert on this...will operate next Monday. Then, when your mother recovers from the operation, he'll start the chemotherapy."

"Oh." Kate is a master of one-word answers. Her face sometimes says a lot, but I couldn't see how very sad she really was. She seemed comforted by my taking charge of things—although I guessed that she didn't believe my explanation. I was not lying to her. I was lying to myself.

Rapidly multiplying cells *are* more responsive to chemotherapy. Lezlie's malignant ovarian cancer cells had, however, been multiplying unnoticed for weeks—long enough to fill her with the liters of fluid that Dr. Wakins had drained from her abdomen.

It was such a change for Kate. She'd had a wonderful life. She was playful, inventive, and successful in everything she had attempted from downhill skiing competition to 4-H public speaking.

She was eighteen and involved with her first boyfriend, Dana Marsh, who endeared himself to our family, and especially to Lezlie. Arriving home from Boston Hospital, I would sometimes find Lezlie talking with him on the telephone. "Whose boyfriend is Dana?" I liked to ask her. "Kate's...or yours?"

Lezlie and I worried more about Craig.

Parents, like latency-aged kids, sometimes need to classify things—to try and give order to life in a world of chaos. Here were Lezlie and I, the psychiatrist and erstwhile pediatric nursing instructor, differentiating our kids as if we were comparing types of trees. Kate was the birch—strong, resilient, and striking in appearance. Craig was the maple—solid, predictable, vulnerable. Kate was tougher. Craig was smarter. Kate kept her own counsel. Craig's thoughts were an open book, like his dad. Kate had a network of support. Beyond our nuclear family, Craig was on his own in life.

There was some truth to these observations. We had discovered that Craig had attention deficit disorder in the mid 1970s when the condition was first recognized. "They finally have a name for what Craig has," I told Lezlie. He was distractable, disorganized, and offended peers by blurting things out. He misplaced virtually every item that was not attached to him.

Craig was also gifted. "Even the teachers don't understand him," a fourth grade classmate said. He was also very loving, empathic and sensitive like his grandfather Bruce who, at Christmas, needed more presents than anyone else.

It was Craig's peer relations that caused his greatest pain. During summers, at our lake, the clusters of children would open for Kate, but close as her brother approached.

"He is one of the 'Outcasts of Poker Flats,'" I said.

At last when Craig reached grade five, we found the perfect independent middle school for boys. The Fenn School encouraged independence—*Sua Sponte*. It encouraged fairness and demanded tolerance. A boy that broke that code was likely to spend some time at the Headmaster's Office seated at "the bench," gentle discipline though it was.

When Craig graduated grade nine with four awards, I could not stop my tears. "It's a strange thing for me to say," I told Lezlie on the day of Craig's graduation. "It's really odd, but if...if we lost Craig...if something happened to him...I would feel that he'd lived a full life."

"I agree," she said.

Now in April, 1994, I kept Craig up to date about his mother's illness. We spoke to one another by telephone at least once daily while he completed his premedical studies at Oberlin College. Craig had always said what he thought. With him, as with me, one didn't have to guess. His communications about his mother's illness were intense, intelligent, and insistent. Craig, the Eagle Scout, could not accept the idea of a world without Lezlie. He began a computer search. Was his mother getting the best of care? Were there new treatment protocols that her doctors and I had not as yet discovered? Of us all, Craig's emotions were closest to the surface. His would later prove to be the most adaptive response.

I could not let go of Lezlie's care. I knew her as if she were me. Dr. Watkins agreed with my preference for Marvin Appleton as anesthesiologist. Amos used him for the most demanding procedures and I had once scrubbed in with them for a liver transplant.

I saw Amos at surgical rounds on the Friday before Lezlie's operation. "Lezlie's going to the OR on Monday," I told him.

"Thanks for telling me," Amos said. "I'll look in."

Amos did look in.

On April 25, 1994, Millard Watkins performed a six-hour debulking operation, and he did it with technical brilliance. After Lezlie's operation, I met her in the recovery room as Dr. Appleton wheeled her in from the OR. She was still under anesthesia, not yet breathing on her own, but she gripped my hand when I spoke her name. Then her pain broke through. Dr. Appleton gave her morphine. He helped transfer her to the recovery room bed. For a brief time she was exposed. I thought about her modesty and her comments that she had never wanted to be naked on an operating room table.

Dr. Watkins came in. He showed only the slightest trace of fatigue. I admired his energy and assertiveness, some of the same characteristics that I had only recently found so annoying. "It went well," he said.

"What did you find?" I asked.

"The cancer originated in her right ovary. There was some seeding of the peritoneal cavity and some spots under the diaphragm and near the liver that I was able to remove."

"There was no spread beyond her pelvis?"

"No. We biopsied several nodes."

"Thanks!" I said. I wanted to hug him. Millard had been the right surgeon after all. I was beginning to see the power of medicine and the reverence that we give selectively to physicians. It is a revocable gift.

Lezlie had been assigned a room on Trowbridge 15. It was strange to see the floor where I sometimes consulted. It was a new but unwelcome perspective. The private service had always seemed elegant and elite. As a visiting specialist, I had always felt like an interloper, an ordinary character from an ethnic middle class background…nothing fancy. Then, with Lezlie recovering from her six-hour operative ordeal, I was not sure who I was. I felt rumpled…as if my white shirt were staging a retreat from my trousers…rumpled…overweight…old.

I found my way to Lezlie's room—the room that would receive her from intensive care. "Good God!" I said. "What are you doing here?" I said to Max and Alice Dewer, two of our closest friends who stood awkwardly in the room.

"We won't stay long," Max said. "We just didn't want you to be alone."

I had ten thoughts at once. Among them I was most aware of gratitude…awkwardness…pain…and pride. It was disorienting to be welcomed in this elaborate setting and under such momentous circumstances. I was also proud. This was my hospital. The elegance of the surroundings became a metaphor for Lezlie's anticipated care.

I nodded gratefully to my friends.

There was another person in the room. I had never thought of Natalie Ralston as beautiful and was embarrassed to be suddenly aware of her this way.

"Max...Alice..." For an anxious moment I could not retrieve Natalie's last name. "This is my friend Natalie...Lezlie's private duty nurse."

Natalie stood graciously through this hesitant introduction. She was striking in her starched white uniform. I looked at her, then at my friends, as if apologizing for my unexpected attraction to this remarkable young woman.

I had worked with Natalie in the intensive care unit. I admired her nursing skills. She was a graceful woman, but there had been no special feeling about her. One of Lezlie's close friends had been Natalie's nursing instructor and suggested that Natalie would be the best person to see Lezlie through her first two to three postoperative days, the time when she would feel most helpless.

"We're going to leave now," Max said. "But we want you to call later. We want to hear about how things are going, if that's all right."

"Yes," I said, a bit absently. *How wonderful to have such loyal friends...*but at the same time I was aware of such strange thoughts. *Wasn't this the way it happened in a novel? The soon-to-be-bereaved husband would fall in love with his wife's dedicated young nurse?*

What would it be like if Natalie and I marry? I was daydreaming about the awkwardness of our having dinner with Max and Alice! *Owen!...This is not a scene from a Victorian novel. You really are nuts!* Still the idea of a Victorian novel did have a certain appeal...Lezlie was from Victoria.

I turned and saw the floor nurses wheeling Lezlie into the room. She was still in her post-anesthesia sleep—but arousable. *She's made it!* I thought. *This will work out all right.* My momentary musing was such embarrassing nonsense.

Natalie got to work.

7

RANDOM THOUGHTS

○ ○

Everyone thinks of himself, and he lives most gaily
who knows best how to deceive himself.

—*Crime and Punishment*
Fyodor Dostoyevsky

"Are you staying the night?" asked one of the floor nurses. Pauline was a pleasant thirtyish woman with pale blue tragic eyes and sandy blond hair tucked back in a bun.

"Yes," I said tentatively. "Is that all right?"

"Of course. There are some things for you to wear," she said, directing me to a utility room. She waited there with me as I fumbled through the clean stacks of pajamas and thin cotton robes. I felt like a schoolboy.

"I think those should fit," she said. "I'll make up the bed for you." I followed her into Lezlie's room. Pauline strode to the couch and delivered its hidden bed like a newborn.

I changed self-consciously into the freshly laundered hospital clothing—striped like prison attire—then hung my white shirt, blazer and tie as if I were putting my identity in storage. I was undergoing a metamorphosis—like water to vapor. Before that time I used to visit the floor as a medical consultant. "I wonder who Dr. Surman is here to rescue," one of the nurses once said. Now, after Lezlie's surgery, it was I who needed a life preserver.

The nurses greeted me with kind but humorless smiles. This had been their way with my colleagues who had come to Trowbridge in the past for treatment of close family members or for their own medical care. I remembered how remote from them I had felt. They were like fellow soldiers who had been wounded in action. I had identified with them and felt compassion, but there was an invisible wall between us—the wall of disparate experience. In life's game of 'capture the flag,' they were the prisoners.

I did not like this new identity but welcomed relief from the professional demands that were temporarily suspended like my tie and blue blazer. As I settled in for the night, I was aware of so many conflicting emotions. Millard Watkins had seemed confident after Lezlie's surgery and she was resting now in a post-anesthesia sleep. A competent surgeon had freed us from the cancer. Lezlie's illness was now under control. She would recover from the operation. There would be a few days of postoperative pain...I would help her through that...and then we would have our lives back, as it was supposed to be. It was time to get on with the children's high school and college graduations. After that would be the beginning of the gentle mid-life reprieve that couples plan for, so they can reclaim their private time together.

Liberated at last from the anxiety of getting Lezlie to the right treatment, my focus now shifted to myself. I became aware of a competing stream of consciousness in which I was stripped of my bulletproof vest of denial. It occurred to me then—painfully—that for the first time since boyhood I was frightened of being left. *Will she leave me?...And then what?...What will it be like without her?...Will she really leave me?...Is that possible?...Yes...It doesn't seem possible....*

I recalled how as a boy of nine or ten I had often lain in bed, in the Milton bedroom with cowboy wallpaper, and compulsively repeated my nighttime ritual of prayers: *God bless Mother...God bless Dad...You have to say it four times.* I had to say it right—to check that it was right. *God bless Mother...God bless Dad...You said that...Now you have to say it again—four times...I did that...Just say it again and get it over with—four times...four times.*

Those were the childhood rituals of fretful fantasy. Now, in Lezlie's hospital room the thought of my possible loss of her was real. There were no magical rituals to rid me of this doubt; only the familiar medical rituals of hospital life.

Like a pendulum, my thoughts swung from reassurance to doubt. I was alternately engulfed in the tragedy of Lezlie's cancer and in a state of disconnect. The fear was palpable, then distant. Boyish thoughts—some quite silly—allowed the kind of momentary regression that sometimes happens in the midst of trauma. It occurred to me, as I slid between the cool starched sheets, that it would be a good practical joke if Pauline had Frenched them, as my bunkmates had sometimes done when we were boys at summer camp. I laughed silently at this welcome distraction. No one could know this secret escape—but the temporary relief was quickly pursued by self-recrimination. *How strange*, I thought. *Here is my life's love…perhaps awakening to intervals of pain between the clouds of anesthesia…and I am back at Camp Manitou.*

A soft glow of city lights mixed with the shadows. Lezlie seemed so remote. We were in the same room together and for a fleeting moment, the setting reminded me of our weekend love escapes at downtown hotels. This was no hotel room. The two of us were in it together but we were living in different realities. I lay in bed in a comfortable position with my head by the window and my body perpendicular to my wife's. Her hospital bed seemed to be at the other end of a Pullman car. At her end was a sterile intravenous drip of normal saline and a pump for self-administration of morphine. At my end, the remoteness and the comfort of cool sheets protected me from knowing what painful dreams she might encounter. Hers was now the world of disease; mine, a surreal spectator's world from which I reached out and then retreated.

Deprived of my glasses, I watched in a blur, as if through cataracts, while Natalie Ralston performed her private nursing duties. She was a wonderful nurse—caring, precise, and able to provide the comfort and safety that I did not know how to give my wife just now. Natalie's whites, starched like the sheets, were illuminated against the darkness. She was angelic.

It surprised me to view Natalie in this way, much as it had when I found her with Max and Alice before Lezlie's return from the operating room. I had always been fond of Natalie and had admired her nursing skills and dedication, but that was the sum of it. She was a handsome woman, but certainly not a heart throb. I could recall no special attraction or romantic feeling for her. There was, however, something distinctive about her, something that now proved galvanizing. What was it? I observed her with fascination—her poise. Her nursing cap caught my attention. She seemed to wear it proudly. Its distinctive style, like a coat of arms, symbolized the school of nursing where she had trained. I squinted at the cap, but it became a marshmallow that bobbed absurdly as she tended to Lezlie's post-operative needs. What was her role in this drama?

She looks so beautiful, with or without the marshmallow, I thought. *What is the matter with you, Owen?…How can you think like that?…Is this normal.?…*

Do others think like this while lying in their dying wife's hospital room?…What makes you think that she's dying?…She's not dying…She has had an operation—a successful operation…I hope she's okay…I want her to be okay…I want God to know that I want her to be okay (if there is a God)…If there is a God, I don't want Him to take her away—to make her leave me…to teach me a lesson for dreaming for a moment about another woman who is like the beautiful young woman that Lezlie was so many years ago…two decades.

That was it but I knew it then only slightly. It was an illusion. Natalie had become for me something other than who she was. It was like traveling along a road and seeing an object that becomes a car, and then an object again as you come near to it. Natalie was becoming Lezlie—not Lezlie in the present, but before, a long time before, in Montreal. Natalie had that same professionalism and warmth, the classic good looks and smile. The woman I was seeing without glasses was my wife of a long time ago leaning across the bed of my wife in present time.

Men think this way, I reassured myself. *Or do they?...What of the patients you've treated? What of their husbands—the ones who've sat lovingly, painfully, at the bedside? What would they think if I were exposed with these thoughts?*

I looked across at Lezlie's rhythmic breathing and wondered again what moments of pain might be breaking through. I felt helpless. I was aware of an odd feeling in my chest where my heart was, as if a knot of guilt were forming like a clot. *How would you know what anyone thought? You are a psychiatrist—but who admits these things?*

You're just another guy, I told myself, attempting to dissolve the clot. *But I don't want to confuse God about what it is that I really want. I want my wife...this wife...the one with ovarian cancer. I do miss how she was twenty years ago, but she is still the same one...I do not want her to go away from me.*

This was the way that I thought now...of Lezlie...then of Natalie...as if she were a new Lezlie, like the old one that I fell in love with gradually when we were young.

There was guilt, but also a liberating warmth in this glorification of Natalie. The process reminded me of my pre-medical undergraduate years in Montreal and how I had felt about the good-smelling bilingual nurses who gave me tender alcohol rubs at The Royal Vic during a three-week hospitalization for double pneumonia.

I remembered my father's gentle admonition when he had discovered me in the midst of some boyhood diversion. "You're going backwards," he would say.

I am going backwards. How odd.... I recalled how as a high school student in Milton, I had fallen passionately in love with another Natalie, a beauty pageant winner two years my senior. I would wrap my arms around her in nighttime fantasy while wrestling my libido to sleep. I had asked her to wait for me to grow up so that I could marry her, like Eugene Gant told his first love in *Look Homeward Angel*. I had often wondered what direction my life might have taken if those first imaginings of marriage had come to pass. My flirtation with Natalie Stillman ended one summer night on a South Shore beach, as I lay beside her and found my hand against her soft inner thigh. There was no resistance—although I looked repeatedly for it—expected it—as I replaced the tentative upward progress of my fingers with gentle kisses.

Pop!…There was nothing more than that. Only a sound—a popping sound—no odor—just an angelic little fart! "Sorry," Natalie said…And that was it.

What would have come of our making love? Would Natalie Stillman and I have married? If we did, would she be sick with ovarian cancer? Where was she now? Perhaps she was divorced—not a chance—or her husband might be dead.

We cannot know how it would be if our passionate daydreams became reality. Most likely there would be disappointment…an unanticipated pop. Fantasy is a bubble, doomed by the pinprick of reality. And what of reality? Would my life with Lezlie, the real life—the wonderful life—twenty-eight years of it—end like a youthful fantasy?

Ovarian cancer, spreading like a garden weed…choking out the beauty and all the effort, all the love, succumbing to a vegetative anarchy. After that I will be alone with foolish daydreams…What then?

I thought of my earlier encounter that evening with Max and Alice. They were old friends who had shared all of the important milestones—pregnancy, childbirth, independent schools, the failing health of aging parents. What would Max and Alice say in their private moments about my transparent reaction to Natalie as she settled Lezlie after her return from the recovery room? *At some point soon I would be alone—but Max and Alice would not be alone. We will be friends, but friends in a different way—because Lezlie will die and I will be alone, but they will be together.*

As I looked again now at Lezlie—across the chasm between us, I saw no sign of her stirring. *What dreams is she having?…Certainly not self-centered adolescent dreams…It must be because I was an only child….*

How disappointed she would be if she knew what an idiot I was…I love her, but I am still an idiot…definitely an idiot! Maybe she too has disloyal thoughts like mine about Natalie…No…She would never think this way…She thinks that I am her everything. She is my everything, too…I hope she is okay. But I don't want this to go on endlessly, in hospital beds…Forgive me!…She would forgive me…But that only makes it worse.

I wondered what my patients would think if they understood my wish for a clear outcome: recovery or death—no in-between. My entire professional life was about *in betweens!* As a doctor, I specialized in treating people with catastrophic illness. It was my goal to help them with the pain and to help them find new meaning. Why did I think that I was exempt from this suffering?

I remembered, shamefully, a discussion with a Sherborn neighbor whose wife had undergone not one but two liver transplants at one of the Harvard teaching hospitals. "I have some idea of how horrendous this must be for you," I said to him one day.

"Not at all," he replied. "Doris and I find joy in every day we have together."

Where was *my* fortitude? Didn't I always tell the transplant patients about the uncertainty, the risks of infection and rejection, the ups and downs from medication side effects? Did I abandon my patients to Nature's rollercoaster, then retreat to level ground for myself? I have always been afraid of roller coasters. It is painful to discover the dry hole of hypocrisy when one has spent a long time drilling for something in nature that burns clean.

All of these many thoughts occurred in rapid sequence. Only minutes had passed. Then, as sleep approached, my denial won out. Denial is the mind's hiding place. You can bury the fear and mine the fantasy. Lezlie's pelvic cancer, the "not-Frenched' sheets, Nurse Natalie, the pregnant couch, Pauline, the tragic-looking Scandinavian...all images in a dream. *It's going to be okay*, I told myself. *Millard is one of the best cancer surgeons in the country...It will work out.*

In nature, man alone can contemplate death. In life, man alone deceives himself in dreams of immortality and in revisionist reminiscence about events long past.

8

A CANCER WAR

o o o o o o o o o o o o o o o o o o o o o o o o o o o o o o o o o o o o
When trouble comes,
it comes not as single spies but in battalions.

—Hamlet
William Shakespeare

I think of her illness often, even now, four years after the first of her abdominal surgeries. Sometimes the memories are fogbound, and sometimes—if only for an instant—the remembering of it all is vivid and the emotions are still raw.

Memory of Lezlie's cancer war is the most vivid when my patients' stories lead me to reflect on things past. Then their stories mingle with my own life experience and I can see in sharp focus as if her illness has been a laser operation that gave me new sight.

In March, 1999, a longtime patient, Susan Canby, calls to set up an office visit.

"I'm just under a lot of stress," she says. "My back has been bothering me. I'm sure it's psychological." Susan is an erstwhile professional golfer who developed a lucrative career selling life insurance to Boston's business elite. She had initially enlisted my help after her father's death from lung cancer. Susan was on the golf circuit at the time, but the game lost meaning for her when she could no longer share it with him. Susan met with me weekly as she began her new career and then a new relationship that led to marriage. It had been two or three years since I had last seen her.

"Why do you think it's psychological?" I ask. She rarely complains of ill health. "Are you having any other symptoms?" People with psychological self-mastery sometimes prefer to think that physical ill health is imaginary.

"Well, I have been a little short of breath, but only when I overdo it."

Susan has always been energetic but never short of breath. She agrees to see her primary care doctor. Dr. Gentilly arranges for an abdominal ultrasound. "It shows the presence of a large grapefruit-sized cyst," he tells me. "There also appears to be at least a quart of fluid in the pleural space beneath her right lung." *No wonder she is short of breath.*

Ten days after her telephone call, Susan meets me in my office. She seems more like a close friend than a patient. I am pleased to be able to help her; also, I remember and was comforted by the concern she had expressed during Lezlie's illness. "I'm all right," she says now, leaning nervously toward me with her hands gripped firmly on the arms of her chair. She wants me to hear about the surgical opinion she had received and see that she is coping.

"Okay," I say. "What did he tell you?" *He* is Millard Watkins, Lezlie's cancer surgeon.

"Watkins looked worried," says Susan, nodding as she speaks as if agreeing with herself.

I study her intently and see the slight bulge forming in her abdomen. The association with Lezlie is unmistakable. *Susan Canby has ovarian cancer.*

"Are you all right?" she asks. Sometimes Susan asks if I am all right when she is troubled.

"Yes," I say.

"Just checking…" she says. "Well, he really looked worried!" she adds, purposefully. "After our meeting he gave me a hug and kissed me."

"Millard Watkins?" I say. "He kissed you? You're kidding!"

"No…He spent a long time with Bill and me. Dr. Watkins couldn't have been nicer. Anyway, here's the drill: it's almost definitely ovarian cancer. It could be benign, but basically he needs to get it out and do chemotherapy. I have a fifty per cent chance of living five years. What are you thinking?" she asks without a pause.

"Oh…I have a friend, a guy, who had a big cyst like that behind his bladder and it turned out to be perfectly benign." *You are talking nonsense, Owen.*

"Yeah…well…Consider the worst and prepare for it is how I think," she says.

"You're right," I say. *Which one of us is the psychotherapist?*

"Look. I plan to live. I mean I'm going to make the best of whatever it is. But I told him, 'I have a great marriage and we need you to help Bill and me have a lot more time together.'"

"How did he handle that?"

"Watkins was great…really great!…I mean, I've been his patient…I really love him…I almost wanted to say, 'Look, what is…is.' I don't want him to feel in any way responsible. Anyway, that would interfere with his ability to focus on doing the best job he can for me…. 'Here's the drill,' I told him. 'Tell me what to do and I'll do it!'"

There is good reason for Susan's faith in Millard Watkins. Years earlier he had detected and cured her of a potentially lethal cancer that another specialist had mistaken for a benign growth.

"Wow!" I say. "You really know how to talk to him. Millard is wrapped in five layers of barbed wire."

"Well…no wonder. Look at what he has to deal with. But I'll tell you, he really cares. You can see it. He really looked worried. He was just terrific."

"What happens next?" I want to know. I am thinking about Millard Watkins and the experience we had had together four years earlier with Lezlie's cancer. *He did the best he could.*

"Well, Monday, he's going to take the fluid out of my chest. Then I'll go home and he'll operate on Wednesday. He cleared out his whole schedule for me. I tell you, this guy really cares!"

"I like the way you sound," I say. "I think you'll do okay. I think you'll do fine! What did he tell you about the chemotherapy?"

"I don't know the names—I mean, it's one thing at a time—but I am going to lose my hair. And I just found somebody who really knows how to color it…It costs a hundred forty bucks. Gee, was I mad when I found out! I told Watkins, 'Why didn't I learn about this a week ago? I wouldn't have had my hair dyed!'"

Throughout the day I think about Lezlie and then about Susan. I stop in the middle of my evening rounds on one of the Trowbridge floors. The long corridor, identical to the one I so often paced, is empty. I take a deep breath, turn toward the walnut-paneled walls and sob.

My wife's debulking operation on April 25, 1994 had been successful. The postoperative course of that first admission was a nightmare. There were three complications. Two were inevitable. One was potentially avoidable. The possibly avoidable one, the kidney failure, might not have occurred had she received more intravenous fluid with the Cisplatinum chemotherapy. I do not know. In future years, however, the quality control would improve—even with the same surgeon and the same medication. They might be the same, but the treatment process would be different.

Awakening at six o'clock on Tuesday morning, April 26, 1994, postoperative day one, I was surprised to see Alex Godley, my childhood friend. In the long spotless white coat of a senior attending physician, he stood at Lezlie's bedside and leaned forward. He lovingly touched her hand and told her in his soft, always respectful voice that he had spoken with Millard Watkins. "The operation went well."

Lezlie nodded slowly at Alex's voice filtered to her through the sedation. Her own voice was a whisper. I wanted to interpret and to respond for her, but Alex's steady gaze made that unnecessary.

I felt sticky and unkempt in my prisoner pajamas, and heavy, as I was in the March family photograph. The hide-a-bed threatened to creak beneath me as I stirred. *It is Alex,* I reminded myself, and relaxed a little.

After a few days she will come home with me. There will be a respite…we'll catch our breath…then chemotherapy. It will be scary, but manageable. I thought, almost whimsically, of the Taxol she would be receiving and pictured it flowing from the yew trees of her native British Columbia—like sugaring off in Vermont.

Dr. Watkins next appeared with his team. He entered her room in the way that rounds customarily occur on a surgical service. The attending physician appears like a visible Elijah, the Passover prophet who comes to steal the matzah (the *ah-fee—c'oh-min*) that Jewish families pretend to hide from him during the seder.

It was a familiar routine. Millard would examine her abdomen and expose the wound to search for infection as if it were a villain lurking behind a curtain. The surgeon would ask how things were, hoping that they were fine, and sometimes pretending they were fine when they were not.

I felt distant during this process. As I sat on the side of my loveseat bed, there was a surreal remoteness to it all. I had been a hospital patient twice in the past, but never a family member in residence. This was different. I was twice a stranger; once with my wife, who now seemed to occupy another dimension of being, and also with my profession.

It was strange to be on the other side of morning rounds, the observed rather than the observer. *This is what a plainclothes cop would feel like if mistakenly arrested.* The tragedy for Lezlie and me was that it was not a mistake.

Millard nodded over Lezlie's wound, as if he were blessing it. He asked if I wanted to look as well. I arose awkwardly, then gazed dumbly at my wife's violated abdomen. I prayed that it would heal in a scar as had the incision that followed her melanoma surgery seven years earlier. There are scars and there are *scars*, in the way that there are military expeditions with definitive success and others with a muddle of trailing destruction.

Millard was encouraging but reserved. I watched his face as if I were a cryptographer; however, the code of Watkins' expression, well framed by his manicured beard, was undecipherable. For a brief time he seemed almost shy. *Maybe it's because I'm a psychiatrist...No...I wish it were that...It is because her chance for recovery is slim.*

The surgical team left us to the unknowable. I washed and returned to Lezlie's side. A flow of bile coursed through the nasogastric tube and the long connecting tube that drained her small bowel. It would be three or four days before she could take food by mouth.

Of all the procedures she encountered, it was the invasion of nose, throat, and esophagus that came closest to making me feel her discomfort. Seated at Lezlie's side, I remembered too well the irritation, the copious salivation, and the persistent nasal discharge that I had experienced as a medical student. When my fellow students and I had practiced nasogastric tube insertion, I was the subject of the experiment and suffered from our neglect to lubricate the tube.

Pauline was on duty and came in to help Lezlie wash herself, performing activities of daily living. ADL's is the medical shorthand. "Is that a rash?" Pauline asked.

I hadn't noticed it.

Lezlie nodded. "I'm a little itchy," she admitted. She was somewhat more alert and watched the nurse with the professional eye of a former nursing instructor.

"I'll get an order for some Benedryl. We'll see if that helps."

"That one knows what she's doing," Lezlie said, in a dreamy voice, after Pauline exited. It sounded funny to hear her say it, as if she'd taken a momentary station break to comment on the delivery of care.

That was her first complication. She was allergic to morphine. Later she would be allergic to Demerol, to Percocet...to opiates in general—whether natural or synthetic.

On that first postoperative day, I could almost feel the long tube that drained her bowel, but it was the rash that most alarmed me. The cardinal rule of cancer care is to maintain effective pain control. To do that requires strong narcotic analgesics and she would prove allergic to them all. Without pain control, she would be like Sarie, the woman from Kansas in *The Grapes of Wrath*, stricken with cancer on the road to California. "I'm pain covered with skin," was how she said it.

9

POSITIVE THINKING

o o o o o o o o o o o o o o o o o o o o o o o o o o o o o o o o o

*The mind is its own place and of itself can make a hell of heaven,
a heav'n out of hell.*

—*Paradise Lost*
John Milton

I believe in magic. As an only child, it was my boyhood refuge. Sinbad the sailor, magic carpets, genies, magic wands, Superman…these were my pretend tools and companions. I loved to explore the margins between what was and was not possible, to gaze intently at a family room lamp and focus ever so hard to try to make it levitate.

After medical school, I found a mentor, Klaus Zeal, a fabulous teacher clinician who was also a master of medical hypnosis. "There are three great feats," Dr. Z told me with enthusiasm. "To fly without wings, to talk to animals, and to heal with the laying on of hands." Unlike the traditionally passive analysts of his day, he entered the lives of his patients like a fireworks display.

Lezlie had shared my first adventure with hypnosis during those earlier years of my psychiatric training. "When I count to three, I would like you to picture a pleasant scene," I began in an affected monotone.

It was a simple induction and I never expected it to work. Then I noticed that she was behaving strangely. She extended her arms as if supporting a weight and looked at me with an absent kind of gaze.

"Where are you and what are you experiencing?" I asked hesitantly.

"Victoria," she said confidently.

"What is happening?"

"Party..." she said, "...in the garden." Then she extended her left arm toward me with its imaginary weight and reached delicately with her right hand for something—*God knows what*—that she seemed to want to give me.

Foolishly, I reached for the invisible item. *This is ridiculous. She's putting me on. I don't believe this. Where is she? What in the world is she doing?*

"You're at our wedding reception," I guessed.

Lezlie nodded. *She isn't faking. Now what do I do?*

"I'm going to count to five slowly (*slowly will give me time to think*). When I reach five, your eyes will open and you will be perfectly alert, relaxed and awake...Okay...one...two..."

Lezlie peered back at me with the same pleasant glazed look. Then she shook her head. *She's refusing to wake up...God!...Maybe this wasn't such a good idea...What if...?*

"Okay, I'm going to count to ten—I mean five—again and this time you will wake up. Okay...one...two...three..."

She shook her head again. *This isn't funny,* I thought. *What if she won't come out of it?...What will I tell her parents? 'Don't worry; it's a little error. Your daughter is going to be in a trance for the rest of her life'?*

"Okay," I said, with a diminishing sense of authority. "You are a wonderful hypnotic subject...This time you will open your eyes at 'five'...Otherwise..."

Otherwise what? You'll have to call Klaus. He'll think you're nuts, or worse, irresponsible. "Otherwise, I won't be able to do hypnosis with you again."

That worked! Lezlie opened her eyes. She looked like the same old Lezlie. *Thank God...I'll never do that again.*

We did use hypnosis again—often. It seemed to rid her of migraine headaches, but the ultimate event would be her first labor and delivery with Craig. "This is the only contraction...There is only one," I told her with each labor pain. "And when it's over you will have no memory of it...Good...It's strong and effective...Now it's subsiding...Good!...Think of a pleasant scene..."

Twenty-five hours after we arrived at Boston Hospital, she gave birth. Craig, barely alive, required resuscitation. The cord had been wrapped around his neck.

"How long do you think you were in labor?" I asked her the following morning. She was resting comfortably. The baby was fine.

"About three hours," she guessed.

I laughed and laughed. "You may think it was three hours, but it was twenty-five. I'm exhausted!" She had felt pain and had required an epidural near the end, but it was tolerable and our use of hypnotism had resulted in amnesia. She remembered almost none of it!

Now in 1994, in the spring of her ovarian cancer, we could always do hypnosis for pain, I thought. It was still postoperative day one, and it seemed endless. Pauline had given Lezlie the Benadryl and the itching had subsided. It was a short-term solution. The pain, the morphine, the itching, the Benadryl would recycle.

There was another reason to try hypnosis. Advocates of complementary medicine believe that *imaging* can help the body destroy cancer. I had used it frequently with patients and colleagues. There was Noel Forsythe, for instance, my colleague who had overcome an aggressive cancer with radiation and chemotherapy. Noel, an accomplished sailor, learned to perform self-hypnosis while imagining a microscopic harbormaster tuning up his immune defenses to destroy the cancer cells.

If nothing else, the process of imagining a cancer shrinking or under attack was a boost to morale. Hope might not cure, but every practicing physician knows it is hard to obtain a cure without it.

Now I began our familiar ritual. "I'm going to count to three," I told Lezlie. "As I do, let your eyes close and picture a pleasant scene. We could be in Victoria with the children…" Lezlie closed her eyes and imagined being in Victoria with her brother Rick. Hypnosis was surely not a panacea, but it seemed to help a little.

The second complication came at the end of that first postoperative day. It began as a low grade temperature. "She could have some *atelectasis*," Pauline said, referring to compression of tissue at the base of a lung that often resolves with a return to activity.

How is she going to get up and around when she's sedated with morphine and Benadryl and surrounded by IV's?

"I feel a little short of breath," Lezlie said in a weak voice. I watched her chest rise and fall and timed her respiration. Her breathing was more rapid than it had been and was taking greater effort. "I don't like it," she said.

"I'll ask if they want you to have some oxygen," I said. I knew why she looked so weak, but in another way her weakness perplexed me. People you love are supposed to be a certain way—not some other way. *She's such a strong woman. This doesn't make sense. She must be sick…very sick.*

It became important to me that her medical caretakers knew how unusual it was for Lezlie to look like this. They might think, "Well, this is the way this lady is. If so, then she is not sick…Maybe she lacks resolve, is giving in, or worse yet, giving up." I wanted to let them know, but would they listen—really listen? I thought about the surgical patients I had cared for over the years and how important it seemed to relatives that the team understood what the patient was like at baseline. I had been aware of that, but not of the intensity. I had never fully appreciated the intensity of those fears. *That will change now*, I thought, sardonically. *My wife dies and I become a better doctor.*

"I'm concerned," I told her nurse. "Lezlie's not herself. I know it's partly from medication, but she seems confused, more than I would expect at this point. She's normally very strong. I always tell people, 'You don't mess with Lezlie.'"

Pauline smiled.

"Really," I added. "And her breathing is a bit labored."

"I'll let them know," she replied. When she returned, it was to provide Lezlie with oxygen by nasal cannula. *She is a good nurse...what a relief.*

I felt helpless. Oxygen, Benadryl, hypnosis, loving nursing care, outstanding operative technique...but there was still something wrong. The low grade temperature, the weakness, the mild confusion...She must have a wound infection. *But what more can I do? I can't wake up the entire hospital and tell people, "Look, my wife has a wound infection. You've got to start her on something."*

I would have to wait. A surgical service can't function on the basis of a family member's intuition, even if the family member is a physician...**especially** if the family member is a physician. There are too many emotions that color perception when a loved one is ill. Also, a surgical service works like a military organization. There is a clear chain of command and an established routine. Disease is like war. One must choose between order and chaos. If she had an infection, it would declare itself. *I know all that, but I don't have to like it! So this is how it is....*

I would continue to fight this battle within myself. I knew that all the years and the times I had been able to help my family medically—especially to help Lezlie—had given me a sense of omnipotence. One learns to contend with that in psychiatric training. Nonetheless, I had always prided myself on my medical intuition. I had felt that way even as a young medical intern in Baltimore when I made rounds with fellow house officers. I could *feel* what was going on with the patients. It was a secret skill. Taking good care of one's patients takes more than practical knowledge and bedside manner; one must be able to recognize it when people are truly sick, and not just uncomfortable. It is important to relieve suffering, but, also, it is vital to make the right diagnosis.

Next morning, postoperative day two, the fever increased. At morning rounds, Dr. Watkins and his team reexamined her surgical wound. It was infected. Dr. Watkins cultured, then drained the infected site and ordered an antibiotic—Ancef.

Why does this have to happen to her? I wondered. I thought again about my transplant patients and the infectious complications that frequently occurred because their immune systems were compromised by anti-rejection medicines. We taught people to expect such complications. *But why Lezlie? She is not on immune-suppressing medication.*

I looked at my wife while her morning nurse applied a fresh dressing. Sometimes we see but we don't see. We have a concept, a picture in our head of how someone is, and we expect that to remain the same, or if it does change, to do so slowly. It hurt to *really* see Lezlie. How fragile she appeared. Free of the bloat from the ascites, she was indeed frail. I could see the weight loss by the prominence of her bone structure. Her complexion was sallow. Her muscle tone was diminished. Lezlie was very sick.

Now there was a new worry. "What's going to happen about my chemotherapy?" Lezlie wanted to know.

"I haven't asked anyone about it," I said. "I guess it will have to be delayed until the infection is under control. Do you want me to ask?"

"No," she said.

"We'll ask together."

Lezlie nodded. The way we talked was so different now, as if we really were at war with her cancer and embattled at the front line. At first I thought it was just her, the weakness and confusion, that kept us from the fluent exchange that was part of our life together. It wasn't only her, I learned. Slowly I began to realize that our conversations were displaced by the pace of events. As a couple we were one together and I was the healthy executive part. Like Samuel Beckett's characters, we were two aspects of the same entity. I would think repeatedly of Vladimir and Estragon in *Waiting for Godot*. Our children were immediately in touch with these events but one step removed, like a Greek chorus.

"I hope they know what they're doing," Craig said, when I telephoned him at Oberlin College. I called daily to keep him informed.

"We know what we're doing," I said, immediately regretting the pointed tone of my response. I wanted him there with us, and at the same time wanted him to stay where he was. His critical thinking was too bright a light.

My identification with Craig was powerful. Craig and I spoke with the same unfettered openness. We analyzed things in a similar way; we each had a native tendency to connect empathetically with other people, and we were both incompetent athletes. Why then was I feeling this annoyance toward him?

It was his portable spotlight. Craig's candor was now a burden because he made me see my own suffering.

It was easier with his sister. Kate visited daily after school and drove back on her own in her mother's Volvo, when I slept over with Lezlie at the hospital as I had for the previous two nights.

In a timely way, Katie had announced that year that she preferred to be *Kate*. It was an epiphany in her development and it came in time for her to take on a very new role. As I watched her together with Lezlie in the days and weeks that followed, Kate would have a new role as caretaker. She would become her mother's helper and protector, as if their daughter-mother relations were reversed.

"If there were one personality I could choose for myself, from all of the people I have met," I had written when the college entrance advisors asked for a parent's letter, "it would be Kate's." It was not to say that I favored her over her brother—it was more of a father's admiration for his daughter. *Equanimity* was the word that best described her, I thought. I did not know then that her appearance of calm was like a line of credit. She would pay later and at a greater cost.

There was another change that I began to notice. The children were less in my thoughts. All of our lives were different now. Before, everything that Lezlie and I did was focused on Craig and Katie. Now our family's focus was on their mother. Everything else came second.

My professional life took on a peculiar new routine. After spending a night with Lezlie, I would shower and shave in her hospital bathroom and puzzle over the safety bars, the elevated toilet basin, and the call-for-help cord that made me feel like an undercover agent in a country of sick people.

When fully dressed in customary work attire, I would take the elevator to the first floor and traverse the lobby to a second bank of elevators, then ascend to my office. It was a surreal process—the shift from a twenty-five mile commute to transportation by Otis elevator. I did have a momentary feeling of superiority and chuckled to myself about colleagues battling the early morning traffic.

10

GRAPES OF WRATH

o o o o o o o o o o o o o o o o o o o o o o o o o o o o o o o o o

By the pleasant lyres
And the siren's song, I conjure you
To cease your anger
And not touch the wall
That the bride may sleep in deeper peace.

—*Spiritual Canticle*
St. John of the Cross

On April 30, I returned from a day trip to a medical conference out of town. I felt refreshed but also guilty about my day's absence. I had always told family members of my surgical patients to pace themselves—that they would be of greatest help to a loved one if they took some time off. It is so much easier to advise others. I had parked in town a short distance from Boston Hospital and taken a cab to the airport, so it was easy to look in on Lezlie before heading to Sherborn for the night. Her wound infection was well under control and she was regaining strength. Dr. Watkins had begun chemotherapy. At last this was her chance to fight her disease. Alice Dewer stayed with her during her infusion as did her brother, Rick Humber. Rick had arranged to take a month's leave from teaching and came to stay with us on the day after her operation. He was determined, capable, and very loving.

It was her fifth postoperative day. Her bladder had not yet recovered and a Foley catheter remained in place to drain it. As Lezlie reviewed the day's events, I glanced at the transparent plastic container suspended from the bed rails. There was a small amount of urine—about 100cc with a clear light color.

"Have you been making much urine?" I asked.

"No...I don't know...not much."

I called for the floor nurse. Lezlie had produced only 300cc in the preceding twelve hours. I knew that kidney failure is a rare complication of chemotherapy with Cisplatinum.

Should I call Watkins? Once again I had discovered a complication before he was aware of it. He must have thought her urine output was adequate when he last made rounds. It was now 10:30 at night. Instinct told me that Millard would do nothing until morning. He would think I was overreacting—an anxious husband.

Of course I *should* have called Millard. He had told me to call him anytime. *But does he mean it?* I was also beginning to lose confidence. Dr. Watkins was the best. I kept telling myself that. But was he the best for Lezlie? He took too much responsibility on himself. I thought of General Patton charging across Europe in his armored division. I admired Millard's dedication, but I needed to have more than a one-general army. I was used to team medicine—with all of the specialists in place. Millard played solo.

Was I taking on too much? Doctor husbands are the most difficult. Everyone knows that! But her urine output is 300cc. Anything under 500cc in twenty-four hours is a sign of kidney malfunction. I've got to do something...God! What if she needs dialysis?...Well, if she needs it, she needs it. We'll do whatever we have to do. What would it be like to see Lezlie chronically ill with a disease that had always belonged to other people? What the hell do people do whose families don't understand about this stuff?

I called hospital information. "Please give me Dr. Witherspoon's home number." Dr. Witherspoon was the transplant surgeon.

"I hate to get you in the middle of this," I told my friend, "but I'm afraid that Lezlie is having some Cisplatinum toxicity."

"What is she getting for intravenous fluids?"

"Not a lot...At least I don't think..."

"I'll speak to the nurses."

"Thanks. I can't tell you how much of a relief it is..."

"I'm glad to help, Owen. That's what we're here for."

I felt myself shaking as I walked back into Lezlie's room. "It's okay," I told her. "I called Dr. Witherspoon."

"What can she do?"

"Anything she has a mind to."

Pauline was back on duty for the second shift. She had such a gentle way. She simply walked into Lezlie's room and sped up the IV. With more fluid, Lezlie's kidneys would open up. They did.

My intervention had been timely but it had a cost. When Lezlie's creatinine level came back the next day, it was 2.0. At least for that moment, 35% of her kidney function was lacking. It would improve steadily. The insult was mostly reversible and her urine output gradually picked up, but my relationship with Watkins would never be the same. He was the doctor, but we were both taking care of my wife. No physician finds that acceptable.

"There's always hope with ovarian cancer," Bob Best, my oncologist neighbor, told me when I next saw him. It was a phrase he would repeat—enough times to make me doubt it. I told him about Lezlie's kidneys.

"Kidney failure with Cisplatinum occurs in five percent of cases," he said. "I don't see it with my patients because I keep them well hydrated."

Good old Best! If he thought it, you heard it. He's just like Craig. "Does it ever come back...the kidneys?"

"Sometimes. Not always...not all the way back."

At least you're not crazy, I told myself. It was one of those lose-lose situations where I was glad I was right but wished I weren't.

I began to blame myself for mucking things up with Millard and in another way for not better monitoring her fluid intake. *If I had canceled my meeting and stayed in town I would have picked it up sooner...or maybe not.* Next I wondered about the hospital floor. Lezlie and I had chosen the luxury of private care. Should she have been on the cancer service? They would have been especially vigilant about this potential complication...or maybe not.

Self-blame, I reminded myself, is a way of attempting to get control as if by assuming responsibility you can go back and change something. So I concluded that the kidney failure was a result of medical error. Or was it? Doctors don't like to talk about their mistakes even when they admit them to themselves. It's part of the training—a deficiency in the training. Medical students are selected for competitiveness and are taught to strive for perfection. It is nonsense. There is no perfection in medical care, but for young doctors in training, errors become a source of shame. It's part of the system—not a good part.

I decided that Bob Best needed to be involved in Lezlie's chemotherapy and insisted that he be consulted.

"Fine," Bob said. "I'm glad to help, Owen, but you can't keep second-guessing Millard."

"Well, then, he's got to start getting things right," I said. "I understand that Watkins needs to be in charge of his case, but if I discover a life-threatening problem, I'm going to do whatever it is I need to do for her. You would do the same."

Best looked concerned. He could see that I was heading for a conflict with Watkins, who prided himself on his ability to provide total care for his patients. In most cases—almost all cases, perhaps—Millard's approach would have been fine. His way was an acceptable standard of practice and had the advantage that one person and one person alone, the man or woman in charge, could be on top of every aspect of a case. There was also a full complement of surgical residents and fellows who elected to train with Dr. Watkins—to take advantage of his wisdom before he returned to Canada. Millard wasn't truly on his own.

I complained to my friend Max. "It's a kind of *deux ex machina*. He writes the orders and bingo! Everything is great."

"Isn't that what the doctor is supposed to do?"

"Hell, no. This is a goddamn teaching hospital. There are consultants. Even the consultants have consultants."

"I hate to say it, but as a friend…" Max said, somewhat sanctimoniously, "do you think you're a little too close to this? I mean…"

I said nothing. I didn't have to. We both laughed, but I couldn't let go of my anger. It was there to stay, and not just with Max.

In my office, I often dealt with this type of emotion, but this wasn't just the office any more…it was me. I recalled once confronting one of my patients about her anger that was getting in the way of important relationships.

"Yes, I'm angry," she had said. "I have a whole *skein* of it!"

Maybe I am the problem, I thought. I could have called Millard that night instead of Dr. Witherspoon. Lezlie was no longer complaining about Millard. Neither was Rick. What did Rick think?…Probably that his brother-in-law was losing it.

Bob was right. I needed to give Watkins a chance.

11

HE NEVER HAD A CHANCE

o o o o o o o o o o o o o o o o o o o o o o o o o o o o o o o o o o

*Instead of blind submission to the incipient or
advanced stages of disease, rise in rebellion
against them.*

—*Science and Health with Key to the Scriptures*
Mary Baker Eddy

I struggled for some sort of middle ground. I wanted to let go, to stop trying to direct the march of events in Lezlie's illness and in her treatment. I wanted to make things right, to do whatever we could do for her not only at the cutting edge of medical practice, but also through force of will. *Could these objectives be compatible?* I wondered. Life is consistently inconsistent and so is the advice we give and receive. Once, while counseling a clergyman overwhelmed by the stress of his illness, I had advised him to "let go" of the struggle and trust to the "process" of his health care.

"We have a name for that," he told me, with some apparent relief. "We call it 'surrender.'"

Which was right?...to let go?...to be tenacious? The margin between life and death is where the greatest battles are fought. Serenity resides in knowledge and acceptance of what we can and cannot effect, but heroism is the unrelenting determination to stand against the odds. No enemy is defeated by force of will alone but none succumb without it.

I could find no middle ground.

Lezlie's brother Rick visited daily with his sister while I saw patients. I wondered what they talked about. There were so many old stories we had all shared.

"You know, I couldn't stand him," Lezlie had once said of the sibling her mother openly favored. "I really wanted to get rid of him. When Rick was three and I was six, I told him that if he believed hard enough, he would be able to fly. There he was one day, standing in front of an open window on the second floor, ready to jump. 'Stay right there!' Mother shouted. She had looked up and seen us as she walked into the yard."

"I remember the time that Mom got furious at Lezlie because she couldn't spell Oregon," Rick had recounted. "She came running through the house looking for an ashtray that said 'Oregon' on it. There was Mom, right behind her."

Mostly the two of them were sitting quietly in Lezlie's room when I dropped by for a quick lunch on the Trowbridge service, or when I joined them after finishing up in the office for the day. There was really no great need for words. The stories had become silent sharings. It was like that, too, with Lezlie and me when we sat together in the evenings.

I would come to Trowbridge 15, catch up on the day's medical events, and give Rick lengthy status reports about Lezlie's condition before Kate arrived with her mother's yellow Volvo and headed back to Sherborn with her uncle. Often I thought I'd said too much. I could see it in a look of puzzlement Rick sometimes had.

I needed Rick to know exactly what was happening. It was *my* need. I was trying to overcome the fear and uncertainty, to be in charge of events that none could master. I was vigilant about her treatment. Looking back, it was as if Rick were watching the play while I whispered my analysis like a theater critic seated at his side.

I knew that in an unexpected, irrational way, I felt responsible for Lezlie's misfortune. It was a feeling that led me to recall the time that Lezlie and I had vacationed in Bermuda and I had almost killed us both on a Moped. The bike was stiff and unresponsive, not at all like the motorcycle, the Honda "Dream" I had briefly owned in my youth.

I had confidently collected the motorbike near the Princess Hamilton Hotel where we were enjoying an idyllic week of rest and sunshine. Soon we were off on a breezy jaunt, driving on the left side as the Bermudians do. The bike was slow. I pushed it harder. *This is more like it.*

"Hold o-o-o-o-on!" I yelled. As I leaned into the curve of the road, I realized I was driving too fast. The bike wheeled off at a tangent like a spooked horse. Across the right lane it went, then into the rocks and gravel at the shoulder of the road. We bumped along as I held on with all my strength, trying to regain control. We were headed for a cluster of boulders the size of ten-pin bowling balls. I squeezed the brakes hard. The bike skidded to a stop. Over the handlebars we went, with Lezlie holding on to me as if I were a surfboard. I struck the loose gravel and slid across it with Lezlie still astride me. I remember thinking, *What am I going to tell her father?*

Uninjured, Lezlie attended me lovingly for four days as I recovered from the road burns like a fallen chariot racer. Somehow it was like that now with her cancer. I so wanted her to have that safe landing. I felt responsible as if it had been my duty to reach in for her ovaries before one of them turned cancerous.

Maybe I was trying to convince Rick and myself of how much I was doing and had done for her medical care. When things were going well, I was enthusiastic and determined. When things went badly, as often occurred, I groped for explanations and sometimes bemoaned the shortcomings of her surgical care. My conflict with her surgeon grew like the cancer.

"They're all good people," Rick said one day as we walked the Trowbridge 15 corridor together. He was a solidly built movie-star-handsome but unpretentious man. "They are trying hard." His communications were brief as if reserving his strength to hold back the tears.

A few days after the insult to her kidneys, Lezlie regained some strength. With characteristic determination, she did laps in the corridor—pulling the IV pole about as if it were a placard for a political campaign. Then she weakened again.

"She has a little temperature today," Pauline said. It seemed incredible to me that all of this was occurring in a single hospital admission. I had seen it before with others who suffered the complications of catastrophic illness. *So that's what it's like.*

"Why are you doing that?" Lezlie wanted to know. Her voice was faint again.

"You have a little temperature. I just want to have a listen to your lungs. Is that all right?"

"If that's what you want to do." Lezlie sat forward and helped me lift the back of her hospital 'johnnie.' Rick stepped out of the room.

"Hmmm."

"Hmmm, what?"

"Just hmmm."

"Don't be funny."

"I'm sorry."

"Is it okay?" She was perspiring.

She looks sick, I thought, *sick as opposed to not feeling well, but not a big deal.*

"Sure, it's okay. Does it hurt?"

"Does what hurt?"

"When you breathe in…Try it…Take a slow deep breath…Yes, like that. Does that hurt?" I thought about my own experience with pneumonia, how weak

I had been and how it hurt when I took a deep breath. It hurt at the end of breathing in, as if someone were pinching my lungs with a set of tongs.

"Yes...not a lot..."

"I think she has pneumonia," I told Pauline. I was grateful that she was on duty. If I were worried, Pauline knew there was something to worry about.

"Is Dr. Watkins on duty?" I asked.

I thought about how he had said, "Just call me. I'm there. Just call me." *He actually believes that—believes that he is always there. No doctor can always be there. If he just didn't think he had to do the whole damned thing himself.*

"Let's see. Mmmm...no...Dr. Jenkart is covering," Pauline replied.

I had forgotten that Millard was out of town for the day. Dr. Jenkart was the new surgical fellow. His would be like the theatrical role of understudy. *He'll think I'm second guessing...He will want to wait for Millard's return at morning rounds before making any changes in her care. You've got to trust him, Owen. You've got to give him a chance.* I debated with myself.... *Trust him...Don't trust him...*like a kid picking at a dandelion.

"I don't know, Pauline. As long as Millard's not around, I'd feel a lot more comfortable if we called Jane Newhause." Jane was an infectious disease consultant with whom I had worked for several years. Her judgment was impeccable.

"Do you want me to page her? I will if you want me to."

That was exactly what Watkins did not want me to do. Here was the patient's husband calling in his own consults. *But this is my wife!*

"You don't mind?" I asked the nurse.

"Don't be silly. I'll do it right now." Pauline's expression was like a yellow traffic light. "It's okay to keep trying," it seemed to say, "but don't expect too much." *Why does she always look so damned tragic?*

"Why?" Lezlie wanted to know.

"Why—what? Oh...the x-ray. Jane Newhause ordered a chest x-ray...to make sure there's no pneumonia. I don't think there is.... Just want to be sure." I was talking like Lezlie's primary care physician. *You're being a jerk. Lezlie just thinks you're showing off.*

"I don't want to go anywhere."

"It's okay. I'll go with you."

The corridor by the x-ray department was cool. While waiting, I thought of the loneliness and coldness that other patients might experience there. "If you don't have pneumonia now, you will before they are through with you," I commented.

"Can you get me a blanket?"

"Here's one."

"Another one."

"Is there another blanket?" I asked the attendant. "Thanks…Here's one. Is that better?"

"Where do they put the dead babies?"

"What?" I could barely hear her voice.

"Those…you know…the dead ones. Where do they put…" She was delirious.

"You're in the x-ray department. There aren't any babies here. It's okay. It looks like you may have a little pneumonia. Jane will order something for you."

"How do you know?"

"The radiology tech showed me the films. There's a little area of consolidation."

"What?"

"A sign of inflammation…Don't worry. Jane will take care of it."

We returned to the floor. I paged Jane Newhause and informed her about Lezlie's delirium. *Encephalopathy* is what I called it.

"We'll start her on some Unisyn," Jane said.

"Watkins will have a fit, but I just don't think this is something to fool around with," I said.

Jane did not respond immediately. Her silence made me wonder at first whether she thought that my bothering her was out of bounds. "I'll call the fellow," she said. "Don't worry about it."

I quickly fell asleep in Lezlie's room. The antibiotic had been ordered and was running in. Lezlie had some oxygen in place. She seemed more comfortable…sleeping. It would be all right.

Awakening in the morning in my usual state of sticky disrepair, I was aware of Millard Watkins making rounds with his team. He said nothing, but it was clear that he was very displeased. His patient was receiving a potent new medication, and he apparently knew nothing about it until he arrived on the floor.

"Jane Newhause thought it was best to treat her pneumonia," I said, somewhat meekly. "I was worried last night so I called her. You were off call…and…I hope that's not too much of a problem." I swallowed the end of the sentence.

Watkins shrugged. He was clearly not interested in my explanation. *But why? Sure, I called Jane, but the fellow must have discussed it with her and presented the information to Millard when they began morning rounds. The fellow doesn't have a big ego. Besides, he's there to learn and Newhause is one of the best infectious disease people at the hospital—or anywhere. It shouldn't be a problem…But…what if the fellow hasn't spoken with Jane? That couldn't be possible. Jane said she'd call him.*

*Jane **always** does what she says she's going to do. Watkins is angry. How angry? Whatever amount of anger, he's doing a pretty good job of covering it up.*

"Lezlie was delirious in the x-ray suite. There was consolidation on the chest film," I added. It was a final attempt to make peace with the cancer surgeon.

"I saw the x-ray this morning. They always overread those things at night," Millard said as he left with his team.

I couldn't blame him for being angry. Control of Lezlie's medical care was being wrested from his hands. *That is the way it has to be,* I thought. *Obviously he doesn't think she has pneumonia. But she does have pneumonia. You don't get delirious with fever and chest rales and pleurisy-type pain, and shortness of breath, and not have pneumonia...But he doesn't believe it.*

Next day I asked Jane about her communication with Millard's resident. "He never called me back," she said. "I did page him." Watkins would never know that she had made that effort. Soon it would not matter what he thought. Things between us were headed for disaster.

Years later I summered in Victoria. I sat with Rick and his family at our friend's lake. We sat on the deck, sipping a cool Molson and looking out over the private expanse of unspoiled Canadian forest. It had been a long time—over three years—since we had seen one another. He told me now, "I saw how you looked at Dr. Watkins when I first met him in her hospital room. It wouldn't have mattered who he was. He never had a chance."

I felt sad as I heard him. What would Lezlie say if she were there for that conversation? I knew what she'd say. If she were there, our experience with Millard wouldn't matter anymore. That would be in the past. We would be grateful for the present.

Rick was right. Watkins did not have a chance. It wasn't because I was bad or that he was in any way unskilled...It was because it was a bad disease. Lezlie had a bad disease, and nothing about it had gone right.

There was a benefit in knowing what I did know about her suffering, but it also was a burden for me and for Watkins. After the pneumonia incident, there were three more doctors involved in Lezlie's care: Dr. Witherspoon, the kidney surgeon; Dr. Best, the internist who specialized in cancer care; and Dr. Newhause, the infectious disease expert. It was not unusual to have multiple consultants in a major center like Boston Hospital, but it was unusual for this surgeon, and it was very unusual that they each were called in by the patient's spouse.

12

THE APPLE

o o o o o o o o o o o o o o o o o o o o o o o o o o o o o o o o o o
*He told me I would be surprised what suffering a man could
endure when he had no alternative."*

—*Faith of My Fathers*
John McCain

At last, after what seemed forever, Lezlie came home to Sherborn. Our family life reawakened like her perennials. The late spring weather was sublime. The forsythia made its sunlit appearance; the daffodils, the crocuses…and in May, the flowering crab apple trees, like prom queens in white and pink. The contrast to her two weeks in the hospital made our earlier concerns seem so overwrought—almost comic. Nature plays jokes when tragedy commingles with beauty. They are not funny jokes.

Back from Oberlin, Craig prepared for college graduation and his first year of medical school and Kate put the final touches on her last year at Concord Academy. The house in Sherborn was once again alive with activity; trips to the lake, movies on the VCR, family visits with my parents, and the children's customary wisecracks about my impromptu piano solos.

"Can't you do it softly?" Lezlie wanted to know. "You play so loud."

"You're just like Harry," I complained. "Whenever I used to ask what he'd like to hear, Dad always said, 'Play Far Away.'"

We had devised a special game for our black Lab—a kind of canine hockey. "Get in your nets," we would tell her. Shadow would crouch in the doorway between kitchen and front hall, then dart about like a star goalie as each of us in turn tried to kick a yellow tennis ball past her. Or she would lie on her back, with her black lips loose around exposed canine teeth.

"She looks like an alligator," I told Lezlie.

"She looks exactly like an alligator," Lezlie replied. "I can't stand the thought of losing her someday." It was a statement she would often repeat.

"She should have at least six more years," I said.

"Well, that's not very long," Lezlie countered. "I think we need to get another dog. Besides, Shadow needs a companion. It's fine in the summer when everyone's around, but after that she's alone all day."

The new dog was called "Bean," an energetic black Lab pup that hurtled about the house like a loose puck.

"I *bean* here before," I complained.

Lezlie's strength increased. She and Kate would shop together and bring back translucent kerchiefs that replaced the wig that Lezlie found to be so hot and cumbersome. Things were okay for a while. I continued my work at the hospital, but for the first time in years I was home for dinner. My colleagues were wonderfully supportive and I would tell them about Lezlie's illness, repeating the same stories as if I had become comfortably octogenarian.

One afternoon, my beeper sounded while I was finishing up a session in the office. As a consulting psychiatrist, I checked on each of my pages and responded when it was necessary to do so. I never liked it when my beeper went off. It made me think of myself as if I were one of those unfortunate experimental mice that the research psychologists had tormented with aversive conditioning when I was an undergraduate. The pager's intrusion was worse now that Rick and Kate were caring for her mom. I hate emergencies but none were as hateful as the ones that occurred at home.

I excused myself and answered my page. It was Kate. "Mom's having bad stomach pain," she said.

"Let me speak to her," I said.

"Ooooh!" Lezlie said. "It's really awful!"

"How long have you had it?" I could feel the sound of her pain high up in my abdomen, as if my heart were delivered into it by obstetrical forceps.

"About an hour. I can't talk."

Kate took the phone. "Mom thinks it's the apple she had after dinner. It didn't go down."

"I'll meet you at the emergency room at Leonard Morse. Do you think you can get her there okay?" I didn't want to say that it wasn't the apple. *We're not in Eden* was the thought that came to mind.

"Yes," Kate said.

Admission Date: 29 May 1994

> *Chart Entry:*
> *The patient complains of sudden onset of midline abdominal pain after eating an apple at approximately 6 pm on the day of admission. She had been tolerating multiple small meals, but had severe vomiting on the day of admission. She initially went to Leonard Morse Hospital, but was transferred to Boston Hospital for further care…Initially conservative management was attempted with nasogastric tube continuous suction, intravenous fluids, bowel arrest and pain control…*

The apple was not the problem. Millard had warned us that ovarian cancer surgery could sometimes be complicated by fibrous adhesions—string-like scar tissue—that binds the bowel and sometimes can obstruct it.

The diagnosis in her chart was "partial SBO"—incomplete small bowel obstruction. When it failed to respond to medical measures, there was a new, more ominous diagnosis: "SBO"—complete bowel obstruction. She would need repeat abdominal surgery to relieve it.

The worst part of it for me was the dizzying process of this illness. She needed surgery for the cancer and surgery for the complications of the surgery. Then there might be complications of the new surgery. That would require still more surgery. *What a stupid and inadequate way to treat disease. In a hundred years, it will be different. They'll look back and say, "Boy, were those guys dumb!" If only we could wait a hundred years—or fast forward. That would be a good trick, like A Connecticut Yankee in King Arthur's Court except with time moving ahead for Mark Twain's blacksmith instead of back to the sixth century.*

The worst part of that second hospital admission for Lezlie was the fear that she would miss Kate's June graduation. That was as painful as the bowel obstruction…more so.

She needed a transfusion of blood and platelets, the microscopic sandbags that protect the blood vessel walls from minor breaks. A double lumen port-A-cath line permitted the simultaneous delivery of intravenous nutrition and medication that flowed in together like merging traffic. Fluid contents of her bowel trickled through the long drainage tube. She was thin and gaunt, but unwaveringly determined.

"I'm going," Lezlie said, at last. She was determined to make it to graduation.

"How?" I asked. I knew, though, when she said it that it would somehow come to pass. It was always like that with Lezlie.

"I'll work it out," she said…and she did.

The graduation took place in a storybook setting on a broad expanse of green in front of the school chapel. It was a clear June day.

Kate had invited her boyfriend, Dana Marsh, and his mother. She was in Boston from Ottawa, a kindly red-haired lady with a fair sensitive complexion. Just prior to the ceremony, I had purchased a green chameleon-embossed Concord Academy umbrella and it opened above her now like a mushroom cap. She sat in a penumbral light between her son and me. It was the place where Lezlie should have been. I looked around and felt surprised to see so many healthy middle-aged women. Why had they been exempt from disease and not her?

My parents sat with Craig several rows back in the mottled light of a gnarled and ancient oak tree. Theirs was an uneven mixture of joy and sorrow—joy for the beauty of the day, sorrow for their daughter-in-law and the cancer that had invaded our lives.

Above the crowd of family well-wishers in sun-baked metal folding seats, the upper limbs of the old oak parted in front of the second floor library window where Lezlie sat—unseen.

I pictured her in my thoughts, as I always would, with her thin drawn face overwhelmed by the brown wig—it was a shade too dark—and the oversized tortoise shell frames that made her look like a little girl in grade school glasses. The ravage of ovarian cancer mocked her beauty. It would be easier for Lezlie to be out of the public eye. It was easier for me, too, as if I too were diseased when at her side.

Natalie Ralston was with her. Having given up a vacation day to be there, she organized the essential medical supplies as if preparing Lezlie for a sea voyage. Dr. Watkins happily wrote orders for an afternoon's leave of absence, and Pauline disconnected the tubing that tethered Lezlie to her IV apparatus. The long tube remained in place, draining the liquid contents of her bowels to rest them, although that would not prove sufficient to obviate another operation.

A buzz of voices rippled through the crowd. Supreme Court Justice Harry Blackmun had arrived and would soon give the commencement address. The senior class began its proud passage from the chapel to a stone patio that abutted the three *senior steps*. A random display of cameras flashed like fireflies amidst the cluster of chairs. An elegantly dressed lady seated to my right stood part way up while holding her hat in place with one hand and leaned gracefully forward to better see her son. I knew that she worked in publishing, but restrained myself from telling her about my first novel. It was to be an epic, like James Joyce's *Ulysses*. It would begin in the bathroom with the dream I'd had seven years earlier on the morning of Lezlie's operation for the melanoma...the cancer she beat. It would end with her recovery—with a YES! *Owen, it's a good thing you are a psychiatrist*, I thought. *You need yourself!*

After the procession, Mrs. Marsh and I ascended the steps to the school library where Lezlie had actively volunteered. The two mothers had spoken by telephone, but they had never been together.

"This is Lezlie," I said. "I'm glad that you are finally getting to meet each other."

They greeted one another with the pride and style of allied generals. "It's so nice to meet you," Dana's mother said in a forthright tone of voice that betrayed no apprehension about Lezlie's medical condition. "Kate is so beautiful."

Lezlie stood and smiled. Natalie Ralston was beside her. What a wonderful smile it was. Her eyes were full of life and mirth, as if she had been a ship's stowaway who had safely reached port. It didn't matter that she was in a hospital gown and robe, that she was so frail in her auburn-colored oversized wig, that a medical appliance collected the yellow green juices of her small bowel. Her smile and the joy in her eyes made all of that unimportant.

"Isn't it exciting?" she said.

13

LITTLE LEZLIE

o o o o o o o o o o o o o o o o o o o o o o o o o o o o o o o o o o

Two men examining the same question…bring minds impressed with different notions, and direct their inquiries to different ends; they form, therefore, contrary conclusions, and each wonders at the other's absurdity.

—*The Adventurer: No. 107*
Samuel Johnson

I had always called her "Little Lezlie." She was so thin—just under a hundred pounds—when we first met at McGill. It was a healthy kind of thin. I would weight lift at Molson Stadium, a block up from our Aylmer Street apartment building. Afterwards I liked to show off. Bending at the knees, I would slip my arm through her legs and hoist her over my shoulder in a fireman's carry—then march heroically up the three flights of stairs to my apartment.

I thought about that often as her weight continued to fall during her second Boston Hospital admission. "You look different," I would tell my wife in those endless days on Trowbridge, "but you are still the same little Lezlie."

"I'm a sick little Lezlie," she said.

That image of her will never leave. I am seeing it again vividly on April 9, 1999, at Susan Canby's return appointment. Susan has improved sufficiently from her debulking operation to plan a return to full-time work. I feel a profound tenderness for my patient as I sit across the blank office space that separates her from me and peer ahead into the past.

"People tell me they like my new hairstyle," she says, laughing.

"Yeah. I was thinking how to ask you whether this was yours or the new wig." I remember that Lezlie never liked her wig. "Too hot!" she used to say.

"I decided it's time to use the wig," Susan says. "It's coming out in clumps. I thought it would bother me, but it doesn't."

Susan's operation has gone remarkably well. She recovered rapidly on Millard Watkins' surgical service. I did have a brief scare when I went by to look in on her on postoperative day three. She wasn't there. "She went home," one of the nurses said. "She was doing aerobics in the corridor." The first phase of chemotherapy began ten days later.

"What do you think?" Susan says.

"You look good." I say it because she is so spirited and on top of it all. Also, despite the similarities in her appearance, Susan's cancer has not spread to her pelvic lymph nodes. There is reason to be hopeful because of that, and also because of a new and highly potent chemotherapy protocol that Bob Best is considering for her. "If it takes a nuclear bomb to kill her cancer, then give her the bomb," I told Bob. "That's what she'll want."

"The nurses said you were doing aerobics," I tell Susan.

"I was doing some stretches," she says. Her smile—always big—looks even broader on her new face.

It is the face of illness...a cancer face.

It is like seeing Lezlie seated across from me, as she had been after the very same kind of operation. Susan is alert, focused, and her mood is good. Her weight is down decidedly, and her complexion is beginning to have that white pallor that I never became accustomed to when Lezlie had this disease. Susan's cheeks are beginning to look somewhat hollow and her eyes look out with the intensity of a ground observer in an air war campaign. The weight loss, the pallor, the wig that looks too big for her face...it was that way with Lezlie.

"Why is your right eye wet?" Susan Canby wants to know.

"Oh," I say. "That's just me. It's always been that way when I meet with you." It is true. Sometimes in the course of the psychotherapy I do, there is a unique feeling that I experience like sharing a moment of epiphany. Sometimes in the course of treatment there are no such moments. Sometimes there are many. Susan is one of the ones with whom there are many.

"I know."

"This is different than it was with Lezlie," I say. It *was* different...the same, but different. It was the same disease and the same look, but Lezlie wasn't doing aerobics in the corridor on her second postoperative day.

"I can tell you think I'll be okay," Susan says. "You're only crying in one eye."

Sometimes the margins blur between what can and cannot be done for an aggressive cancer. There are unexpected outcomes in medicine; the potentially fatal cancers that spontaneously resolve, the patient who recovers uneventfully with aid of the very same treatment that may have failed for most who undertook it.

One difference in Susan's care especially pleased me. I was surprised to learn that Dr. Watkins had asked Bob Best to select and manage the postoperative chemotherapy protocol.

"He's learned," Bob said. In fact, it was now part of operating procedures for cancer care at Boston Hospital. The surgeon was in charge of the operation and perioperative care. The oncologist managed the chemotherapy protocol. Millard would bring the new procedure protocol with him when he assumed a tenured professorship that had been offered him in Western Canada.

The French have an adage that I have always liked: *Le plus ca change, le plus c'est la meme chose* (The more it changes, the more it is the same). I think now, however, that nothing is ever *really* the same. It may look the same, but that is as far as it goes. *Looks like* and *is* are no more the same than illusion and reality.

As Lezlie faced her second abdominal surgery for bowel obstruction, I felt a profound powerlessness. It was a solitary experience, as much as I tried to link arms with the children and with Rick. I knew that each of them was also feeling that same aloneness.

Boston Hospital: Chart Entry:

> *The patient was prep'd and on 6/11 went for exploratory laparotomy with lysis of adhesions, in which she had a gastojejunostomy tube placed as well. Findings were significant for peritoneal studding of the right diaphragm...The patient developed postoperative fever on day #2 to 3. The skin was opened and noted to have a pocket of pus and discharge, midline along the incision. The patient was initially started on antibiotics...With opening of the abdominal incision, and drainage of the pus, however, the patient's wound clinically improved quickly...*

The discharge summary was sterile. The wound was not sterile. Lezlie had a wound infection...again. Dr. Watkins and Dr. Jenkart, the surgical fellow, took down the suture line to establish drainage. Later, I stared blankly at the freshly exposed wound as Pauline redid the dressing. *My God*, I thought. *Dear Lord, it looks like the Grand Canyon. What have they done to her? What have they done to my dear, sweet Lezlie?*

"Hi," I said as I sat beside her and took her hand. There were beads of sweat on her forehead. It was from the fever.

Lezlie nodded her head. She didn't talk. It was as if she had removed herself from the destruction of her body the way prisoners of war do from their captors. The pain was back. She was in another of the procession of narcotic analgesics. It would be a day or two before the itching began again and the Bendryl. That had been the pattern of her allergic reaction to opiates.

"I guess it will have to stay open and granulate in from the bottom," I said about the incision.

"He said that," she answered. The wound would heal from its exposed base. It would be a slow process, but it would heal.

I thought about the beautiful summer weather that continued. When we got her home again, could she be in the garden? The wound would heal but she would be encumbered by the healing process. *It will be slow. It will take all summer.*

I could feel my anger toward Millard. It was building again. *It's not his fault, Owen. You've got to get on with it. This is what it's like. All the consults you've done, all the years. This is what it was like for the patients you saw and their families. I didn't know. Did I help them? Yes,…and now you'll help them more.*

Millard left town that afternoon. He was gone again. I felt a strange relief. "She's still febrile," I said to Pauline.

"Yes," Pauline said. I thought about how often she must have cared for her patients over the years. *How many of them died? A lot…Does she think Lezlie is going to die? Yes…Will she die? No…Yes…Maybe. Her cancer is more than eighty percent fatal. Then she'll die. She could be in the twenty per cent. That is unlikely. Don't give up, Owen. Don't let her give up. It's all you have.*

"Here we go again," I said to Pauline sardonically. "Off goes the surgeon. Up goes the temperature curve."

Pauline listened patiently—lovingly, I thought. Lezlie was dozing again. That was good.

"I'm sorry, Pauline. We'd better let Jane Newhause know about this."

Pauline nodded. "I'll take care of it," she said. "Don't you worry yourself about it."

How wonderful she is, I thought. *They are all wonderful—the nurses, the surgical team—all good people. And Millard? Is he a good person? Yes, he is, but such a godawful pain-in-the-butt.*

"She needs IV Vancomycin," Jane Newhause said.

"Watkins will be nuts about it."

Jane shrugged. "That's what she needs." She wrote the order.

Would Millard have started the Vanco had he been there? I didn't know. It was his hope that good drainage would be sufficient to cleanse the wound. *Maybe he is right,* I thought. *No, he's in denial. He doesn't want this to be happening. She's having every conceivable complication. This won't heal without antibiotic treatment. That's why I called Jane…Was it the right thing to do? Of course, it was…It was the right thing to do. Watkins will have to live with it.*

Millard would choose not to live with it. It wasn't denial. He was convinced that strong antibiotics were trouble and should be avoided in Lezlie's situation. Strong antibiotics can lead to infection with resistant strains of bacteria. In many instances, he would have been right to hold back, but then Dr. Newhause would not have begun them. This was her field of expertise. More than that, for Jane…her life's work.

"It's good to see you walking around," Natalie Ralston said. She had once again done private nursing for Lezlie on the night shift, for the first two days following the new operation. She continued to come by and look in. I continued to be embarrassed about noticing her.

Lezlie smiled. It was that same broad smile that Susan Canby would have almost exactly five years later.

"My CA 125 is down," Lezlie said. The CA 125 was a good measure of cancer activity and had improved with two cycles of chemotherapy. As bad as things had been, she was getting stronger.

"She's pretty tough," I said. "No one messes with Lezlie."

Lezlie rolled her eyes.

Natalie laughed.

"He's ordered lamb chops again," Lezlie joked. On the private service one could order virtually anything, and broiled lamb chops were the best. It was a celebration of sorts.

Craig was back from Oberlin now. His grandmother and I would join him at graduation ceremonies later in the month. My father was having his own challenging time in his ten-year battle with transitional cell cancer of the bladder, but it remained under control. Lezlie did not talk about attending graduation this time. She was a William James kind of person, the ultimate North American pragmatist.

Rick had returned to Victoria after spending a month with us. He would rejoin us when the school year ended. He was indefatigable and loyal beyond measure.

Kate came by and we all raided the private kitchen together. It was another privilege of this type of private care. When Kate came to the hospital she did so joyfully. "You must be proud of your children," the nurses would say as did our friends who visited. It gave Lezlie and me a good feeling to have Craig and Kate so selflessly involved. It was a good part of a bad thing.

"Well," Millard Watkins said when he returned days later. "You look like a lady who needs to be out of the hospital." He did not talk about the antibiotics, but when she went home, he discontinued them. He did not need Jane Newhause looking over his shoulder. He was the cancer surgeon. He had been here before.

14

HANDCUFFS

o o o o o o o o o o o o o o o o o o o o o o o o o o o o o o o o o o
Each man kills the thing he loves. By each let this be heard.
The brave man does it with a sword…the coward with a word.

—*Reading Gaol*
Oscar Wilde

Lezlie was at home again. She managed the abdominal wound with little comment other than to note that it looked clean and it was healing. There was no lamentation for Lezlie—no "what if's" or "if only's." Instead, she turned her attention to Bean, the new black Lab puppy. I thought it a terrible nuisance to have a puppy when there was so much to be done. But it was a clear pleasure for Lezlie and a favorable distraction for the children—not that they were exactly children anymore. Tragedy is like a fracture, a break in the structure of living. After a fracture, new bone forms in a spindle shape that unites the separated parts. Then a reshaping occurs and it is stronger. "What doesn't kill makes me stronger," was how Frederick Neitzche said it. It was one of my father's favorite quotes.

Craig and I left for Oberlin with my parents after Lezlie's second homecoming. It would prove to be a short homestay. We could not know that then. Things were better and we lived day to day.

Craig continued to learn as much as he could about ovarian cancer. He knew that Lezlie's chances for recovery were poor. Of all of us, he seemed most open to that truth. Lezlie did not talk about death, as if it were not an option for her. Her work was not yet done. She had always said of death that it happens "when your work is done."

It was hard for us to be at Oberlin without her, but the graduation went well. I watched with a sense of triumph for our son. He had sufficiently overcome his attention deficit disorder to be nominated for Phi Beta Kappa. The little boy that his mother and I had worried so much about was awarded high honors in neuroscience. More than that, he had entered manhood, which comes to boys who truly value others beyond the extension of personal need.

Craig had become active in the Oberlin mentoring program. Craig, the boy who liberated housebound moths on summer nights in Sherborn, had spent hours helping Jesus with his studies and advocating for him at the local middle school. After graduation ceremonies, the family of his "little brother" invited us to a farewell barbecue.

"We will miss him," Mr. Esperanza said. He shook my hand warmly and gazed steadily at me in a kind of visual punctuation.

Mrs. Esperanza nodded in agreement. "You son huz bin wun'fill wi' Jesus." She pronounced her boy's name as if she were saying "Hey Zeus." She regretted that my parents were unable to attend—it was too much for them—and she was sad about Lezlie.

The Esperanzas put out a full spread—ribs, chicken, hot dogs—enough food for a Red Cross relief effort. A neighbor lady and one of Jesus' friends came by. There was a gentle honesty to their lives that reminded me of John Steinbeck's advice: When you are most in need of help ask someone who is poor. *It would be nice to live next door,* I thought.

We returned to Sherborn and to our family's evolving routine. Lezlie's illness seemed to have a kind of chronicity that became a part of the way things were for us all. It is like that with illness. One adapts. I had known that before—but not so well.

My work was a refuge. The best approach to feeling powerless is to lend power to someone who needs it. My colleagues would stop and join me in the office when the door was open. They said little but listened a lot. My patients were equally thoughtful. Sometimes I wondered if I were performing optimally for them, but I learned that there is a subtle boundary between the personal life of a professional and the public's appraisal of the professional's worth.

I recalled an interview I had over two decades earlier when applying for a prestigious resident training program. "What do you think," the interviewer inquired, "about people with psychiatric problems who wish to become psychiatrists?" My interviewer had a prominent facial tic. His office was bare and I thought it seemed depressing. "I think they shouldn't afflict patients with their own problems," I carelessly responded. I was not accepted into the program.

Now, I called home frequently to check on Lezlie. "How are you doing?" I asked one day. She had been home from the hospital for no more than a week.

"Not great," she said. "I have a temperature—just over a hundred. The visiting nurse is coming later. She can check it for me again."

"I think we should let Dr. Watkins know," I said. "I love you."

"I love you, too," she replied.

"He's in the OR," Millard's nurse said when I called him.

"I'm not sure how important he'll think it is," I said, feeling awkward about invading his busy schedule, "but Lezlie has a low grade temperature—100.2 It's not very much, but she has a history of infection and we're following things closely."

"He'll call you," the nurse said. She knew the case.

"Have him call Lezlie," I said. "Her number is…"

"We have it," she said. "He'll be sure to call her."

It was a busy day. Sherborn is an hour's ride from the major Boston hospitals. I arrived at home a little before 6:30. Prior to Lezlie's illness, I often got home at ten or eleven o'clock at night, occasionally later. Now I felt guilty about arriving after six. Often I felt I shouldn't be in the office at all. It made me feel especially guilty to know that I wanted to be in the office.

Georgia Brook, the visiting nurse, was still with Lezlie when I arrived. Lezlie looked ill, feverish. "Did Dr. Watkins call?" I asked.

"He said to bring her in the office tomorrow. He'll be away lecturing. Dr. Flowers—I think the name was—will see her." Reginald Flowers was a nationally known attending surgeon who often swapped coverage with Millard. I did not know Flowers well, but had liked what I'd seen and heard of him. Unlike Millard, Reggie also had a general gynecology practice. That was even better. *Perhaps we should have used him in the first place.*

Tomorrow she'll be dead, I thought. I did not have to say it aloud. Georgia could see it on my face. Lezlie was too ill to notice. She was anxious—atypical for her—and her pulse was slightly elevated.

"What is her temperature now?" I asked.

"One hundred point five," Georgia said.

"Can you check it again?" I could feel myself shaking inside. It was part fear, part rage.

"I did," Georgia said, "just as you were coming in…"

"I'll call Dr. Flowers," I said. "Can you stay a few more minutes—is that okay?"

"Please," Georgia said. "I want to do everything I can." She meant it.

"Oh, hello…Reggie?" I spoke into the phone, surprised that Dr. Flowers responded to my page in less than five minutes. "This is Owen Surman. I think

Millard has told you about my wife. You're covering for him, right? Great. Well, her temperature has gone up since he spoke with Lezlie's VNA nurse a short time ago. Now it's over 101....You may know she has had a recent wound infection and is off antibiotics. I think she needs to be seen as soon as possible...Okay...Wonderful. I'll bring her right to the emergency room. Thank you so much. I can't tell you what a relief it is. Well, I'm glad you think so, too. We'll be right there."

"We're going to the ER," I told Lezlie. She looked alarmed. I had momentarily forgotten that she was no longer processing things the same way I was. She was too sick.

"I don't want to." She began to cry.

"You have to," I said, incredulous. I could not recall when I had last seen her cry. It was something she did very rarely. *What if I can't get her to go? Nonsense.... Just take her...and do it quickly.*

Georgia hugged her and wiped the tears and the sweat from the fever. She helped us to the car.

ER's are fast when you are dying, slow when you are not. Dr. Jenkart came by. It was four a.m. "We're going to admit her," he said, matter-of-factly. It could as well have been four in the afternoon. Good surgeons make it look easy. "I'll get a consult from Jane Newhause in the morning."

"I'd like you to call her now," I said.

"Now? But..."

"Don't worry," I said sardonically. "Jane will be upset if you don't wake her up for this." It was true.

"It's okay," Jane said. "I'm glad you called."

"Can you imagine waiting for tomorrow? She'd be dead...I don't know what Watkins is thinking about. He's giving a lecture somewhere. Who cares?"

"I've ordered IV antibiotics for her," Jane said. "I'll be by to see her soon." Jane's hospital day started at six a.m.

"I love you, Jane. You've been so wonderful all through this. You know he stopped the antibiotics that you ordered for her wound infection."

"We'll take care of it," Jane said.

Later that morning Lezlie was once again safely on the Trowbridge private service. "I don't understand Watkins," I said to Pauline, who continued to be Lezlie's primary nurse. "Is he trying to kill her?"

"I don't think that," she said. She was comforting as always but her expression had a "let's get real" element to it. "Although this certainly is hard for you both."

"What do you think of Reggie Flowers?" I asked.

"Well, I'm a bit prejudiced…He's my doctor, but I think he's good. He's very good."

"I know he works closely with Alex Godley. Alex is an old friend from our childhood days in Roxbury."

"Oh, I didn't realize you were from this area," Pauline said pleasantly. "Dr Godley always looks in on Mrs. Surman. I know he's very fond of you both."

"I'll call Alex," I said. "I've had it with Watkins. We're getting rid of him," I told Lezlie. "He's through."

Lezlie was feeling better. Her fever was breaking. The IV antibiotics were running in. *Just in time*, I thought. *Just in time.*

She nodded. I looked twice to be sure I wasn't imagining it. She didn't say yes or no…just nodded. "Can we do that?"

"What do you think about Flowers?" It sounded silly, like I was asking about funeral arrangements. *Cut it out, Owen.*

"Fine," she said. "I like flowers."

"You always have," I joked.

"Yes," she said. Then she smiled. "I know you'll take care of everything. It's why I don't have to be afraid."

I squeezed her hand and cried.

"Reggie? Did Alex Godley talk with you? Oh, he did…good. Look, I'm sure you can understand. Can you take over Lezlie's care?" I had spoken to Alex with Lezlie's approval. It would be a bit awkward for him but he was her gynecologist. He wasn't a cancer surgeon. Flowers was both.

"Okay, Owen," Reggie said. "But you'll have to tell Millard first. We go way back."

"Sure," I said. "I understand that he is technically brilliant, but right now I'd gladly pay his one-way plane fare to Canada." I immediately regretted the comment and wondered if Flowers, too, would think of me as an interfering husband.

Once again Lezlie was recovering. I was amazed at her resilience. *She never gives up*, I thought. Once again the kids were in to visit. We had gotten a rush order on my photos of Craig's graduation. Craig and his mother went over them together like a quarterback and his football coach. I ordered the broiled lamb chops.

"Yes," Watkins said, when he came back to town. I telephoned him as soon as I could. "I know she's back in. What we have here is an FUO, a fever of unknown origin. Changes?…What kind of changes?"

My face flushed. I could feel my heart rate accelerating. *It's those Eastern European genes*, I always told myself. I had always marveled at Lezlie's graceful way of expressing discontent. She had that old English waspy grace that I so admired. *We are who we are,* I thought. *You're not a WASP, Owen…*Lezlie was an aristocrat for us both.

"I've asked Reggie Flowers to take over Lezlie's care," I said. *Why are you doing this,* I thought. *Don't you know that in the end it won't matter? Yes, but it matters now. I know he wants to do what's right for her but….* "Look, Millard. It's a tough case. I know it's not easy on any of us…"

"Yes…" His voice sounded hurt but icy.

"We just have a problem working together. I need to be actively involved in my wife's care and to have my colleagues whom I've worked with for twenty years…longer than that…involved. You like to run your own show. That's just the way it is. I understand that. So I think we need to part company and move on."

"I don't understand what you're speaking of. Which colleague are you referring to?"

"Jane," I said. "I'm talking especially about Jane…Look. Lezlie had a wound infection—two of them. Jane began her on Vancomycin. You came back from the Mayo Clinic or wherever it was you were lecturing, and you stopped her antibiotics. Now she has a fever. It's not of 'unknown origin.'"

"Jane Newhause doesn't have all the answers…" Millard cut in.

I think he should stop. Why doesn't he just give this up? I'm not just a colleague who is questioning his judgment. I'm the husband of a woman who is going to die. Maybe it would be better if she did die now and avoid the pain of what's coming. I don't know. If I hadn't called Flowers it would be over. I don't know what to think. It's grief—pure anticipatory grief. I'm trying to be respectful about this, but…

"I know about infectious disease. I did a rotation in it for a month. These are dangerous drugs, especially Vancomycin…You…"

"Millard…" I paused to think about what I was about to tell him. *He did a rotation twenty years ago and that makes him as much of an expert as Jane, who is respected internationally?*

"Years ago, as a medical student," I continued, "I wanted to know if I'd make a good surgeon. I met Gilbert Adams. He was chief of surgery at Boston Hospital and was annoyed at me for dividing my loyalties between two summer jobs. Professor Adams' advice to me was 'it's better to do one thing well than two things half-baked.'"

"And?"

"There's one thing that comes first for me, above everything else, and that's my family's welfare. I will do anything…go to whatever lengths to do the best for Lezlie that I can."

Millard was speechless—no doubt white with anger.

It's his own fault. He could be more gracious than this. Why doesn't he just get on with it? He knows Flowers…. Who cares if he steps in for whatever time she has left?

His composure was gone.

"It's a privilege not to care for your wife," Dr. Watkins said. "My hands have been tied from the beginning!"

There. He's said it, said what he felt. You're a psychiatrist, Owen. His ego has gotten ahead of him…What? Did you hear what he said? No Boston doctor would make such a comment. This is an outrage.

"Millard," I said. I wondered what was coming next. It wouldn't be something that I'd stop and give a lot of thought to. "When I was a medical student, I spent some time doing research in one of the surgical labs at Harvard Medical School. I enjoyed the surgery—really liked it…It just wasn't the right field for me…But when I did the wound closures, I put in my sutures—one at a time."

I heard Millard catch his breath. He gasped. It was over. What I'd said to him in medical code was "I've taken better care of dogs." It was a sadistic comment. I could have said nothing more cruel. Did he deserve it?…No. I was angry beyond reason…More than that. As we spoke I pictured Dr. Jenkert taking down the suture line to drain the infected wound from her last operation…saw a single continuous suture line that came out like a slip knot…saw the wound red and raw gape open like a sliced watermelon. Did Millard help take it down? I wasn't there. Should he have placed individual sutures? I didn't know.

15

TO HAVERFORD AND BACK

o o o o o o o o o o o o o o o o o o o o o o o o o o o o o o o o o

The conclusion I've come to is the cosmic force of timing. That's the lesson I learned…There's a celestial clock with gears within gears and wheels within wheels and individuals spiraling through life. I don't know if I can explain it, other than when it's time, it's time…

—*"Nov. 22, 1963: The Day I Died"*
<u>The New York Times Magazine</u> *November 21, 1999*
Vaughn Meader

It is November, 1999. Susan Canby called last Friday—the fifth—and left a message on my hospital voice mail. "Hi! It's Susan." Her messages always begin that way, as if she were about to reveal some new discovery as vital as life itself. "Things are great. We're back from Hawaii. Everything is fine. Dr. Best checked my CA 125. It's under ten! Everyone is thrilled; they were practically dancing at the clinic. I'm really in remission…"

I know she has been doing well. Susan has finished a grueling course of chemotherapy, the "three-by-two" protocol—three courses of treatment each with two cytotoxic agents. "And I only missed three days of work!" she said in our last office visit.

"This is a bad time for you," Friday's message continues, "but it's good to hear your (recorded) voice. Give me a call when you can and we can set something up."

A bad time? What?…Oh! She remembered…Incredible. For a moment I feel guilty, as if my lapse of memory were an act of infidelity. It is the anniversary of Lezlie's death. Five years. I had put it out of my mind this morning. The reality of death is unimaginable and it feels best to leave it that way. There comes a time, however, when you are closer to the end than to the beginning...or a time when it is past the end for someone dear to you. For Lezlie, it is five years past the end.

The remembering hasn't ended. It seems like nature, too, has been leaving voice mail. That same Friday night, Gordon Chambers called from Victoria. I have not heard from him in several months. November is also the anniversary date of Sandra, his wife's death. Sandra was Lezlie's childhood friend who died fourteen years ago of pancreatic cancer. I often think about how similar the two cancers had been, both deep in the abdomen and elusive to early detection...both killers.

Gordon and I are an odd match. I, the intellectual...he, the erstwhile international rugby player. Emotionally, we are brothers-in-law. There is never much to say...perhaps a joke or two...and some talk about our children.

On Tuesday, November 9, I see my friend, Alex Godley, the gynecologist who diagnosed Lezlie's cancer and dutifully visited her at 6:15 each morning of each hospital stay. I am waiting in the coffee line when he greets me. "Owen! How good to see you," he says. "You know, this is so strange. I was thinking of you last weekend. We haven't seen each other for a year. My wife has been after me to clean up my study...You know I keep all my work there...And, while sorting through things, I saw the videotape of Lezlie's funeral. You had given it to me, and I kept it, but suddenly there it was...Tell me...how are you doing?"

"How funny life is," I say. "Last Friday was the anniversary of her death."

"No-o..." he says.

I watch Alex's face intently, like a tracker, searching for the memory traces of what we two had shared during her illness...the pain...the conflict with Watkins...the relentless progress of the cancer...I remember how he would look at me during the bad times, as if my appearance was a naked window to the deepest feelings of helplessness.

"Did you see the *Boston Globe* on Monday?" I ask. "The Health Sciences section was all about ovarian cancer."

"Yes," he replies, self-consciously, I think, as if acknowledging the inadequacy of what we could do for her then. We part without mentioning lunch. We have always been planning to meet for lunch, but it has been seven years since we actually dined together. Perhaps now we didn't mention it because there was a reason not to meet—a reason beyond the demands of our schedules. I think that neither of us want to revisit that other time. There is also the matter of my writing. I have told some of my colleagues about this memoir. I have not told Alex. It would be like stepping into an emotional wind tunnel.

Judy Foreman's article in Monday's *Globe* reads, "Cutting edge drugs are a must in treating rare cancer." It addresses the challenge of early detection and the discouraging rate of cure in those with advanced disease. Foreman is nonetheless optimistic..."Better chemotherapy drugs, however, and equally important, a much better understanding of how best to combine and administer them, are beginning to make a dent in those numbers..."

As I study the piece, I recall Bob Best's words, "There's always hope with ovarian cancer." Now I think there is much more hope. I wonder if Craig, too, has seen this article. Of the three of us—Craig, Kate, and me—Craig has had the hardest time in each of the Novembers since his mother's death. He is the most demonstrative about his grief and he sometimes seems perplexed by the renewed vigor of my activities.

On Sunday of this week, Craig joins me for dinner with my mother at her gracious retirement home. He is angry...accused me of avoiding the topic of his mother's death. I recently returned from a speaking engagement in Japan and am eager to share the photos I had taken. Craig says, "You're running."

"I'm not running," I answer. "Damn it! This is my job. This is what I do, Craig. I'm living my life." It is easier now to see Craig when it is just the two of us. If we are with his grandmother or if Kate is with us, then it is a family time and Lezlie's absence is most evident. Families with trauma have a memory for it that bubbles to the surface like a sea monster. I hear of it in my practice...stories of holiday get-togethers that revive the old grief, the conflicts, the failed expectations.

"I don't care. I need to talk to you. I need to know what you're thinking—how it's affecting you...I'm just doing what she said to do with you," Craig replies. Then he repeats his mother's advice. "Yell at him...Harass him...Tell him he's wonderful...Tell him he's the greatest in the world...Tell him he's the weirdest in the world."

Craig looks like a shipwreck survivor...disoriented, fearful, grateful to be alive...searching for something to hold to...grieving. He speaks in her voice with words he tape-recorded during his mother's final hospital admission, before she came home to be with us as long as she could. *How much of it has he memorized*, I wonder.

"What if **you** died?" Craig says.

My mother listens and quietly shakes her head. "I miss your grandfather, too," she tells Craig. "But I don't always talk about it." Twenty months after Lezlie's death, Dad succumbed to the bladder cancer that he had fought for twelve years.

I excuse myself from the table and lead Craig to a private sitting room. I try to console him. "It's no use," he says, sobbing. "Nothing helps. She'd dead. It's awful."

Later, after I return home, I find a copy of the written transcript I made of Craig's interview with his mother: "So I leave you to partly watch over yourself," Lezlie said. "I want you to support Owen the way you always have…No differently. Don't change…Tell him you can't believe he said that. Tell him that was the best thing he ever said. Just be always with him the way you are now because that's what really helped him…"

I cry as I read it. I have never stopped thinking about Lezlie. *Do the children know that?* I wonder. I do tell them.

Lezlie was the craftslady who knit together the elements of our family. We were separate now. "When she died," Craig says on Sunday, "you said, 'I'm your father and your mother now…'"

"I'm not your mother," I say. I listen with an empty feeling and wish that I could be her, too. The separating of us all is a part of the way things must be. Growth is a mixture of loss and fulfillment.

In August, 1994, near summer's end, Lezlie and I visited Haverford with Katie and helped her organize things in her dormitory for the start of freshman year. Later she would poke gentle fun at me. "Can you imagine?" she would tell her friends in my presence, "There we are on campus, and he decides to lie down on the grass, stretch out, and read his *Barron's*…"

That was the fun part of our reminiscence…It was a hard time. Lezlie had been in Boston Hospital a third time in July—that time for infection. She had a viral infection called CMV and a more troublesome gastroenteritis with debilitating diarrhea from a bacterial infection, *clostridium difficile. C diff* is a known complication of antibiotic treatment in susceptible hospital patients…Millard Watkins had not been crazy when he said that antibiotics were dangerous. It is just that there is often no successful alternative.

The CMV (cytomegalovirus) and *c diff* responded to treatment. It was the third time she had spent two weeks at Boston Hospital. The great chasm in her abdomen was healing—bridged with healthy tissue—but the bad run of complications had been a huge ordeal. When Lezlie came home that third time, she looked like someone who was running out of life. I wondered if she could see that in herself. She rarely spoke about dying. When she did so it was not about her going but about my being left. Also, she was determined to help Katie get settled at Haverford. She managed to do so with that undying force of will that had seen her through the Concord Academy graduation.

At Haverford, Lezlie attended Katie's introductory lectures and met the faculty. Among them was Kate's dean, a gentle, competent woman who welcomed us as if there were no other students that required her attention. I had a few minutes with her in the office before Lezlie arrived for the meeting. "I'm sorry," Dean Truman said.

"Have you seen this disease—ovarian cancer?" I asked.

"Yes," she said. "A famous person who had it—Gilda Radner—was my friend."

It was comforting for us to know how very supportive the Haverford faculty would be. But for me, Lezlie's dying became even more palpable. *She really is going to die*, I thought.

Later that day, we helped our daughter complete her move. The room was small but recently redecorated. An ample-sized window looked out on a cluster of green Pennsylvania pines. "It's a great view," I said, optimistically. Lezlie nodded mechanically in agreement. Her expression was unsmiling, uncharacteristically vacant, as if for a moment she were somewhere unreachable.

Kate left to join classmates for lunch. For the only time in our marriage I felt alone while with my wife. Her face remained impassive for a time as we walked, silently, on the blue green grass between Katie's dormitory and the smooth macadam that also flanked the school's cinder track.

We were quiet together for a time…seemingly separate…Then, she convulsed in tears. Lezlie's small classically oval face folded in itself beneath the canopy of her wig. Her chest—wasting with her body's fight against cancer—heaved between gasps of despair. It was tragic. We knew but never said it aloud…She would not see Haverford again.

In mid-September, Kate returned to Boston for a weekend visit. Lezlie's bowel was again obstructed and she was receiving nutrition intravenously. She looked tiny but resolute. As we drove to Logan Airport to meet our daughter, Lezlie wore her wig that always seemed too big for her thinning face, and she carried the motorized unit that pumped a nutritional mixture into her blood stream through a permanent catheter (PIC Line). The apparatus reminded me of a lawyer's attache case and in an odd way, it imparted Lezlie with an air of authority.

July 19 of that year had been our 25th wedding anniversary. I had thought that it might also be our last. I wanted to give her something—something with a permanence that she herself could not experience. An emerald seemed like the right thing. Lezlie was not one for adornment. She had a lovely diamond engagement ring, a strand of pearls, and a good necklace that had been the gift of family friends. She dressed in simple classic clothing…I would give her Talbot's gift certificates at Christmas time. It was the only way I could induce her to spend for herself…The idea of the emerald appealed to her, however. It was the Irish in her, we thought, from her mother's family. The emerald green of Ireland…James Joyce's green, of all that was earthly and beautiful. An emerald would be just the right thing.

It became a summer's project and I embarked on it intently like a collector of rare artifacts. Finally, I telephoned the family friend who had assisted us with Lezlie's diamond engagement ring. His store was in the city center, on Washington Street, once the site of stately old movie theaters: the Loews Orpheum, the Paramount, the RKO Keefe. As a boy, I visited them with my mother after a day of shopping. The street runs from the border of Chinatown past the pornographic display of the "Combat Zone" to the retail district and the historic landmarks: the Old South Meeting Hall, the Old State House…The area is near the route to Logan, so we arranged to see the jeweler on the Saturday of Kate's arrival.

Joshua Gold, the jeweler, was a kind, diminutive man with large expressive eyes and a gentle endearing smile. Years later, he would recall the event. He had seen then—everyone could—that my wife was slowly dying. I remembered his caring—delicate—approach to us and wondered how it had affected him. "You made it easy for me…I'll never forget it; it really touched me," he would say of the experience. "How beautiful it was."

It was a Columbian gem that Joshua had found for us, eight-carat and perfect to the naked eye. Lezlie beamed.

Lezlie and I told Kate all about the anniversary present. Kate knew from telephone exchanges that Lezlie was losing ground. The visit with Kate was wonderful. She stood by her mother like a loving giant. This lovely six-foot tall character with deep blue eyes and long brown hair who turned heads without noticing…How kind and selfless she was. She knew exactly how to be with her mother. "I'm coming home," she told us. "I've thought about it and decided. It's what I want to do."

"Do what you think will be best for you," Lezlie and I told her that weekend in her freshman college year. She said it was best for her to be at home with her mother. That was when Katie became Kate. It took a while for me to get used to it. She is Kate for me now.

Lezlie's bowel obstruction had become increasingly difficult to manage despite the parenteral nutrition and the nasogastric tube that drained fluid from her GI tract. Her strength was ebbing. We arranged for an elective readmission to Boston Hospital. Bob Gentilly, her primary care doctor, was also a gastroenterologist. He arranged to admit her through the Trowbridge service on the Monday following Kate's return to Haverford.

The trip back from Logan was exhausting. Lezlie's every separation from Kate was grievous. Like a soldier who carried on in battle despite near fatal wounds, Lezlie was spent. She had mustered what strength she had. The ring...the visit with Kate...the parting. On the way home from Logan, the bowel trouble worsened. The drainage through her nasogastric tube became more viscous and darkly bilious. She began to vomit small amounts around the tube...The smell was feculent. I felt so sad for her.

It occurred to me momentarily how I had imagined as a medical student, when learning about this kind of disease, that I would kill myself if my intestines were obstructed the way my wife was now experiencing it. I had tried to imagine what it would be like to have cancer. *I can manage the pain*, I thought. *If my bowels become obstructed, I can manage that, too. But what if the vomiting is so severe that it smells like what is supposed to come out at the other end? Then I would end it. How? Get a gun? But I would be too sick to have a gun...I would need the gun before I was too sick to get one...But I don't want one when I don't need it...I might panic and use it when there was still a chance for cure...*

Lezlie did not seem to notice the odor. She was too sick.

"I'm taking you to the Emergency Room," I said. "You need to be admitted."

"I want to go home," she answered, tearful, eyes pleading. "They can admit me tomorrow." We were driving through the Sumner Tunnel.

"Well," I told her, "You can go home now, but it's a long walk...I'm going to the hospital."

In the ER, we were greeted by John Chang. He was the director of emergency services at Boston Hospital. There had been a Grateful Dead concert at the Boston Garden, and the city's emergency rooms were crowded with the acute complaints of the group's aging admirers.

"This stinks," Dr. Chang said. He is tall for an Asian—six feet—and has a kind face and warm demeanor. He spoke in a stage whisper. "It just stinks."

I began to cry...I still do when I think of it.

"You are doing the right thing," he said. Dr. Chang lifted the telephone and called admitting. "There's been a mistake," he said. He spoke with only the slightest accent. "The Surmans *aw* here for admissions *too-day*...I believe *theh* is some error...It is *too-day—not too-morrow*. Admission is expected."

There was a pause in his discourse. The record indicated admission was for Monday. Under such circumstances the patient must be worked up in the emergency room before transfer to the medical service.

Dr. Chang turned to me and winked. "I <u>am</u> the director," he said into the phone. Lezlie would avoid the confusion of the ER and go directly to the floor and the nurses who loved her.

"This will be our little secret," John Chang said.

16

AN ARABIAN PRINCESS

o o o o o o o o o o o o o o o o o o o o o o o o o o o o o o o

The gates of hell are open night and day;
Smooth the descent and easy is the way;
But to return and view the cheerful skies,
In this the task and mighty labor lies.

—Dryden
Quoted in The Rambler *135, September 10, 1751 by*
Samuel Johnson

Boston Hospital…Admission Date: 10-2-94
Principal Procedure: 10-12-94: Panendoscopy and placement of a G-tube
History of Present Illness: This 51-year-old woman was admitted because of
abdominal pain, nausea, and vomiting in a patient with known ovarian carci-
noma. She'd been admitted two times for a small bowel obstruction requiring
lysis of adhesions in June…She has been increasingly plaqued [sic] by abdominal
distension, nausea and pain after eating and vomiting. Three weeks prior to
admission she was treated for partial small bowel obstruction with nasogastric
tube. This subsided acutely but she has continued to have recurrent symptoms…

On Sunday, October 2, Lezlie settled in on Trowbridge 15. Her relief was immediate and her comfort improved greatly on October 4 after Dr. Flowers tapped her abdomen and removed acitic fluid that had reaccumulated in her belly. My wife had come back to us again and the engulfing cloud of tension began to dissipate. With continued intravenous feeding and bowel decompression, Lezlie's strength improved. Her complexion was no longer gray but china white. Her large loving eyes were lustrous again. Seated in bed with oversized pajamas, legs tucked gracefully beneath her, she had the appearance of a delicate but energetic young princess.

The nurses playfully referred to the room we now occupied as The Penthouse. It was a big well-lighted room with a picture window view of the Boston public gardens and swan boats like the ones that had transported me through childhood. "All this," Lezlie said, "and I'm not even Saudi Arabian."

Our family came and went…one of us sleeping over in a folding bed…taking meals, as if this were a hotel suite or actualization of an Art Buchwald tongue-in-cheek cost saving plan for condominium conversion of hospital rooms.

I was proud of this affluent setting but also guilt-ridden. When I married Lezlie, I was aware of her family's cancer history. Arthur Humber, her grandfather, had died in his forties of a spinal cord malignancy. I was convinced that my wife would die before me, and at an early age. Lezlie, for her part, always insisted she would outlive me. We trivialized death by speaking of it this way as if engaged in some eccentric competition.

Then in 1987 she had the melanoma. I was certain I would lose her. At that time, we agreed, for the children's sake, to increase her life insurance. We applied, but she was ineligible. Then, in 1993, I seized an opportunity for catastrophic health care coverage. If one of our family were stricken, the medical coverage would be virtually unlimited. Now, I could take solace in this prescience. I told our friends about it…You wouldn't call it boastful—but almost that, as if some small act of governance could mitigate the horror when nature unbolts the gate to anarchy. One cannot—ever—assemble or direct the parade of coming events, but there is power in the predicting of it. There is, however, a penalty for prediction when it proves accurate (although most often it does not, and even the effort of foretelling proves futile). If I knew it I should have prevented it! I felt privileged for affording her this level of care but gut-wrenching guilt for my failure to insist that she protect herself from gynecologic cancer. *It isn't your fault*, I told myself. *It's an act of Nature…I'm not in charge. Haven't I always said that to my patients: 'We're not driving; Nature drives!' Yes…but you could have told her…I did tell her…when she had the ultrasound for the ovarian cyst. 'Take them out,' I said. She said no. I can't run her life…But I should have discussed it…Things were busy then…The children were applying to schools…After that I had planned to talk more with her about it—when we were living alone together…to talk with her more urgently about a hysterectomy…not only because of the ovarian cyst. She'd had those fibroids that were so damned unpleasant for her and so impeding for sex…Was that selfish? Yes…No…*

We would have a new life together and sex would be part of it as it was in the first life we had together before the children…Perhaps it was selfish. Alex was her gynecologist—one of the best…He said she didn't need an operation. That, too, would have risks. Did I want it for her or for me, or for both of us? Maybe for all of those reasons…I should have spoken with her and Alex. Would she have let me?…I should have asked. There was no resolution for this guilt. There is no resolution.

The principal medical concern now was whether another operation might relieve her intestinal obstruction. Reginald Flowers, the cancer surgeon who was also a gynecologist, ordered an MRI scan and carefully reviewed the findings with Dr. Gentilly. *Alex would have wanted us to see Flowers in the first place—instead of Watkins—had Flowers not been lecturing out of state. But he is here now,* I thought, *and if he had been here then it would have been the same debulking operation that Millard did so brilliantly.*

It would now be a pivotal choice for Reggie Flowers. If successful, an operation to divert her bowel would improve the quality of her life. She would be able to eat again. Possibly there would be opportunity for a fresh approach to this implacable cancer that was like revolution inside of her. I searched the medical literature, then telephoned M.D. Anderson Hospital about the immunological treatments that would soon begin phase one trials. We would think of something. If, instead, the surgical outcome were unfavorable…if the cancer proved to be extensive, it might be impossible for Lezlie to heal. That would destroy the quality of the life she had. "I don't want to do something just for the sake of doing it," she said. "If it's not going to do any good, then there's no point to it."

Rick Humber, Lezlie's brother, was with us again. His wife, Dianne, would come later with their children. Lezlie's mother, Anne Humber, was in town now and staying over at the Wellesley Inn. Craig had begun his first year of medical studies, but he was in Worcester and only an hour away by car, the gray Volvo we had given him for safety. When Kate returned, our family presence would be complete. We all agreed that I would go to Haverford to help her begin her leave of absence.

It was difficult to leave town, but I secretly welcomed the chance to get away for a day or two…like coming up for air. My life in Boston was fragmented with the battle for Lezlie's survival, the family needs, the clinical work at Boston Hospital. My emotions were fragmented as well. I grieved in private moments but otherwise distanced myself as much as possible from the same emotions. My appearance was another matter…unchanging…self-absorbed…sad…at times even distracted. *Am I impaired,* I wondered. I needed my medical practice. Did my practice need me? It was a recurrent concern. I reasoned, though, that tragedy is a part of life and that my personal tragedy would allow me to share my patients' hardships in a deeper and more spiritual fashion. It did embarrass me somewhat to recognize that in my office the support now flowed in both directions. Later it would no longer embarrass me. It is the humanity of psychotherapy that promotes change as much as it is the method. I should have learned that in my residency from a teacher, Aaron Lazare, who later became chancellor at the medical center where Craig was now training. But in the end—for us all—the best teacher is Life itself.

One of my patients, Will Smythe, was an unexpected source of spiritual guidance. Will was a pro ballplayer who had decided to leave the brutality of football for a job in computer sales. "No game, no pain," was what we said about it. Will is a Christian, not a gladiator…a big, gentle, fair-complexioned man…powerful, modest. At the gym, he benched 450, but you had to ask him. Soft-spoken, he had a trace of South Georgia in his voice. "Be careful when you lean against the wall," I liked to tell him. During our work together, Will had introduced me to the writing of C.S. Lewis. Before leaving for Pennsylvania, I purchased Lewis' book, *A Grief Remembered.*

I read C.S. Lewis' work on the USAir flight to Pennsylvania. It inspired me. After landing, I collected the pearl gray Taurus that I had ordered from National Rental Car and drove to the Wyndham Hotel on Lancaster Avenue, about two miles south of Kate's campus in an area the Philadelphians call "Mainline," as if its affluence were like a heroin addiction. Along the way, I stopped for some toiletries and purchased a hard-backed journal that I would carry about like a jewel case. Next day I began the diary while sitting on a bench at Haverford College in the gentle Pennsylvania autumn. It was bright and sunny, with a cool wind that chilled for moments, then left…revisited…left again, like an errant tax collector. I felt refreshed, then disconsolate. I was all right…alive…intact. Then I thought of how it was the twilight of Lezlie's life. Nothing in our lives is ever just one way and no other way. *Evening Journal: A Surfer's Pastime* began the diary:

It surprised me when I telephoned Lezlie last night—from an empty hotel room—to hear the same music in her voice despite the morphine and the Benadryl. Her dying has been like her living and our relationship goes on in its unique way. The wait for grief is like a surfer's pastime. The waves have several forms and arrive in barely predictable sequence…It has been a beautiful fall nonetheless…"

That was the way it was for me…everything normal…the freshness of autumn before the leaves have all fallen…the symphony of student voices…then spasms of grief. I folded the book and called Lezlie from my portable phone. I told her about Kate and how things were going at the school. It was customary for me to debrief myself with Lezlie, but it occurred to me—self-consciously—that I had gone into quite a bit of detail before asking how she was. *Just like an only child*, I thought. Her voice was so strong and clear. I had repressed awareness of how very frail she was.

I watched Kate closely during my visit for any indecision she might have about returning to Boston. There was none. She was determined to come home and care for her mother. It was important that we be frank about Lezlie's prognosis. Kate understood that her mother would die and that we couldn't know when the time would be. There was a sadness in my daughter's eyes. Mostly it was her mother's cancer that affected Kate, but I knew as well that she felt the loss of the political science courses she had to forfeit. Kate said little. I had learned not to intrude on her thoughts. We worked together, methodically, through the process of clearing out her dormitory room, then met with Dean Wise, her faculty advisor.

"Kate and I will drive up to Boston this afternoon," I informed him.

"Would you like to hear about a support group?" Dean Wise asked.

Kate smiled and shook her head without actually saying 'no.'

"I have to be careful about her," I replied, appreciating the offer. "We think so much alike. I have to remind myself that there may be aspects of this that are different for her. She thinks like a forty-year-old…" Kate was not the only one who avoided group support. I would not know until much later that it was a mistake to deny our need for psychological support.

"Yes," he said warmly. "I was new at the school when I met her and wondered if she were a senior." Kate listened and smiled self-consciously.

"Our brains work the same," I said. "I once asked her if she ever lay upside down and imagined walking on the ceiling. 'Yes,' Kate said. 'And when you get to the doorways you have to step over.'"

Dean Wise laughed, gently, respectfully.

"You do have to step over," Kate said, waving her arms to clarify the point. It made us all smile.

Kate and I had lunch at the International House of Pancakes. "Death of a parent," I told her while we stood together for a time in the parking lot, "is not only tragic, but inconvenient." Later in my second journal entry I wrote, "Kate laughs with her mother's music…I do not feel alone…"

On the trip home, I talked to her about her mother and what I anticipated for her last weeks with us. "We'll be certain that she doesn't suffer. If pain becomes a problem, we'll call Hospice, start intravenous pain medication, and stop the intravenous nutrition."

Kate nodded…silent…pensive…without tears.

"I'm not taking her back to the hospital," I said.

"You're not?"

"Only if there is something that must be done for comfort. If the gastric tube stops draining and she needs a new tube placed in her stomach through her nostrils." It was a graphic account, but it was a brutal disease. As it once had been for Will Smythe, Lezlie, a devout Christian, was now a gladiator called upon for battle, not with lions or human assailants, but diseases of the self. The last of these foes is the penultimate challenge.

I reminisced with our daughter as we traveled back to Boston. "At night," I said, "no matter what time…twelve…twelve-thirty, your mother would get into a newspaper story and we'd argue about turning out the lights. And then she'd start some deep discussion about world events…"

Kate laughed.

"I'd always say, 'Shut up…good night.' After a time she began to answer with the same phrase. 'Shut up…good night,' she'd say."

We checked through airport security. "What a nuisance," I said.

"At least you know the man behind you won't be able to shoot you on the plane," Kate said.

"You're right," I laughed, ignoring the little girl sound that had just come into her voice. "You know, as long as you are somewhere in the world, I'll be all right."

As we returned to Sherborn, I thought of one of my patients. Elsa Froemahn—a genteel elderly Austrian-born lady who had escaped the wrath of Hilter but lost her family to the camps—had shared some of my many stories about Kate. "She has an old soul," Elsa had told me. Patients—and friends—identified in differing ways with our family's story. For Elsa, it recalled the final farewell and backward hand wave to a mother too encumbered by arthritis to leave Europe in the invasive spread of Nazism—which was itself a cancer. Like Kate, Elsa had been a *de facto* adult, catapulted into adulthood, blocking out the pain of loss and focused on the immediacy of what had to be done. It would be my pattern—my error—to see Kate more grown up than she was. She took so readily to the responsibility of caring for her mother. Childhood was gone for Kate; adolescence packed away like summer toys.

"I speak to so many people," I told Katie that same day, "who have not found love. They spend years and years in situations that are devoid of it. But once you've had love, you know what it is. Life is an incredible teacher if you can listen to it. It's a little like baseball…If you've never had the experience of a perfect swing that connects the bat and ball, you don't know what to do with it." The words were awkward as I spoke. "I think you'll have a great love," I said.

"Thanks," she replied.

"Well, there's chance involved. But there's choice, too," I said. "Having had the experience of love in your life, you know what to look for…"

17

PAIN RELIEF

○ ○
There is no sun without shadow, and it is
essential to know the night.

—The Myth of Sisyphus
Albert Camus

We were together again. Kate had interrupted her studies. Craig had begun medical school but found a way to be with us. I marveled at his ability to attend to his work as well as to his mother. Rick, ever solid, organized the household with Kate while I was at my office, a short walk and two elevator rides from Lezlie's bedside. I was relieved by this proximity but vaguely guilty.

I remained actively involved in Lezlie's medical care. There was no more personality clash, no more doctor conflict, although I continued to think about Millard Watkins…to reevaluate what had transpired between us. I talked about it with my colleagues who dropped by my office with words of support. I was surrounded by psychiatrists. I told them I would enlist Millard's help again if we were back at the beginning of things. It was true. He would leave Boston Hospital for Toronto in January, 2000, but I would use him now—again. Not even Reggie Flowers could surpass Millard's technical skills. He is that good at what he does well. It is a problem we all have. Someone is good at a thing so we expect that person to be good at related things. Life is not like that.

For friends at the office, my tragedy was important but not dire. It had been that way for me when friends had family illnesses. By nature, I am a person who denies—most of us are, to some extent. It was different, however, for one of my colleagues, psychiatrist Tony Bellavia. I could see it in his face when we talked. I do not think he had ever met Lezlie—possibly for a moment at a department Christmas party—but he identified with us in a way that comes only from personal experience. Tony was remarried now but had lost his first wife to a rare form of malignant sarcoma. Elsa was twenty-three years old when her cancer took hold; Tony was a medical student. It was pain that I saw now in his expression…the pain of her pain. There had been a lot of it. Pain control was less of a priority in those times. Medicine was more for the conquest of disease than for the relief of suffering and doctors worried unnecessarily about narcotics addiction—as if that really matters when Death is at the doorstep. It is so easy to look back in disbelief at the flagrant stupidity of it, but like Plato's cave dwellers, we cannot see beyond our field of vision.

One of the great worries about Lezlie's situation was her allergic reaction to each of the narcotic analgesics she encountered. Up to now it was sufficient to blunt the allergic response with antihistamines. There would come a time of greater pain. I remembered how our family had several years earlier seen Kathleen Turner in *Cat on a Hot Tin Roof* at the Shubert. I remembered "Big Daddy's" off-stage screams as the insides of his belly were choked by cancer. *It can't be like that for her*, I thought. *I will not allow it to be like that…How will I prevent it? I didn't know…*

The answer came from a gifted pharmacist who like Alex Godley had been a childhood friend. Harry Demonico is an unimposing youthful man with a warm but steady gaze and a searching analytic mind. He works for Partners now, the Boston teaching hospital consortium.

I saw him one day when he came to consult at Boston Hospital. I told him about the pain management problem with Lezlie. "Do you have any ideas?" I asked. He was headed into the hospital as I was leaving. We stood together for a time as if frozen between footsteps in the lens of a camera. I wanted to be unemotional and spoke as if it were a casual curbside request.

"There is a drug," he said, "Stadol…It's a mixed agonist antagonist…" That meant it acted in some ways like morphine and in other ways, the opposite of morphine. "It blocks the Mu receptors."

"The what?" I asked.

"The Mu receptors. There is more than one opiate receptor. The Mu receptor is responsible for some of the side effects we encounter with morphine…nausea…histamine release."

"Is it strong enough to help her pain?"

"No," Harry said, "but it might block those receptors. Then you could administer morphine."

"Is this written up somewhere?" I asked, doubting but hopeful.

"No…. Just clinical wisdom."

"Let's write it up." I said it with the studied nonchalance that doctors use to distance themselves from suffering.

"Okay…"

I called Reggie Flowers, told him about Harry and his suggestion.

"Sure," he said, "no harm in trying…"

"It sounds a bit far out," I told Lezlie, Rick, and the children. "But, who knows? Harry's pretty smart. If he thinks it'll work…maybe…" *Maybe not*, I thought. What then? *Something else…*

Next morning, Pauline gave Lezlie the first dose. I went to the office and saw my morning patients. I looked in on her dozing in the early afternoon. "How is she doing?" I asked.

"Good," Pauline said. I paused, looked at her questioningly. "Really…" she added.

"Great," I said, amazed. "No itching?"

"No itching," Pauline said, smiling now, watching the relief unwrinkle my face like an iron on cotton cloth.

"No rash?" I asked, walking closer to Lezlie's dozing form—apparently pain free.

"No rash," Pauline said, her smile broadening…almost becoming a laugh.

"I can't believe it," I later told Harry. "I'll never forget this!"

At last we could effectively control Lezlie's pain…and the greater pain that would be coming. Years later I would review the literature on Stadol and write to *The New England Journal of Medicine* about Harry Demonico's discovery. The *Journal* had published one of my letters in the past, but not this time. Their policy prohibited publication of personal accounts.

I still do not know what Lezlie thought then about the prospects of her dying. "I don't want you to be alone," was all she said about it.

Then there was Natalie. Looking back now, it seems crazy, but that is how it is when life becomes chaotic…It is inevitably crazy. Normal behavior would be even crazier! Natalie was suddenly in the picture once again.

It happened this way: I was scheduled to travel to Virginia to give a talk on—of all things—medical ethics. Natalie is from Virginia; her family was there, and her mother was ill…and…The confusing part of it was Lezlie's role in it all. She and the friend who was Natalie's erstwhile nursing instructor agreed that Natalie should go to Virginia with me to be sure I was all right.

On the day prior to my departure, I saw Natalie, formerly not at all beautiful, but very beautiful now, in her starched whites and the same nursing cap that had looked so much like a floating marshmallow on the night following Lezlie's first operation—the debulking procedure. Natalie was there now at Lezlie's bed-side...and Lezlie, apologetic because she was unable to go with me as we had planned before this terrible illness, looked relieved that I would have companion-ship.

So it occurred to me then that this was part of something that had been willed...perhaps ordained...that Natalie and I would become lovers. There would be this transition as there might be—at least in fictional accounts—when bereaved husbands fall in love with their late wife's caretaker...and that Lezlie saw it that way...wanted it that way...that it gave her some peace of mind that I have someone with me were she to die. Later, I would confide with our close friends Max and Alice about this poorly-processed thought. "I don't think she was thinking that way," Alice would tell me.

As we prepared to board the plane, I asked Natalie if she would like to sit with me. Lezlie was not going, of course, and there was a seat next to me...and that was fine with Natalie. On the way I felt her leg against me...like Lezlie, Natalie had...has...great legs, and I could feel them—one of them, that is—and didn't know then, not until much later that it was not Natalie at all that thrilled me, but the extent to which she became for me a reincarnation of the Lezlie I had known...bright and vibrant and loving in those youthful Montreal years.

I heard Natalie mention that she was "in a relationship." I felt a wave of disap-pointment. *Foolish*, I thought. *Well, she didn't say it's permanent...Maybe they're not getting along. Maybe they're about to break up.*

Later that day I was in my hotel room. Natalie was at her mother's home. It was late—about 10 o'clock. I was daydreaming about Natalie, about marrying her after Lezlie's death. Then I picked up the telephone and called Lezlie at Bos-ton Hospital. I felt so lonely for her. I spoke with Reggie Flowers, who was there—like me, he kept late hours. He told me what I dreaded but expected...that she was inoperable. The results of the abdominal MRI were that her bowel was inoperable. He could go in, of course, and explore her abdominal cavity, but to no particular benefit other than to do something. That was what Lezlie and I had agreed not to do. So often in medicine people feel compelled toward futile intervention that causes more trouble.

It is true, I thought. *I knew it all along...but now I really know it. Lezlie—my wonderful loving dearest of all people in the world—will die...just like that. Poof! Gone, as if she had never been there at all, and all of it but for the children could just as well have been a product of my imagination.*

I called Craig in Worcester. "I haven't finished preparing my talk," I confided. "Would you like to listen while I review my notes?"

Craig was concerned for me; fearful, no doubt, that the next day I would embarrass myself. It wasn't just a talk; it was a keynote-type presentation. He listened patiently, lovingly, as I stumbled through my note cards. And then he was gone and I was once again alone, terribly alone.

It was one o'clock in the morning. It would take another hour, at least, to complete my preparation. At last I was finished. The clock registered 2:45. Time was no longer relevant. The rest of my life was like one long broken line, disappearing over the horizon into God knows what. I began to cry. It wasn't a soft kind of crying. I listened to myself, wondering if I could be heard beyond the walls of the hotel room that were impregnable and prison-like in appearance. It was not just crying…I howled. "Lezlie!" I yelled. "Where is my little Lezlie…" My body doubled over on my abdomen like a pita bread, and I convulsed in tears. It was all over.

I walked into the morning conference hall the next day as in a dream. My colleagues consoled me and wondered, I imagined, why I had not cancelled the lecture. Natalie had come over to listen. She was striking in her tailored suit. Did they think we were having an affair? What did they think?

The talk was the best I'd given until then…as if my whole career that I had shared with my wife were suddenly crystallized into a single moment of passion. As I spoke, I was aware of Natalie listening to my lecture, and I thought what any foolish man would think…that she would fall irresistibly in love with me, but there was no relief in the thought. It was all so damned sad.

After the talk, I walked from the conference room with Natalie at my side. I had always been scrupulously faithful to my wife and would remain so. Still, it pleased me to have an attractive woman at my side. Natalie's appearance was striking and there was a seductive quality about her that she was unaware of and that made one think that no one in her life was more important. I craved like an alcoholic in withdrawal. I don't remember what I said to Natalie…something very embarrassing if people…that would convince people that I was a jerk. It was something to the effect that I, while alone the previous night, had imagined that she and I had married and that she, too, had become ill. There was a silent moment in which I watched Natalie's face change. She said I had misinterpreted her feelings.

We flew back separately to Boston.

Two weeks later I told Natalie that for a time I had become her fantasied lover. "I respect you and want to have your friendship," I said, "so this is 'phase three,'" meaning that something else would come of it all that wasn't our being lovers, but more than our being just friends.

She had stopped by my office. I read her a poem that I had written about Lezlie. Natalie cried and agreed that it was passionate.

"What you have done for me is life saving," I said. "One of the advantages of being fifty is that one is aware that these feelings can be experienced with more than one person. What you gave me, without knowing it, is a kind of hope. I've started to work out again. Kate tells me if I'm going to date I have to lose weight." Natalie laughed affectionately. "Fantasy is the fertilizer of life," I said.

We all knew then that Lezlie's death was imminent. Lezlie knew it. There had been a rapid succession of talks after Kate and I returned from Haverford. "If you are hesitant to go in, that's all I need to hear. We don't want to end up with a mess," I had said to Reggie Flowers. He had nodded...listening, emotions in check. I was reminded of how Jane Newhause had spoken of him. "When things get rough," she said. "Reggie gets calm. That's the kind of man I like."

Lezlie had nodded her head silently when I reported back to her. I could see how deeply disappointed she was...sadly realizing for the first time, perhaps, that life would end for her soon. *How soon*? I wondered. *How soon does she think? How soon do I think?* It was imponderable.

Kate, too, had nodded decisively after I had told her of my discussion with her mother's new surgeon. Kate is a realist—then and now. Her response and her mother's reminded me of an Italian immigrant I had once met in consultation. He was terminally ill. "When it's end, it's end," he had told me.

It was "end"...or was it? Perhaps there is never just an end but also a beginning of something else. Lezlie would go in one way, but stay with us in a new way. Ron Johnson, an expert on bereavement had taught me when I was in psychiatric training that "people don't die—they just go underground."

There is a transition between the certainty of living and the acceptance of dying. When there is such acceptance, there is a kind of emotional purgatory. The cartoon character stands still in space beyond the edge of a cliff and awaits the fatal fall. That is where things were for us in early October. There were choices, however, even in this purgatory. There remained a moment to live in...if only a moment. After that we would go on with our lives. Before it was over and before I began my desperate search for a new life, there would be a time for us as a family that was like none other. Most important was that we manage the pain. The first priority was comfort. The second priority was to get Lezlie back home not so much so that she could die there as that she could live there before she left us.

18

IN THE VALLEY OF THE SHADOW

o o o o o o o o o o o o o o o o o o o o o o o o o o o o o o o o

And I shall dwell in the house of the Lord…forever.

—Psalm 23
Holy Bible

It is December 18, 1999, but the weather here feels like early fall. The price of oil has been rising despite the unseasonable temperatures, but natural gas is cheap, so I acquired a contract on the New York Mercantile Exchange. It is a break from the life and death struggles that surround me. One of my patients died yesterday…of cancer. He came in short of breath with a belly full of fluid after a month or two of feeling ill. When the patient was admitted, Amos Archer said if he were a woman it would most likely be ovarian cancer because it had come on so fast. Even now, five years after Lezlie's death, I cannot escape the tentacles of ovarian cancer, even when the cancer patient is a man.

I am at the bedside when Amos taps the man's abdomen. He doesn't have any pain; he just breathes hard and fast and says he feels hot. "Get me a fan," he tells us. "Please get me a fan." He is afraid he is going to die. Amos says when we leave the room that it looks like the man is going to die.

It is a strange morning. I return to the office at 9 a.m. after rounding on the surgical service. Rounding is a bit like changing television channels with the remote control. In one room someone is getting better…smiling, happy to be going home. The next person is comatose on a ventilator. The next person is being prepped for an operation. There is not much talk about the man who has died except to say that there has been a postmortem examination. In a week or two we will look at a projected image of the pathology slides.

My first patient calls to cancel. Then someone from a local pharmacy calls. She wants to know about Mr. French's prescriptions. I tell her I don't treat anyone named French. She says he said it was Dr. Surman.

"Maybe it's Therman?" I ask.

"No," the pharmacist says. "The patient spelled it."

"How?"

"S-u-r-m-a-n," she says in a friendly voice.

"It's a great mystery," I said.

After seeing my ten o'clock patient, I get another call from the pharmacy. "About those prescriptions," she says. Her voice sounds like she's been told a good joke. "It was another Dr. Surman across town." There is a pause. *Another Dr. Surman,* I think. "Craig," she says. "Your son."

Craig calls at noon. "Are you in with a patient?"

"Yes. What's up?"

"I just wanted to give you a hard time," he says.

"Oh," I say, embarrassed.

"I just want you to know that I'm here doing the same things you're doing." Craig sounds like the pharmacist—like he's heard a good joke.

I forget that he's in his second year of psychiatric training. It is not about competence. He proved that long ago when he rescued me from my own undoing—fooling with an overheated car radiator that exploded in my face. He was thirteen at the time. He began first aid and called for an ambulance as the skin blistered then peeled from my face. He took me to a washroom near the toll booth on the Mass Turnpike. "Stay there," he instructed. "Keep putting cold water on it." Without his quick thinking, I would have needed skin grafting.

He's like me in so many ways. It's just that my brain hasn't caught up to all of his achievements.

In those October days five years ago, when Lezlie was preparing to leave Trowbridge 15 and come home to us, it seemed to be harder with Craig. His emotions were more on the surface. Craig had never done well with change, and death—the ultimate change—was outside his orbit of tolerance. He was angry...palpably so...kind, loving, always the Eagle Scout, but full of ire about his mother's fatal passage.

"You're being unrealistic," I would tell him impatiently.

"What about immunotherapy?" he asked. He, too, had been searching the medical literature.

"I spoke with Bob Best," I told Craig. "He says it will just make her sick."

Next he focused on his mother's diet. What kind of fatty acids should be in her hyperalimentation? Long chain?…medium chain? His Oberlin College experience led him to think like a neuroscientist. He wanted Lezlie's doctors to protect her nervous system as much as possible to keep her with us in the most important way. I arranged for Craig to speak with one of the nutritionists. I wanted to help him and also to spare Lezlie's physicians from the intensity of his emotion. Perhaps I wanted to spare myself.

Craig and I deliberated in a private place on the Trowbridge service. My mind was racing. I needed—urgently—to make him know that it was no longer a priority to extend his mother's life but to palliate her suffering. "Look," I said. "If you were with Jesus when he was on the Cross, would you have purged his bowels to relieve liver failure?"

"Yes," he said…angrily…confused. Then we were silent together. I told him how much I loved him. I, too, was angry but had not yet recognized how truly angry I was that his mother was about to die…that I was unable to stop it…angry, too, that Kate's educational insurance policy would not even cover the cost of tuition because it was her mother's cancer, not an illness of Kate's that required the leave of absence. I was angry at Watkins…angry at myself about not encouraging her more actively to have a hysterectomy. There was a kind of symbiosis in my relationship with Craig. We often seem to have the same feeling, but it takes him to express it for us both.

I rejoined Lezlie after Craig and I had spoken. "He says he wants to record an interview with you," I told her. I said it ironically, if not quite sardonically, in the way one distances oneself from an idea that is expectedly unpopular.

"That's fine," she responded.

"You're sure?" I was surprised, then felt I'd done Craig an injustice, that I might have presented it in a more constructive way. Still it seemed like an odd idea…a reach…an attempt to preserve some part of her, if only her voice.

"Yes." She seemed at ease with the idea.

I breathed in slowly and exhaled like a smoker but without a cigarette. "Okay."

Lezlie knelt effortlessly on her hospital bed. Craig returned. The nurses finished taking vital signs. Rick was there, too, sitting quietly…watching his sister, knowing she had very little time. Only Kate was absent, doing those essential household errands with Lezlie's mother. It wasn't so much that her grandmother was helping her as it was that Kate was finding a venue for her grandmother. Anne did not do well in hospitals.

Craig plugged in the recorder. It began to hum faintly. "This is October 10th," he dictated. "We're on Trowbridge 15. My mom's room…number 21."

"You'd better put the year because when three generations from now listen to this, it's nice to know the year." Lezlie gestured with her hand like a porcelain princess, animated by magic.

"Tomorrow is Grampa Bruce's birthday, wherever he is, so…I'm here, Craig, and my dad Owen…" he continued.

"Craig is twenty-two years old," Lezlie told the tape recorder, "and is all decked out in a green tee shirt with a black dog on the front of it that I bought him years ago…like three. It says 1991 on the back of it. Lovely jeans with holes in the knee and frayed cuffs…and spanking new sneakers that his grandfather Harry bought him. Owen is here…"

"In nondescript formal attire," Craig interrupted.

"Pretty well put together," Lezlie continued, laughing. "He's actually looking pretty good…no ink stains anywhere just at the moment."

"Been working out…" Rick said. "Sneakers in great shape."

"Took off his favorite tie that's all frayed," Lezlie said, smiling, "but we can't do anything about that because they're not making that wonderful tie anymore, so he has to continue to wear this frayed tie until whenever it falls off. And we're honored to have, on Canadian Thanksgiving, Richard Bruce Humber, here from Victoria—three thousand miles away—visiting us on Trowbridge…Boston Hospital…and somebody else can talk now."

"Lezlie's looking great," Rick said, his sonorous voice threatening to choke. "She's got her new gray top on with the zipper down the middle…and I'd like to keep her warm. Things are pretty darned good here. We're all together."

"Mom looks something like a Buddhist monk," Craig said, with a certain joy in his voice that was loving, "with short hair…sitting in the lotus position and doing a lot of deep breathing. Is there any advice you have for all of us?"

"Well, I can't give advice to my brother and my husband," she said. "But I'm still allowed to give advice to you even if you're twenty-two and that is what—the same advice—that my father gave to me, which is to stay exactly like you are…to just be Craig and nobody else…always. That's the most important thing…"

It had been foolish for me to be angry at Craig. The recording was just what we all needed, if only to remind us as Rick had said, "We're all together."

Lezlie went on effortlessly…talking about the family…how the children were the same or different from her and the same or different from me…encouraging Craig.

"Do you feel like I should spend all the rest of the time with you?" he asked ingenuously, "with you as opposed to taking tests and…"

"No," she said honestly, "because, you see, I feel like you're with me…with me all the time. I've always felt that Craig was with me…"

Rick left the room unobtrusively, because it was getting to be too sad for him. Craig and I remained, listening intently, marveling at what she said.

"As far as…" Lezlie continued, "not that anybody asked, but as far as the fact that I have cancer, I still don't believe it. On one level, I think, because I don't think I could be quite as calm as I am. I'm not an evangelistic kind of a religious person, but I am a religious person in my own way and I always have been ever since I was little. I used to walk up—all the way up the hill—to the United Church from Beech Drive, which is many long blocks…to teach Sunday School. When I was a teenager, I used to sit and teach these five and six-year-olds and it was really super fun. I loved it. And I feel that comforting me…"

19

COMING HOME

o o o o o o o o o o o o o o o o o o o o o o o o o o o o o o o o o
And therefore never send to know for whom the bell tolls. It tolls for thee.

—Meditation 17, Devotions Upon Emergent Occasions
John Donne

On Christmas Eve Day, 1999, I visit the cemetery in Sherborn. The year ending would have been our thirtieth wedding anniversary year. Our black Lab accompanies me to Pine Hill then runs off sniffing frantically as I walk to the rose granite marker with our family name in block capital letters. It is different seeing it now than it was previously. Now I expect it to be there, whereas before it seemed incongruous…arresting…almost startling.

I stand respectfully in front of the marker. To the right beside me is the small spruce where we buried the urn with Lezlie's ashes. I don't cry. It is the only time that I have not cried. I just say, "Merry Christmas, Lezlie…" then watch my shadow—broader at its base and thinner at its apex—straying away to the left across the hard winter ground. The stone too has a shadow and I see that it runs in parallel with my own. I look at it dumbly for a time as if I have never seen a shadow like it and wonder what meaning it might have—if shadows have a meaning. Then I say, "I love you," and leave.

There rarely are people at the cemetery when I go there, and none are here on this Christmas Eve day. Several years ago I had a patient from Yugoslavia whom I interviewed with the help of a hospital translator. She had come to be with her husband who was struggling with complications following kidney transplantation. "Americans don't seem to believe in death," she told me. "I see many beautiful cemeteries, but nobody is visiting them."

There is no other life but for the flowers, the vegetation, and the dog, ever eager to have a run there as if the place has some very different meaning for her. It seems sacrilegious to whistle for the dog, but I think it can't be sacrilegious—at least not disrespectful—if there is no one to hear the whistle. I look about to be sure. Then I whistle. It is a piercing whistle that summons Shadow. I also use it for hailing taxis. Once, when I was a student in Montreal, I hailed a police car that I thought was a taxi. I tried to explain in French, but the occupant of the police car made no better sense of my French than he did of the whistle, which was certainly bizarre under the circumstances.

The dog does not respond to my call. When she is in the right frame of mind, she bounds briskly to me, but there have been many deer this year. For Shadow it is a greater priority to follow deer tracks than to answer my whistle. When she does not respond, I walk to the car with an "I'll show you" attitude and start the engine and drive the car in a circular arc so that it faces in the direction from which we came. I smile with self-importance as she appears on the crest of a rise in the cemetery. She stands bolt upright, tail wagging, looking toward the car with the oddest expression, as if to say, "Well, what is this all about?" I laugh. "Yes," I say to her, "you're coming too."

The cemetery is an odd place for loving, but it's not a bad place. No place is a bad place for loving. I miss Lezlie. I have a new life; she is in it…just invisible.

In October, 1994, she had come home to us from that last admission at Boston Hospital. One of the first things Lezlie did was to visit the cemetery at Pine Hill. I went with her; Craig and Kate went and helped to maneuver the IV apparatus that was the main conduit for her nutrition and for the pain medication that effectively relieved her suffering. I remember feeling tired—weary—wanting to remain in the car, to stay in the driver's seat and close my eyes for a nap, if only for a few minutes.

Earlier in the day I had spoken to Craig at his school in Worcester. "We'll meet you with Lezlie at Pine Hill," I instructed.

"Oh," Craig said, sighing. "Is she dead?"

"No. She is dying, but she's not dead. We're going to visit the cemetery and look at where she'll be interred." I heard myself say "interred." It sounded as incongruous as it had whistling for a police car when I needed a taxi. Nor did I think well of the word "grave." "Interred" seemed more genteel, the better of two discredited venues.

Shadow came, too. She was seven years old then and took an instant liking to the cemetery, but she was remarkably well-behaved as if the significance of this visit were not entirely lost on her. We do attribute more than merited comprehension to canines—at least to our own canines—but Shadow was no longer "just a dog"; she now had the distinction of "dog nurse." Always devoted to Lezlie, she was now glued to her mistress, watching and looking, as if trying to understand why things were different while knowing that they were very different. Shadow was also the chief of comic relief, with her kitchen hockey antics and intelligent expression. She even had her own "friendly dog theme song" which I chanted to make-do melody. We tried so hard then to bring humor into our lives, sometimes more successfully than others. Even the IV apparatus that trailed Lezlie at her cemetery visit like preserved foods after Napoleon's army had a special name. We named the upstairs IV pole Zbigniew Polesky after Jimmy Carter's national security advisor. The downstairs IV pole was South Polesky.

We were not alone at Pine Hill. One of Lezlie's friends, Charlene Robeson, was the town cemetery commissioner then, and she accompanied us with the professional air and good will of a familiar real estate agent surveying home building sites. Sherborn is a small New England town and everyone knew us then. Our minister Ashley Atherton would later tell us later that it reminded her of the last act in *Our Town*.

Pine Hill is a broad expanse of hilly woods...not dense...lots of breathing room between the leafless maples and the evergreens. In the distance from the site of the place that we chose for "being interred," one could see the spire of the Pilgrim Church and on Sundays the church bells chimed hourly.

Kate and Craig—resolute in their roles—looked sadly perplexed but remained loyal to their mother's wishes. The event had an eerie and unreal quality as if Lezlie's tour of Pine Hill had nothing to do with her life coming to an end. It was more like a change of venue, as if Lezlie's was a planned separation and this would be the new place of her residence. I was certain that the children thought the whole thing quite weird, but they were good-natured about it and went along with it as if it were not weird but just the very sort of thing you do with your mother when she is going to die. There was no getting away from that eventuality. Perhaps that was her intent...that Lezlie was making sure that none of us take imaginative refuge from the truth of her passing. Never one for puns, I took some delight in the name of the funeral director from Waterman's. His name was Will Leave. I told Lezlie and the children that it sounded like a comment on mortality. No one laughed.

Lezlie's mood frightened me in a way...the forthright way in which she began to learn of all the options and organize the scene of her dying, as if undertaking knitting lessons. Her face had an intense determined look...her eyes bright, unsmiling now…serious…set back in eye sockets deepening with the wasting brought on by her advancing cancer. She was still strong then, and she strode across the ground, mindless of the intravenous apparatus with which we pursued her…surveying the edges of the cemetery as its grassy composition invaded the surrounding almost endless woods. *How many people can they…we…bury here*, I wondered. I thought of the many people over the years who might come to Sherborn and die here. I thought about it at length as if having discovered death for the first time.

Her mood frightened me because for the moment I was not sure that I knew this Lezlie…*But then, her moods were varying.* I thought of how different she appeared now than just a few days back when Craig recorded her in her last Boston Hospital admission. She seemed so much more at peace then and I imagined it would remain that way throughout her homecoming. Sometimes she was still at peace, but not now at Pine Hill. *Sometime later she would be at peace at Pine Hill.*

"…I've really done a lot of praying," she had said for the tape recorder. "I have, you know…it really helps me the way the family has reacted…the fact that the family has been able to be together, that people have been able to cry. They've been able to cry…then not cry…then cry again." It was the family that mattered most to Lezlie. What did the scene at Pine Hill have to do with family? Was this a final resting place we all would share? Certainly we thought that way as we talked with Charlene Robeson about where we would place the engraved name plates that would mark not only Lezlie's passage but mine as well in some future if seemingly never-to-be time. Or was this to be a mystical meeting place, a kind of parlor…a place to convene and share the indelible memories?

"I feel cheated," she had said for Craig's tape recording, "just because I'm selfish and wish that I could be here and have fun with Owen…and watch you guys from afar…you know…your lives. So I leave you partly to watch over yourself…" None of us wanted that—to watch just for ourselves.

Perhaps the cemetery and the funeral service we would plan together and the Canadian rose granite stone that would reflect the late afternoon sun would become pieces of a great puzzle. I remember those five-hundred-piece puzzles that I worked in my youth. I remember how they would portray something concrete when I completed them…how the varying unrelated shapes became something with a meaning that I could point to as if to say, "and this is what it is all about?"

Then it changed again…We were back on Stoney Brook Road and Lezlie was in the living room on the sofa that could become a fold-out bed when she could no longer manage the stairs to our bedroom. She took the morphine at intervals around the clock. I would administer it...or Kate with Rick's assistance...and Lezlie would doze, then awaken and visit with the family and friends who came to help us.

She was selective about her visitors in order to conserve her strength. Understanding friends were respectful and kept their distance without hurt feelings when Lezlie chose to exclude them. I had always told my patients, especially those who most fear social isolation, how important it was that they not "entertain" their visitors. Lezlie understood that well and was steadfast in making the most of these last days or weeks. *It won't be months,* I thought, then wondered, *Does she think it will be months?*

The living room sofa became Lezlie's command post. Four friends formed an inner circle and became her general staff. They came from the four corners of her life. Alice and Lezlie had become close friends when the two women were first pregnant. They met in 1971 at the washing machine at Charles River Towers, which was visible from Storrow Drive that flanks the river—named for British Royalty—that courses past Harvard to the sea. Jackie was a friend from church. The two women wrote much of the Sunday School curriculum. Elinor, who had been Natalie Ralston's nursing instructor, worked with Lezlie when she taught at Boston Children's Hospital. The fourth friend, Linda, was a neighbor with children whose ages were the same as Craig and Kate. Each of them knew intuitively exactly what to say to Lezlie, how long to stay and visit, and how to offer their help so that Lezlie could accept it without feeling that she burdened them.

The women in Lezlie's life were loyal and loving, the main ones who were her chiefs of staff and the many others who also helped. They brought food, they drove her to hospital appointments, they helped Kate and our family visitors from British Columbia. Alice would later be as close as one could to being a surrogate mother for Kate. After Lezlie died, Linda and another neighbor would visit our home daily for a year to care for Shadow while I was at work.

Like the rest of us, Lezlie's friends were devastated by her illness not only because they loved her, but also in another way: they were women in the same time of life. They were always energetic with Lezlie, realistic within the bounds of reality...positive without pretense. But I could see beneath it all that they were afraid...fearful of losing their close friend and fearful for themselves. Lezlie had been the helper, the adviser, the confidant. She was a young fifty-one and vigorous...the strong one...and she was suddenly imperiled. Sometimes when those closest of her friends came to visit, I thought of the Biblical story of Ruth...*Whither thou goest I shall go...*

It was a sad and confusing time but also it was a loving time. During the day I spent several hours at the office. Rick was at home with Lezlie and Kate. Lezlie dozed off and on with the morphine and Rick would venture into the yard pruning bushes and working at the home repairs I had avoided. "I need to keep busy," he admitted.

I had counseled families about how the end is not predictable. Things get worse and then better and then worse again and at some point it doesn't get better. Now I needed to counsel my own family. "One of these days," I told Kate and Craig, "There will be no more 'little Lezlie.' It will shock us and we will do our best together...call the funeral director, notify the visiting nurse, and telephone Grandmother Anne. It will be incredibly difficult. We'll go through it together..."

Psychiatrists, clergy, social workers...these are the symphony conductors for the chorus of grievers. I adopted that role with our family—or tried to. I did not always do a good job of it. In the same way that I helped orchestrate my wife's medical care, I tried to make sense of her passing, to provide a structure of sorts for the children and for our extended families. I had the hardest time with our two mothers; with Lezlie's because she was too distant, guarded. With my mother because she was too close, too visibly heartbroken.

There was another larger problem that I did not anticipate that blind-sided me. It was the matter of identity. I did not anticipate as I might have that when I lost Lezlie, I would lose so much of myself. I would confront it when I next visited the cemetery with Craig...this time without Lezlie because she would be too ill and without Kate because she would remain at home with her mother.

20

ORIGINS

o o o o o o o o o o o o o o o o o o o o o o o o o o o o o o o o o o o
In love's bond we metamorphose.

—The Examined Life
Robert Nozick

Lezlie's mother came from a hard southwestern background. She was a tall large-jawed woman with prominent but attractive facial features, big hands, and skin that wrinkled like linen. Anne was an educated well-read woman who strove throughout her life to transcend the hardness, but never could. She was full of contradiction. Her mind was keen but she lacked insight. She lived in Canada for most of her adult life but maintained American citizenship. Her manner was robust—bold—but her taste was refined. "Just do your own thing" and "carry on…" were her phrases that I best recall when listening to my memory of her voice. But she never quite did her own thing. That was her misfortune. Anne Barry had dreamed of having an executive career in New York but gave it up for a handsome English Canadian. She raised their two children in Victoria among in-laws from an alien culture. Anne's origins were Irish Catholic. Her husband, Arthur Bruce Humber, was an unpretentious ingenuous man with parentage as fundamentally English as the Humber River.

Phillip Barry, Anne's father, had been a powerful man who quit Ireland to keep his life, then claimed enough American land to give his ranch a place on the national map. Perhaps Anne, too, intended to claim something big. It was never quite clear what that might be…an abstraction no doubt…dignity, perhaps…or prestige—something that would fulfill her potential in a way that occurred uncommonly for women of her generation.

I talk with her still and there is terrible sadness in her voice when she talks about Lezlie. Anne could never fully embrace her daughter, perhaps because women didn't count in the world from which she came. Anne idolized her son. "We had different mothers," Rick would tell me, disconsolately, when I visited him in Victoria in 1997, three years after Lezlie left us. I recalled then how Anne had once referred to him as her "golden egg." She had said it just that way. It was the summer of Lezlie's death. We had dined together at a Thai restaurant in Wellesley. Craig was there, and Kate, with two of her Mountain School friends. Lezlie was still strong enough then and she delighted in the interaction among the young people. Then Anne held forth those often repeated nuggets of family history. "And then I had my golden egg..." she said. It was that way with Anne. The stories about Rick and how he put her "on top of the fridge..." as Anne told and retold about a time in her son's adolescence that only she could remember.

In a time later, when it was closer to the end, Kate was at home with Anne and Lezlie. They were in the master bedroom at Stoney Brook. Kate looked on as her grandmother withdrew her hand from Lezlie's gentle grip. That was how Kate described it...as an act of withdrawal. I was not there to judge it, but even if it were a misperception, there would have been some basis for seeing it as Kate had. That aloofness of Anne's was not for lack of love nor from want of maternal calling. When Lezlie and I had talked about her mother, as we often did, I reminded her that Anne did love her, however remote the expression of love might be. "This is the same lady who kept you warm by the oven when you were born premature on the plains of Alberta," I would tell my wife. I remembered the photos that remained from those years. Anne had dressed in that padded-shoulder, hat-adorned style of the forties. She was a strong woman, good looking, resolute, competent. There had been pictures, too, of Lezlie's dad, Bruce, movie-picture handsome in RCAF uniform. No wonder Anne had fallen for him and given up those New York dreams.

Pictures were Anne's main preoccupation in the last month of Lezlie's life. She spent hours at it, sorting out triplicate photos that we retrieved for her from our disorderly basement. I would see her placing copies in each of three albums that would be for the children and me. It was as if her fear of the future and pain from the past left no room for emotions in the present.

Anne was so interesting...all the stories, embellished over the years like whipped cream on strawberries. How Phillip Barry put his Englishman son-in-law on a fast horse that rode off into the Nevada desert. Anne's father, Phillip, was part real, part myth, and the parts were irretrievably commingled. Phillip, we were told, had come to America as a condition of his release from the Tower of London, but his scene of incarceration might have been at some other location. He had been held there—at whichever place—because of Sinn Fein associations.

According to family fact—or legend—a priest had pleaded for his release. There were stories from Phillip's early ranching years in the American South West…how desperados stole his cattle and tied Anne's father to his horse…how he returned to see them hanged. He sounded bigger than big. He might have lived forever, I thought, were it not for the truck accident on the ranch that took him in his mid-eighties. *How would it have been to meet him*, I wondered, and imagined myself taking the reins of a horse, as my father-in-law had done…then being borne off into the desert.

Phillip Barry came from a man's world, but he favored Anne. She had a tough, smart, independent—actually rebellious—nature, but she also knew the gentle side…she'd made the lace dress for Lezlie's high school prom. In her working years, when I met her, she helped run the Library at The University of Victoria—"The University" was how she said it. "The You—Nih—Ver—Sit—ee," Lezlie would say, imitating her mother. With the same pride that Anne related the Rick stories, she would tell me of how Saul Bellow visited U Vic and how she rescued him, in a manner of speaking, and invited him to her home to tea. First it was tea—then the story changed. Saul Bellow stayed the night…nothing intimate, of course. He had admired her silver collection.

When I arrived home in the evenings to Stoney Brook Road, I found Anne at her picture albums in the dining room. Lezlie's sister-in-law Dianne joined us with her girls: Larisa (six) and Jocelyn (nine), and with my nephew Graeme, who was seventeen. Rick kept active at the landscaping and Lezlie's friends delivered the bounty of food which was magically assembled on dinner plates in a stir of activity while Lezlie rested on the living room sofa bed. I played with Larisa and Jocelyn…told them of my imaginary twin brother, Bill. "Have you seen Bill?" I would ask. "That guy…boy is he weird!"

"Would you like milk or non-milk?" I asked one night at dinner.

"What is 'non-milk?'"

"Every liquid that you can drink that's not milk," I said.

"We'd like milk," they replied.

"Would you like milk in your milk?" I asked. It was fun to play the Mad Hatter.

"Do you want some Seven-Up, Uncle Owen?" asked Jocelyn.

"No," I said. "My non-milk is orange juice."

There was so much silliness. It was such a wonderful way of chasing off fear. We played kitchen hockey with Shadow. I sang her "Friendly Dog Theme Song" and kept score while she guarded her "nets." In between, the girls would visit with their aunt. "Laughter is good for you," she told them drowsily.

The end was approaching. *When would it come?*

"I want Dianne to have my ring," Lezlie said, wanting to know if I agreed with that. "She never had a real diamond."

"Sure," I said, feeling only a moment of possessiveness. "She and Rick have been so wonderful. It's a great idea." Much later I would reaffirm that belief.

There would be the tape recording Lezlie had made with Craig at the hospital…a living record that we have. "I'd just like to say a word here about my sister-in-law, Dianne," Lezlie had said, "who's like a sister. She's an absolute gift—one of the most loving people I ever met. Years ago she taught me how to put eyeliner on when she had a date with Rick. She's my…it's nice to feel…she understands me."

"Oh…no," Dianne said when Lezlie told her about the ring. "I couldn't take that." She was gracious about it—accepted and treasured it.

The famous emerald ring would go to Kate…and the pearls.

Lezlie had something, too, that she wanted me to have. "An orphan to history…" as someone once described the ones like me who had no trace of ancestry in Eastern Europe. I had marveled at my bride's fabulous ancestry…the heraldic Humbers and the Barry forebears who traced their indirect ancestry to Commodore John Barry, Father of the US Navy. I had brought home those prints of Barry and the USS United States from Goodspeed's on Beacon Hill. Lezlie had wanted nothing to do with it. "We don't even know if we really are related," she insisted.

"But your cousin is named John Barry," I had said.

"They made it up," she said.

Nor did she want anything to do with Barry's biography that had been sponsored by the Order of the Sons of St. Patrick. I had retrieved the rare book from the Dover library. It later disappeared. I looked everywhere, ultimately paying the fifty dollar fine.

One day a few days later, Lezlie and I were in the bedroom. She could manage the stairs if only once or twice a day. She made her way to her antique Victorian dresser while dragging along "North Polesky" and the IV fluids. She bent over the upper drawers. She was thin, bony, with no hair, bent like a feather…fragile, but in her way not fragile at all.

"Here," she said, extending her hand with the long-lost Barry book.

"You hid it!" I said, laughing, "You hid it…I can't believe it. You hid it."

I wondered what larger meaning it could have. Lezlie had given her diamond to Dianne, her emerald to Kate, her recorded advice to Craig. I wondered what special thing she had for me. Perhaps it was the ancestors—from her mother's side—that seemed to give me license to my own country's heritage.

The ancestors were wonderful. John Barry, the Revolutionary War hero...Captain of the Alliance...Captain of The USS United States, the same frigate Stephen Decatur would bring to war against the Barbary Pirates. I had shared in those adventures as a youth and pretended I was a ship's officer captured on the North African coast. I escaped in a daring rescue, as the Sultan readied to boil me in oil.

As Lezlie lived those final weeks, I watched her mother, busy at her picture albums, and thought that I was in my own way a lot like Anne. I believed that she, too, had claimed her mate's ancestors...Bruce Humber's blueblood beginnings, and his maternal grandfather, Charles Hackett, whose daring rescue of a foundering American ship won praise and a gold watch from Theodore Roosevelt. Anne displayed it proudly in the living room of her English Tudor home. My mother-in-law...daughter of the turn-of-a-century Irish revolutionary.

How different was that experience from my own with the shards of anti-Semitism that pierced the prose of F. Scott Fitzgerald in *The Great Gatsby*, of Hemingway in *The Sun Also Rises*, even Shakespeare—master of masters—*in The Merchant of Venice*.

My mother-in-law became a pretender to Victoria society much as I later absorbed the relatives—Irish and British—who imparted the panache of the dominant class. It was a silly predilection, but very real. My union with Lezlie had enabled me to cross the boundaries of my ethnic Jewish past. Now my wife was dying and with her those parts that had become parts of me. What better bequest than to leave me with the ancestors?

On October 24, Craig and I revisited the cemetery. We wanted it to be a place we could visit and sit and be with Lezlie in a way. Neighbors had placed a park bench on the adjoining site. There was a rock with a golden eagle and a soccer ball and flag were by the grave where our neighbors had buried their son, one of Craig's classmates.

The granite man, Ed Michaels, came with us, along with Will Leave, the funeral director. "He looks like he was carved from granite himself," I said to Will when the monument man was at a distance.

I thought along with Craig of what Lezlie was and had been at her core. Before our son's birth, Lezlie had worked at Boston Children's Hospital. There was an insignia, a nurse holding a child to her bosom. I described it for Mr. Michaels. Could he replicate it? He said that he could. We would get whatever permission was required and he would etch the insignia on a flat stone marker that would bear Lezlie's name and her dates. I could have a marker for myself…it was cost saving to do it now. I said that would be good. Could he do a caduceus—the staff and serpent that symbolize my calling? Ed said he'd be happy to do that.

How strange this all is, I thought. *Isn't it something for old people?* The men that accompanied us were helpful…knew about all of this. My son and I were strangers in this cemetery land. Leave knew it well; he had lost a young wife years earlier. I was sorry for his tragedy but comforted by his experience. I thought of how it was the same way for my patients with catastrophic illness—how they felt better after meeting others who had survived transplantation. Leave had survived the death of a wife.

I gazed about at the many memorials, the gravestones and markers. *What meaning do they have? Where are the visitors? Do they come alone, unseen?* Much later I would read Howard Colvin's *Architecture and the After Life.* "Man," he wrote, "has known few greater stimuli to architectural and artistic creativity than the attempt to transcend his own mortality." That is what it was…the strangeness. I faced the death of my wife…the death of a part of her identity that had fused with my own. Ultimately I faced my own death. *Impossible,* I thought. *The world exists because I see it. That is ridiculous! The world is the world and I am me…* The thought of my own death made no sense then, nor does it now. *If I die, will it all have been a dream?* I had thought. *And if it is a dream, can I awaken from it?* Do similar thoughts…troubling, unanswerable…deter those who build monuments to loved ones but rarely visit?

Craig and I spoke little then, but we shared everything. He reminded me of a large rock he'd discovered at the corner of our property. He said it was shaped like a chair—a chair rock—and he asked if we could move it to the cemetery. He thought he'd like to sit there sometimes after Lezlie died. I replied that our landscaper could move it. *This is just another piece of real estate. How very strange!* It would be real estate with a gravestone and the family name carved into rose granite with block capital letters.

"Should it say SURMAN," I wondered aloud, "or HUMBER/SURMAN?" Craig said I was trying to be an aristocrat.

21

HOLDING HANDS

o o o o o o o o o o o o o o o o o o o o o o o o o o o o o o o o o o

Nuptial love maketh mankind;
friendly love perfecteth it.

—*Of Love*
Frances Bacon

Lezlie did not visit the cemetery that second time. She was too fatigued, too sleepy. It was hard to tell to what extent the drowsiness was from the morphine that we gave her at intervals to keep the pain under control. The drowsy periods became longer. She was confused sometimes when she awakened, but we could reorient her. I wondered if her diet was too much for her or if the cancer was growing in her liver. I wondered how close we were to the end and remembered the many times that I had attended patients near the end of life...how their families waited, torn between the threat of loss and the threat of wakeful suffering that only loss by death can relieve.

In the evening after Craig and I visited Pine Hill, our family was joined by Georgia, the visiting nurse who still writes and sends us holiday greetings five years later. She changed Lezlie's intravenous solution. I said that I thought her liver was failing. There is a sign of that—called a liver flap—in which the extended hand beats like a bird's wing. I wanted Georgia to see it...that made sense...then showed Craig. Rick watched in silence. Sometimes I felt foolish in his presence...I could see my own foibles and limitations...wondered now if I were showing off in some bizarre way for my medical student son. Why? What weakness of character required me to demonstrate an intellectual control of these morbid events? Rick said nothing. Later I talked with him about the emptiness I knew I would feel when it was over. "I long for its conclusion," I told him, "but realize that there will be an untenable aloneness."

"I will change my life," I told my brother-in-law. "I'll take writing courses…"
It was reassuring to talk with him, even though I felt petty and ridiculous at times
in doing so. I tried to be so firmly in control of the events that spun around
Lezlie's dying. I could see what was happening too clearly. I knew what to
do…the many things that I could do to ease her suffering. It was never enough
and afterward—long afterward—I would feel a terrible sense of inadequacy. Rick
was the quiet observer…the listener. He did not know the biological intrica-
cies…the landscape of illness, but his presence was strong and steady. In the day-
time, he pruned the hedge and fixed our flagstone walkways.

At four o'clock the morning of that same night—late in October, 1994—I
awakened to the alarm. I would set the clock at intervals of three to four hours to
give her the pain medication. Lezlie had reported no pain since 9:30 p.m. Our
plan was to keep ahead of it. For the most part, that proved effective.

It was my habit now to retire early with her, to lie beside her and hold her
hand. I wondered sometimes whether she would die that way. Would I awaken
to find no one beside me but the structure she left behind? It was an awful
thought. Fortunately, I did not think of it often and could dismiss it when I did
think that way. The greater part of those nights was peaceful…remarkably so.
Sometimes I found myself wanting to smile at her, reaching over and stroking her
head lightly while she slept…stroking her balding Buddha head.

I thought about our early days together…always returned to that. I had
known even then, in those challenging years of medical school, that I would
someday look back on it as the best time of our lives together. It was "someday"
now. There was, nonetheless, a fabulous tranquility now in holding her hand. It
puzzled me. In the later years of our marriage, before her illness, I would lie
beside Lezlie, frustrated by the lack of physical passion that menopause had
dulled. "I'm settling," she would say of her body…her widening hips…her uterus
clumsy with fibroids. I would sometimes lie with her then when she slept and
yearn for the younger Lezlie that could build a fire in me that burned clean all the
wooden fragments in my life. We would still have that sometimes in the later
years, but the times were farther between. I was almost always the initiator when
it came to sex, but sometimes she would approach me in the most unexpected
way. In the lake, for example, in the late summer, near the boat landing. I would
be embarrassed, but she would prevail.

That was her paradox, her mystery. Lezlie was the quintessential Anglo-
Saxon…composed, poised, impassive. Then suddenly there would be that wonderful epiphany and she would be alive with unrestrained sexual energy. When
that happened, it would remind me of the time that she seduced me in the mid-

dle of Mount Royal, when we were coupled together in the most basic way…half-dressed, incompletely hidden behind bushes that flanked the well-traveled climbing paths.

I wanted that part of her more as it became less. I suppose that is always the way of it. At times I would think—foolishly, embarrassingly—of how it might be if she were no longer in my life and I were free to find the romance that we had once shared every day. It was a selfish thought. I don't know if it is usual for men to think that way. I'm not an analyst. My patients do not talk to me about such things. They struggle too much with daily limitations of ill health or with the distress of interpersonal conflict…with episodes of anxiety or panic that seem spontaneous…with sleeplessness or depression. I do not know what other men think in their private thoughts when lying in bed at night, hungry for sex. I have no basis of comparison. I have sometimes felt—if only for a moment—that I wanted to be separate from her although I loved her dearly. Now she was dying beside me and all I wanted to do…all that mattered to me…was to hold her hand. The sensuality of that rivaled anything I had known before. Nature brings such irony. Less was now more, as they say, the 'sip more quenching than the quaff.'

"Why is the alarm going off?" Lezlie asked.

"For the MS (morphine)," I said. "I set it for three hours." The alarm was blaring and insistent. I turned it off.

Awake now, Lezlie checked her notes. I had not written down the last morphine dose. *She is a nurse*, I thought. *I remember perfectly well what she's had and when she had it. She is the one who is confused. But she is a nurse…everything has to be charted.*

Lezlie allowed me to repeat the morphine that I injected into her IV, but only after we had discussed it several times. She was awake, but confused. *It's her liver*, I thought. *Liver failure is a good way to die…quiet…dozing…painless.* I did not want her to die. There were times that I did want that ultimate relief from her suffering—but not now.

"Did you get the urn?" she asked.

"Why are we discussing this now?" I wanted to know. It was 4:20 in the morning. I am not a morning person under the best of circumstances.

"Because there is no time to discuss things," she said sensibly.

"Yes," I answered. "Two mahogany cylindrical urns like your father's." It had been seven years since Bruce had died. We had spread his ashes—surprised that they were actually bone fragments—not ashes. We released them into the wind at the cinder track at the University of Victoria. Now it was Lezlie's wish that her ashes be divided, half buried in an urn at Pine Hill, half scattered at the private lake in the Victoria highlands where we had spent our honeymoon in 1969.

"I have both nameplates arranged," I added. "They will be placed side by side."

"I didn't ask you that," Lezlie said. *I forget that she is limited in what she can process,* I thought. "You are saying too much. Just stick with one question."

I repeated to Lezlie about the urn, paused, then mentioned the name plates again. *This is what our marriage is like. I will ultimately have my way.*

"Why is your name going to be there, too?"

"I'm going to die also," I said, "Just not now."

"But," she said, "what if you remarry and in the prenuptial agreement she wants to be buried with you?"

"What!" I said, amazed. She repeated what she had said. "I don't believe this." I could feel the tears welling up. *I've done enough of that for now,* I thought, holding back.

"Are you putting me down?" she asked. Her speech was slurred.

"No...no...no...I'm just incredulous! What am I going to do without you?"

"You'll do just fine," she said. "Things will go on as they do, and I'll be looking in and saying, 'What's he doing that for?' but others will say, 'You can't expect anything different of him at this point,' and they'll accept it."

I laughed, then held her hand.

22

DON'T STICK OUT YOUR TONGUE!

o o o o o o o o o o o o o o o o o o o o o o o o o o o o o o o o o

Time goes by so fast. Nothin' can outrun it. Death commences too early—almost before you're half acquainted with life—you meet the other...

—Big Mama *Cat on a Hot Tin Roof*, Act 3
Tennessee Williams

There are nine days left in February. It is a leap year...especially for me. I am selling the house at Stoney Brook Road. Craig has been slow to come to terms with it, but has joined me today to sort through the furniture. What does he want to take? What can be discarded? What things must I store? He has come at midday. A bright sun reflects off his silver Volvo station wagon. The yard is full of snow. Winter began its chill after an unseasonably warm December. The season now behaves like a medical intern late for rounds, moving furiously about to catch up on lost time.

"I will be angry if you don't take that," Craig admonishes, talking about the American country blue coffee table that Kate made at Concord Academy. "I don't have room for everything," he adds. "You definitely need to take that." Sometimes I think my children have mutinied and appointed themselves as parents. It does not offend me. I have seen it in the office when an adult child accompanies a parent who is elderly or widowed.

"Fine," I tell him, passively, knowing that in the end I will do whatever works best. I feel especially close to Craig now. A few weeks ago, I met with his journal club at the Harvard-Longwood campus. We discussed uses of medical hypnosis and Craig reviewed the paper I had written years ago on hypnosis for treatment of warts.

"We'll start with your paper," he had said. "They are interested in career development...." It was a good session...especially good to see how much at home Craig was with his fellow residents.

The feelings are raw now as the two of us face the loss we have suffered. "I found a note to you from Lezlie. Do you want to see it?" Craig asks. He is seated at the foot of the cellar stairs. He wears a surgical mask to keep clear of the dust. He is recovering from bronchitis and coughs at times as he sorts through the papers that lead back in time like rings of a great tree cut in cross section.

"Sure," I say, then hesitate. I had the same response when he inquired about our wedding picture that hangs in the living room. It has been so long since I inspected it closely. Doing so now creates that familiar emptiness in my chest that used to be constant.

Craig reaches over his shoulder and hands me a torn yellow sheet as I descend the stairs. I read his mother's undated note:

O

cold roast beef in

    foil

hot gravy on warmer

salad-dressing in frig

peaches in frig

bacon on warmer

    Love me

PS give Happy his pills please

I take the note upstairs to my office. The emptiness has returned in me. *Is this poetry?* I look across the polished hardwood floor and search for the familiar volume of Ezra Pound—*The Cantos*—two shelves up from the bottom...dusty...*all the things I must throw out. How does her poetry compare to his,* I wonder, and thumb through the book, another leftover from my University days in Montreal where Lezlie and I shared the passions of unseasoned love.

Lezlie is everywhere in this house...her directions on the Maytag washing machine. "Kate, Kate, Kate turn the dial to 2.4 black for colored clothing...." Her poetry is greater than Pound's.

I am obsessed by my own writing, as if on a mission, as if my dead wife were alive in this process. "I want you to write," she often said. Now I tell Craig I am afraid I will not find time to write…the demands of moving and so forth. "It's a luxury," he tells me. Craig has shared my writing. His comment annoys me.

"It is not a luxury," I tell him. *What is it, then?* I wonder. I know what it is…the house of the memories of the life I had with her.

Yesterday—Craig was here yesterday, too—we stopped in the process of tagging the furniture and labeling the possessions that will remain in the family. I read to him about the Fugakyu sushi bar…he has joined me there…and about his mother and the minister and Bob Best's house call days before her death. As I read to him, I burst into tears. He comes to my side and hugs me and buries his head in my shoulder and cries with me. "It's not fair," he says. It feels good to cry in grief, as if purging an entropic process that pulls on the mind like an undertow.

The children have accepted my decision to move from the country. Sherborn is for young families. It is time for some other family to begin the cycle of their children's growth. The new owners-to-be have a five-year-old son who has asked for the hammock on the screened-in porch. "That's nice," Craig says. "Lezlie would like that."

This interlude with Craig makes me think of the wonderful job his grandmother has done in helping the children deal with the many changes that have followed in the five years since Lezlie's death. Grandmothers are like that. Masons of the mothering trade, they bring the mortar that holds firm the bricks of family life. When Craig was a child, suffering the consequences of attention deficit disorder…when Lezlie and I suffered along with him…his grandmother would come with the strength of experience…that stabilizing force…hope generating…love.

Early in our marriage, when Lezlie and I came to Boston for my psychiatry training and her work at Children's Hospital, my parents found us the brick apartment building in Watertown. Across the street there was a tributary of the Charles River. On the other side of the building was McDonald's Funeral Home, a reminder of the invisible sea that collects the flow of our lives.

Our two-bedroom unit looked out on the parking lot. Lezlie would look for me in the evening when I returned from the hospital in the 1967 used Thunderbird that was my father's gift at graduation from medical school. I remember once looking up at my wife as she held an undiscernible object at arm's length through the living room window. "Your mother brought a pickled tongue," she called out with that unique mixture of humor and disgust that can fly gracefully across an ethnic divide.

"Oh?" I said, embarrassed.

"You told her you missed having it."

"Don't stick out your tongue!"

I drove the Thunderbird proudly in those days. Later we took it with us to Pearl Harbor, then shipped it back to the mainland when my tour of active duty naval service was completed. The car had a checkered career, having spent its first five thousand miles in service of one of the local Mafiosi who returned it to the dealer with no questions asked. Mother's family had been in the used car business and were still at it when Lezlie and I came to Boston. She needed a car as well. Money was tight, and for the appealing price of $100 they provided a solidly built 1963 used Chevy which transported Lezlie safely—if not proudly—until the day the steering wheel fell off. "There I was," Lezlie said, "stopped in traffic with everybody honking at me."

"What did you do?"

"I just opened up the window. 'Look,' I said, and held the steering wheel out of the window where they could all see it."

Laughing, I said, "What happened after that?"

"They stopped honking!"

There was a warm relationship between my mother and Lezlie, but there was always a certain unevenness between them, as there is between bricks that have not settled quite right.

Now, my mother has become the family matriarch and her retirement home condominium is the new county seat for our nuclear family. We dine there together twice a month on Sundays. Between visits, the children call, confide in her, complain about their father.

"I feel that our relationship is closer now," she told me last week.

"Yes, it is." I knew what was coming next. She too was thinking about those last days before Lezlie's death, when Lezlie refused to see her or my father.

"Frankly," Mother began, "I haven't said anything about it, but…"

"Don't," I interrupted. "I know what you are talking about. It is best not to say anything." There is a pause in our conversation, like the silent time between scenes in a play. "I know it was pretty rough when she wouldn't let you see her." I remember vividly my parents' last visit in November, 1994.

It was a chilly day in November. Mother appeared at the top of the long, sloping driveway at Stoney Brook Road. Bent forward from osteoporosis, she was dressed in a plain-colored windbreaker and rain hat. I recall how she stood with the support of her cane. Her face was sorrowful and angry.

We talked outside together, long enough for me to feel awkward and ungracious. "I suppose Lezlie has no use for my aunt's ring," Mother said.

"Why are we talking about the ring?" I said. There was nothing special about it. Mother had given it to Lezlie when I gave her the emerald ruby for our twenty-fifth wedding anniversary. It was symbolic of the link my mother yearned to have with my wife, but this was not to be. Lezlie had always loved her as if from a distance.

"No," I said about the ring. Mother looked as if she were victimized and helpless. I could feel a growing annoyance. Her distress was burdensome to me. My wife was dying. I was impatient with the lamentation of aging parents. Why? I think now it was because they had no right to outlive her, as if the postponement of death were a competitive event in which those who win are sometimes old and sometimes young and lose a little time. "Do you want me to ask her to give it back?" It was a cruel question.

I was angry, too, because I was her son and I was supposed to comfort her, and I could not do it. This was my mother after all, dear to me from fond memories of her undying love. This was the same mother who nurtured my confidence and lessened the pains of childhood disappointments. The truth was, however—we each knew it—that Lezlie would refuse to see her. It was clear, now that Mother's pain from Lezlie's rejection was enormous. It was because the pain was so great—my mother's and my own—that I could not console her. There was nothing left in me for that. Instead I became increasingly irritable. "I can't have you coming into the house like that," I said—it was a cruel admonition—"it's too much emotion. Lezlie can't handle it!"

My mother's eyes welled with tears. "What do you expect?" she said. "I don't know what you want from me." She was crying now—she never cried. My father came and stood silently by her. It seemed to me, right or not, that he somehow understood. He wanted to protect my mom, but understood that there was no choice but for her to let go.

"Pull yourself together," I said to her. My tone was harsh, insistent. At the very same time that the words came out I thought of her age—eighty—and the absurdity and dishonor of this confrontation.

"Maybe I should just go," she said. Along with her despair, she was angry that Lezlie was dying. How much of it was anger at Lezlie's evident intent to exclude her mother-in-law? How much of it was anger at me for failing her? I knew it was all three.

"That's all right," I said. "If that's what you think is best. You're angry."

"Of course I'm angry," Mother said, her face now distorted with tears, framed by the nondescript, flimsy rain hat anchored with a knot beneath her chin.

"Our relationship will go on for another twenty years," I said.

"Whose relationship?"

"Yours and mine. It will go on for twenty years." It was a non sequitur. I was groping for something, not sure what it was, but aware that the bond to my mother would remain when Lezlie's life passed. I was telling my mother that I needed her at the same time I was pushing her away. I felt an awful guilt about it as if, like Conrad's Lord Jim, I had abandoned a ship and its passengers in a storm at sea.

"I would do anything for you." She was openly sobbing. She was a strong, determined woman. I had never seen her like this. My guilt increased my anger.

"Then pull yourself together, right now," I ordered, desperately. "I am a grieving man. This is my wife—not your daughter. If you help me with this I will value that. If you make things difficult with anger and histrionics, I will never forget it." I was shaking inside...almost irrational. Why? It was the conflict, the intolerable conflict. These were my parents. I loved them, but inside the house my wife was dying and my parents would be an encumbrance.

Mother was not crying now. She walked in a steady way, then gripped the wrought iron railing and painfully pulled herself up the brick steps to my house. She entered the family room where Lezlie's mother sat with the vacant look of one who has survived a catastrophic natural event.

I left the two mothers and my father and walked into the living room. I asked Lezlie twice...gently...if she wanted to see my parents. She shook her head. It was too much for her. Their emotions would overwhelm her.

Now, five years later, while Mother is planning for an eighty-fifth birthday celebration, we are revisiting that other time.

"I know how hard it was that she wouldn't see you."

"It was terrible," Mother says. "It was just terrible. Your father and I loved her so much. We never had a chance to say goodbye."

"She loved you, too," I say. It was true. Lezlie did love them. Also, however, her love was mixed with the jealousy and regret that people sometimes have when love for a surrogate mother awakens the intense feeling of lost love from an unaffectionate biological mother. I remembered how, for example, when Lezlie had been well, she had helped me look for a function room for my parents' fiftieth anniversary. As she and I drove to the Dedham Hilton one Saturday morning, she plagued me with unsolicited directions. Finally, I pulled to the side of the road. "What in the world is wrong with you?" I demanded. "You are driving me crazy. I lived in this area for seventeen years."

Lezlie returned my gaze with that air of indelible certainty. "What kind of psychiatrist are you?" she demanded.

"What?"

"What kind of a psychiatrist are you?" she repeated. "Your parents are celebrating their fiftieth wedding anniversary and my father is dead."

It intrigues me, especially as a psychiatrist, how much the thumbprint of past loss and disappointment shapes our response to the important events and relationships in our lives. I wonder if this is part of nature's plan for survival…this powerful—at times unconscious—persistence with which we strive to repair old wounds.

As Craig and I clean house, the loss of Lezlie is intense in my thinking, and I know it is an event that I will carry forward wherever my move takes me. One of my patients, a veteran of the Pacific Theater in World War II has been a source of insight for me. He too lost a wife to cancer after twenty-five years of marriage. Then he remarried and has been with his second wife for thirty-three years. His psychological condition has responded well to treatment. Our visits now are only checkpoints for prevention. Warren Knox identifies with me…asks whenever he sees me how I am getting along. He's referring to my grief that reminds him of his own, now over three decades old.

In our most recent visit I asked about his first wife, Betty. Does he still think about her a lot?

"All the time," he said. "I would give both arms in order to talk with her for half an hour."

23

THE WEIRDEST DYING PERSON

o o o o o o o o o o o o o o o o o o o o o o o o o o o o o o o o
My days sprint past me like runners; I will never see them again....

—*The Book of Job*
Holy Bible

In the days that approached her mother's death, Kate and I talked more about how things would be after Lezlie's passing. We talked about the funeral. Kate said she didn't know what to do about people who might sympathize inordinately.

"You do it this way," I told her. Just the two of us were in the family room at the time. I asked her to stand and face me as if we were two actors at a dress rehearsal.

"You be the person," I instructed. "Now you just do what you learned in life-guarding." Kate took the role of the drowning swimmer reaching desperately to a rescuer. We were reenacting the block-and-parry technique that allows the life-guard to keep from being pulled under.

I took the role of rescuer. Grasping Kate's left elbow and wrist firmly in my right hand, I gently spun her about into the carry position. The process reminded me of those years in her childhood—Katie was about three—when we practiced "college wrestling" in the living room with her mom as referee. Katie would push out with her feet against my chest, and I would be propelled—albeit at my own effort—far across the living room floor...crashing into a wall, plummeting to the floor.

Perhaps Kate remembered that as well. We were both laughing now. "Alternatively, there is the feigned sneeze ploy," I said, "like this: ahhhhhh choo.... Oh! I'm sorry! I must be getting a cold."

We laughed and laughed.

Later that same evening, Lezlie's brother and sister and their children joined us after Rick drove his mother to the Wellesley Inn. We watched David Letterman. He was interviewing Sam Donaldson about the upcoming November 3 Senate race. Before we each retired for the night, Kate and I looked in on Lezlie, sleeping on the sofa bed in the living room. She was alive.

"Are you having a good sleep?" I asked Lezlie.

"Yes."

In the early morning hours, I read to my wife. There were a number of letters from family, neighbors, and friends. One very thoughtful letter came from a friend, Ed Billings, who was an administrator at Princeton. He had counseled both of our children when they began their college applications. Another note—I found it charming—came from a Philadelphia dowager whose son was under my care at Boston Hospital.

We compared skin color in the light of the early November morning. Her skin, now lightly pigmented, looked better than mine, I told her. "You look like you've been to Florida."

Lezlie smiled. "But I haven't been to Florida."

She seemed energetic just then…asked about whether she could take her oxygen—she had portable oxygen, now—for a trip in the car. I suggested more walks in the living room instead, maybe outside if the weather were warm enough.

The love poured out of me. "You're the weirdest dying person I've ever met," I said.

"I know," she replied.

The end began on November 4, 1994.

At 6:30 a.m., I left for transplant team rounds. Lezlie was comfortably awake after a painless night with no morphine from 10:30 p.m. Craig and Kate were alone with her. Their aunt and uncle were off with Jocelyn, Larisa, and Graeme and planned to meet Grandmother Anne in Wellesley at noon.

Transplant rounds were in a large conference room with four lengthy rectangular metal tables pulled together like a patchwork quilt. There was a tacit seating arrangement which unknowing visitors sometimes violated. The team was an assortment of surgeons, internists, and consultants that worked together and often helped each other in their personal lives. It was like a family…spiritually connected…embracing…sometimes funny.

It was 7:40 a.m. One of the liver specialists presented the case of a man with end stage alcoholic liver disease. He needed a transplant, but from the sound of it had not begun to come to terms with his alcohol dependence. I said that we should wait before listing him to cadaveric transplantation and see what our addictionologist recommended.

"If you list him now, I'll need a drink," I said. I was thinking of the chaos and regret that follows when a precious organ goes to someone who is not yet psychologically capable of caring for it. It was a crude comment, but good comic relief, and everybody laughed—we needed to do that sometimes. Then my beeper went off.

It was a call from Craig.

After what had seemed to be a good morning, Lezlie's pain hit at full force at 7:30 a.m. Then she fell while in the bathroom. Craig was there and broke her fall. He thought she'd had a seizure.

Kate took the phone. "Give her another shot of morphine," I said. I was thinking, as I directed her, that time was taking a shortcut past her years of adolescence and young adulthood. There was a sorrow about it, a "this isn't fair" dimension, but Kate could handle it.

This was my daughter whose reliability was a fact of community life in Sherborn; Kate who joked about her three near-death experiences…the near-fatal allergic reaction to a bee sting when we summered one year in Victoria…the Bactrim allergy that landed her in the hospital for a week of IV steroids when she was fourteen…the sailing accident—that was the worst—when she had crewed on her friend's family yacht. The weather was bad, and *Morpheus* had drifted into a catamaran race course with Kate below deck watching the Loran. She had emerged from the cabin just seconds before the pontoons of a big cat struck *Morpheus* broadside and rode across her stern. "Look out!" one of the crew members had screamed over the sound of the wind. Kate had thrown herself to the deck as the catamaran swept over her. How composed she had appeared when I arrived in Marion after racing along Route 128 at ninety-five miles an hour. She was fully in charge of herself—only the slightest bit shaken—despite the close call and an ear injured and swelling from contact with the deck when a pontoon had settled on her.

Now, as we spoke about her dying mother that Friday morning, November 4, 1994, I could picture Kate with her brother in the second floor master bedroom. The sun would be pouring in and Lezlie would be in bed with the IV apparatus beside her. I could feel Kate, competent, organized, thoughtful, but also afraid.

She's only eighteen! "Give her a milligram...up to the line on the syringe...And give her some Atavan under the tongue...Let me speak to Craig."

"Page the visiting nurse," I told Craig. "I'll cancel my day and be there in about an hour."

It took that long to get to Sherborn from the city. Georgia was there when I arrived...and the children were relieved to see me. I telephoned two of Lezlie's doctors, Bob Best and her primary care doctor, Bob Gentilly.

Georgia and I increased the morphine to two milligrams every ten minutes. It was enough to sedate Lezlie and relax her, but she would need more aggressive pain management.

I looked up at the bottle of intravenous solution that replaced her water loss. I knew now from Lezlie's recent blood chemistries that her kidneys were no longer working. That meant that her body would stop losing potassium. Potassium levels are critical to nerve and heart function—too much and she would have a cardiac arrest. That would end the ordeal simply and abruptly. There was potassium in the IV solution. *Maybe,* I thought. *Maybe I should keep it running...It could be a mistake...nobody would know.* Down low in the stomach, I had that feeling that our conscience creates. *No.*

It was a short drive—fifteen minutes—to the community hospital where I sent Lezlie's daily blood work. Professional courtesy is one of those substantial dividends of medical practice. "Just a minute," one of the nurses said, then returned with a liter bottle of IV solution without potassium. This would be the end of Lezlie. It would be hard for us...hard for me. *Can I get her the pain relief I promised? Yes.* If there is ever a time for euthanasia, this was not such a time.

I arrived home in a sweat and hung the new IV solution with the nurse's supervision. I retreated momentarily to the first floor bathroom—bathrooms are the great secret havens of the western world. There was some mild commotion. Then Kate came to the door. "There is some stranger that wants to see Mommy," she said in that little girl's voice she sometimes used in times of high emotion. For a brief interlude, time had reversed itself...had glided back past adolescence to the great safety of childhood. I remembered the stale psychiatric terms that I had learned in residency training: *"regression in service of the ego..."* Yeah!

The stranger was Dr. Miles, the hospice director.... Ellen Miles...*Jesus,* I thought. *Why do I say Jesus? Who cares? God...nature...something...is looking out for us.*

"I have a cold in the recovering stage," Ellen said, so she had postponed a planned visit to our home. Her timing was exquisite. Lezlie would have all the pain relief she needed...that we needed for her.

Dr. Miles coughed, as if to confirm her account of the resolving cold.

"Is that all right?" Lezlie inquired from her sedation. She meant was it all right for the doctor to be there with a cold.

We all laughed, like the others had earlier that morning at transplant rounds.

"Yes," I said. *My God, she's worrying about catching a cold. I can't believe it.*

"Dr. Miles said it's okay."

"Just want to be sure," Lezlie said. She was barely conscious now…heart rate rapid…breathing shallow. *Why is the pain so bad? She hasn't passed any urine. Her kidneys must have shut down. That's why.* I thought of the cancer choking off urine to her bladder.

"Do you think we should put a catheter in her bladder?" I asked Dr. Miles. If the bladder were full, if that were the source of pain, a catheter would relieve it. *If there is no urine in her bladder, then it's what I think it is. Her kidneys are completely obstructed.* I thought about the many transplant patients I had cared for. The idea of Lezlie's kidneys obstructing in this way twisted in me like a fist.

"Good idea," the doctor said.

"How many points does he get for that?" Lezlie murmured.

I felt like crying as I told her softly that her kidneys had now failed.

"You just threw that in," she said.

"I said that it was like going to a good play…one never wants it to end, but it must. We've had a good run," I said, "for twenty-nine years."

"Yes," Lezlie said. Her pain was under control now—three on a scale of zero to ten—and getting better. It made me happy for her.

"Owen," she said. "You're always the wonderful optimist."

24

IN THE SPIRIT PASSING

o o o o o o o o o o o o o o o o o o o o o o o o o o o o o o o o o
Can it be that love, sacred, devoted love is not all-powerful? Oh, no!
However passionate, sinning and rebellious the heart hidden in the
tomb, the flowers growing over it peep serenely at us with their inno-
cent eyes; they tell us not of eternal peace alone, of that great peace of
indifferent nature; they tell us, too, of eternal reconciliation and of
life without end.

—*Ivan Turgenev*
Fathers and Sons

It is three o'clock on the Ides of March, 2000. I am at the office, between
patients. It is a drowsy time in the afternoon, but I will not need to bite my lip, as
I sometimes must when sleep is in pursuit. Alan Abrams is coming by to see me.
His wife, Margaret, a former patient of mine, died just days ago after what
appeared to be successful transplantation—double transplantation—of a kidney
and heart.

I am aware of that inchoate nervousness that I sometimes have before a new
patient's first office visit. I still experience that, even with thirty years of psychiatric practice. I know Alan. I met him with his wife before the operation. He is a
focused, analytic person. They were both management consultants, the type of
people who expect to make things work. Margaret was Lezlie's age, also a Canadian from Vancouver.

There is a call from the front desk. I walk slowly to the lobby and greet him.
Alan's grief is fresh like the first heavy rain of a thunderstorm. Nonetheless, he is
a master of composure. His first words startle me. "I understand now, about losing someone that close to you, and I want you to know how sorry I am," he says.

Awkwardly shaking his hand, I accompany him along the connecting corridor, chiding myself in the process for having shared Lezlie's story with him and his wife. I do not recall why I did that and grope for the context. Psychiatrists are not supposed to share such personal information. Why then do I persist in doing it? *Because all of life is a sequence of stories.* As I listen to others' stories, I reencounter my own.

"I'm all right," he says, "only there are a few things that are bothering me...that I want to talk over with you, Owen." He calls me Owen, repeats my name frequently—personally—as if our meeting were born of an old friendship. His eyes fill with tears. He inhales roughly through his nose.

"I'm sorry. I didn't want to do this," he says, apologetically. I respond by passing a plain, square box of Kleenex. Alan laughs, sardonically, about the facial tissues. "I feel so empty. It's just awful..."

I listen.

"...I just don't know if I did the right thing." He repeats the story of Margaret's death. "At first, she seemed all right...I waited until she went into the recovery room. Then I went home.... I wish I had stayed but I needed to get some rest. She was still sleeping from the anesthesia...

"Well, they called me at four in the morning. Dr. Archer said that she was having some serious trouble...He's a great guy. Did everything he could for her...They told me when I got there, she was..." Abrams paused, his face contracting in on itself, "that she was brain dead."

"I don't know what it was like for you when your wife died. It just was unreal. She looked like...like she was sleeping...peaceful...and they told me she was brain dead...showed me the CAT scan. You couldn't live with that much injury. I wondered...I think this way: if I were them I would have just drilled a hole to let the blood out...anything. Why couldn't they do that? But they said there wasn't anything they could do. I have to believe them. You don't know what to believe...

"I feel so responsible. Did I do the right thing? I keep thinking—I know it doesn't make any sense—but I think it, anyway. Maybe she could, by some miracle, overcome this. She was so determined...and she did make it as far as she did. Why? Why did she get that far...then have this happen? I can't understand why God would do that. I think maybe I shouldn't have let them turn off the respirator. I asked for the neurologist to come back before we made the decision. It was terrible. He tested her...touched her eyeball...her reflexes...nothing...Still, I can't put it out of my mind. Was it right what I did?"

As Alan talks, I think of what it had been like six years ago—November 5, 1994. "I guess you really don't know what it's like until you've been through it," I hear him tell me.

"No," I tell him. "You don't know."

"It's why I wanted to talk to you," he says. I understand that Alan wanted to talk to me—not because I am a psychiatrist, but because I am a psychiatrist who has lost a wife.

Alan wonders—worries—about what Margaret might have felt in one of her dying moments. Could she have been awake, alone in her hospital bed, staring up at the ceiling, knowing that the end was near...frightened? I tell him that it was too soon after her operation for her to be awake. There is a silent visual feedback that comes from within me as I speak the words. I remember Lezlie in the recovery room after her first cancer surgery. She had opened her eyes...had seen me. She did not remember later. No memory had been recorded...as if the mind has its own answering service, and hers was switched off.

I remember now, about that last Lezlie day on November 5, six years past. I remember wondering what thoughts or dreams might part the clouds of her somnolence. The morphine had done what it was supposed to do for her...what she had wanted. I remember how she had slipped into a light coma...how I had stepped out of the master bedroom and cried as if it were the end...but it was not the end. She was still there—alive—when I returned from that momentary recess. I stood by the bedside like a sentry.

I remember how she then awakened...briefly...even spoke to us. I do not remember how many times. One time when she awakened, she said she liked the dress Georgia was wearing. Another time, she wanted to know why I had called her "old little Lezlie."

"I've always called you that," I reminded her. She nodded in response, in a sleepy, tentative kind of way. Someone in the room—I think it was the hospice nurse—told her that she looked beautiful.

The hospice nurse had comforted her...comforted us all. "She is on the fence between two worlds," the nurse had said. "She can see the best of both of them."

I wondered then what thoughts Lezlie might have had. Could she have thoughts?

"Do you think about memories of good times?" Craig had said to his mother when he recorded that interview with her during the last hospital stay.

"I think about good things we've done," she'd said.

"Like what?" I asked.

"Well, I think about trips we've taken. I think about swimming at Farm Pond. I think about walking in the woods at the top of the street. I think about having the two different ski houses that we had. Sometimes I think about the week you and I took off and learned how to ski together. The fact that we took a week—just boom, out of the middle of nowhere, Monday through Friday—and went to Vermont and learned how to ski while we were supposed to be…I was supposed to be nursing, and you were supposed to be a doctor…"

I was a doctor when she was dying. It was a Saturday. We had all been there throughout that afternoon—Craig, Kate, Rick and his family. The hospice nurse and Georgia, who still writes every Christmas, had gone. It was unusual to have help from both sources. I watched Lezlie constantly, watched her sleeping, listened sometimes to her breath sounds through my stethoscope.

It was surreal…happening, but sometimes only *seeming* to happen, as if this were a rehearsal…not even a real play. Then the oddest thing occurred. Shadow began to whimper, then leaped onto the bed where Lezlie lay. It was so very strange. She, too, had been watching Lezlie intently, then began to whimper and jumped, just like that. She had not done that before…never during the seven months of Lezlie's illness. Later, I would talk to the children about it. "She wanted to do CPR," I would tell them. That was later.

I wondered, too, what the children thought there in the bedroom where their mother was passing away. We said little to each other, but spoke a great deal with our eyes…the glances…the dewy stares. There were few words.

"You're a good daddy," Kate said that afternoon.

"Why?" I asked, surprised at the breech of silence.

"Because of what you're doing for Mommy. Another daddy would have taken her to the hospital and said, 'You do it.'" It was another of her magical transitions, like water changing state from steam to ice. Kate the old soul, the adolescent, the child. For only a moment she had become the child again…even younger than her cousins.

We did not know that Lezlie would die that day. She was getting to dying and we were with her on that uncharted journey. The household activities continued like background action on a stage. We had dinner together: Rick, Di, the cousins, Lezlie's mother—who seemed drawn into herself as if consciousness could be retracted like the head of a tortoise—Craig, somber; Kate, with changing shades of mood like colors on a chameleon.

I asked Jocelyn and Larisa about their pets. Had one of them ever died? They told me of a pet turtle that had died. I asked if there had been a ceremony. They nodded vaguely, unsure, perhaps, what that word meant.

"There is a language about illness," I told them. "When someone is sick, people say, 'Joe looked great today. Soon he'll be playing golf again.' But when someone is dying, there is another language. People ask how Joe is and the hoped-for answer is 'comfortable.'"

I told the girls that adults, like children, understand little about death. Grown up people sometimes worry, especially when they are old, what it will be like when their time comes to die. "And what do you suppose they hope to feel like?" I asked. There was a pause. I felt self-conscious about having asked the children that question.

"Comfortable," said Jocelyn, the eleven-year-old.

There are so many things from that day, memories suspended in the mind like great portraits in a gallery. There were strange things and mystical things. Were they real or inventions of the mind? Why did Shadow leap on the bed? It was so sudden and out of context.

At eight o'clock, Paul, my colleague from our years in residency training, came to visit. He had taken orders…become a Jesuit priest, but continued productively, elegantly, in medical practice. When he arrived at the house, I felt comforted by his friendship. He was the Paul I'd known for so many years. He climbed the stairs to the master bedroom where Lezlie was having her final evening of sleep.

Then, an epiphany. Paul—no longer just a friend or the doctor looking confident in white starched coat and stethoscope—became Father Paul now. The silence was encompassing. No photograph could capture its mood.

"You…more than anyone I've known," he said to Lezlie. His unhurried speech was measured. "You've lived your death—presided over it—the way you've lived your life."

"I know she'd like you to pray for her," I said respectfully.

Then Paul prayed, soulfully, with power beyond the power of simple strength and I felt something almost palpable—but not physical—that rose from Lezlie's dying self. I felt it enter my chest and fill me with her everlasting life. Then Paul said to Lezlie that he loved her and I said I loved him. I walked him to the car.

"You've done it the right way," Paul said.

Later as I listened to Lezlie through my stethoscope, I could hear the sound of pneumonia crackling at the base of her left lung as if hairs were being rubbed together between one's thumb and index finger. She remained in a light coma, but it hurt her to be moved even the slightest amount, and each time I felt a crushing feeling of guilt as we increased the morphine dose, now almost one hundred milligrams an hour.

I could hear the muted gallop rhythm of her failing heart. I knew then that her dying was real. I thought of Sandra again, Lezlie's childhood friend...of a photograph I had from a summer in Victoria. We were at Brentwood Bay when the two women waded into the water of the Saanich Inlet. I can still see in the picture I have kept and copied and framed how Lezlie's head bowed as she eased her way cautiously but gracefully among the stones beneath her feet.

Earlier on November 5, the day of her death—Sandra, too, had died in the month of November—I had cried beside Lezlie. "Sandra was your roommate before me and now she'll be your roommate again," I said.

I clung to Lezlie that evening with my stethoscope as if one could draw a person to one's ear through a hollow tube. The children, Rick, Di, and Lezlie's mother stood at the bedside.

"So this is what you were up to," I said to my wife. "You didn't want to be left again; and now that Diane and the kids are ready to fly back to Victoria, you're leaving first."

I was aware of being unkempt, my clothes rumpled. Sometimes I felt silly...as if I had been pretending to be an important doctor about to shepherd them all through a field of grief. My sorrow was like a giant snow bank. I was standing in front of it, gazing at its looming whiteness. Then I could no longer hear her heart. She had died.

An end is never really an end but always the beginning of something else. There was a slow, deliberate flow of activity in the house. The hospice nurse came back. We called the funeral director. I do not recall the feeling of my feet against the stairs as I descended from the bedroom...only that I sat on a love seat in the living room, as if I had been transported to that specific location and none else. The room was dark and I could feel a deep, isolated foreboding. It was a terrible feeling, not like anxiety or fear or even emptiness...more of a dead feeling...an unreal, nothing-exists-in-the-world feeling. It was unlike anything else yet strangely familiar. I thought about death...I had seen it in my practice...it was not new to me, although the death of her was very new. Something else was in the room, from another time. I was five years old then and my grandmother, my father's mother, had died. I could now recall a ghostly feeling of something—blackness—transported through that childhood home.

Remembering my children, I pulled myself from the living room. Kate told me her brother was upstairs with the people from the funeral home that were preparing to transport Lezlie's body. Why was he doing that? It was like the hospital interview again, some attempt to capture everything that she could leave behind...a voice...an empty body. I climbed the stairs, looked in on him. His look gestured me away, told me this was his time, however odd the circumstance of it...Then I descended the stairs again...now alert to my surroundings. The undertaker's helpers soon followed—a tall man and a short youngish woman—both dressed in black. As they bore the litter from the house, I was struck by such a foolish thought...that they looked like bizarrely dressed members of a ski patrol transporting someone injured from the mountain trails. When I told Rick and the hospice nurse about that, I began to laugh. It seemed hollow to me and certainly inappropriate. Then I said to Rick, "I feel many emotions: sadness, deep relaxation, joy for being able to do this for her with dignity. I feel unburdened." *What joy,* I think now, recalling the moment... *What dignity? When death leaves only an empty shell?*

Then I walked to the family room door and followed the stretcher bearers and Craig, who was helping them, to the gaping door of the hearse that now seemed to fill our driveway.

"This isn't Lezlie," I said as the doors closed on her remains, "but the body she lived in." Then we hugged and entered the house together and Kate was with us and the three of us hugged each other...like survivors of an avalanche.

25

THE DOORBELL

o o o o o o o o o o o o o o o o o o o o o o o o o o o o o o o o
Then I closed the door and left the house behind me and
began driving the whole distance of our marriage away
from the suburb towards the city.

—*Eavan Bolland, "A Marriage for the Millenium"*
New Yorker, May 15, 2000

There are so many images. Where do I begin? Life is a museum. It is May 6, 2000. I am once again at the Boston Museum of Fine Arts, this time with my Japanese guests, a senior professor and his protege. In the fall, they invited me to speak at a meeting in Hirosaki. It is my turn to reciprocate. The introductions and the exchange of scientific information are over. We are standing together now but somewhat apart in the Asian exhibit hall. We are gazing separately through glass boundaries at Japanese panels and their ancient themes depicted with delicate authenticity…courtesans at a boat landing…one of the women is intoxicated. The others look back at her.

The professor is contemplative now, almost sad, almost frowning. "Did you know," he asks rhetorically, "that there are few of these antiquities in Japan? Most are in American museums."

"No," I said. "From the war?"

The professor nods subtly. He is a very wise man, a gifted scientist with gray hair and skin that is unwrinkled.

"They are stolen?" I ask.

He shakes his head. "They were sold…some forced. There was no money…"

Now I understand his sadness, or is it longing? The museum holds the past for all of us.

On May 11, I have a postoperative visit with an elderly patient who has undergone hip replacement surgery. The initial operation was planned two months earlier, but she developed pneumonia and after that a bladder infection. Lena is a wonderful white-haired African-American lady, a retired social worker. I knew her when I was in residency training and have met with her at times over the years in times of difficulty.

"You know..." she begins. She has a mild palsy and her head moves when she speaks, like a religious Jew in prayer—*duhvening*. "People don't really understand how lonely it is when you lose your partner in life." She speaks slowly with a precise but gentle voice and pauses briefly at the end of each thought in a way that seems instructive. Her expression is reflective. There is more wisdom than sadness, but the sadness is there, too. That is why her other doctors asked me to look in.

"You understand," she continues, then interrupts her stream of thought. "By the way, you've changed. I hope you don't mind. Here I am an old person telling you when you are an eminent psychiatrist...going to Japan and giving a talk...You used to have sort of a rumpled professor look...and now look how elegantly dressed you are."

I am not aware of being elegant. "Look," I tell her, then hoist myself indelicately so that I am sitting atop the air conditioning unit beneath a picture window that looks out over the Boston Common. It is the same kind of room that I visited when Lezlie was in the hospital. I raise my pantlegs..."Two socks, different colors!"

Lena Frye laughs. "Well, at least there is some of the old you left. I really have no business saying this...Just don't become too much of a Yuppie."

It is my turn to laugh.

"I thought I would be over it after all this time," Lena says, pensively. "It's amazing to me how much I have been thinking and dreaming of Samuel in these past few weeks while I've waited for this operation. You know it's awfully hard when you are old and lose your ability to get around, to do the simplest things."

"You'll get it back," I tell her. "Your problem is that you are a social worker, a helper. You need to take care of people. But you'll get back to that again. It will take a few weeks...a few months, maybe, but you will get your mobility back."

"Well, I hope so," she says, momentarily reassured. "I guess I thought when I broke my hip, 'well, that's it, you've had it!'"

"That's the way people think," I tell her. I say that I had felt that same way years earlier after the burn injury from the car radiator. "I was only in the hospital—on the burn unit—for a week, but when I got out, the whole world looked different, so bright. And when I drove, the car seemed to float on the pavement. I felt so weak. Everything was an effort...and that was after only a week in the hospital!"

Lena smiles. "That's it," she says. "That's how you feel. Well, maybe there's some hope after all...But the dreams...I tell you...they were so vivid. I kept thinking about Sam and about how it was at the end. Was there something different that I could have done? He had a blood clot in his lung and was taking a blood thinner when he fell and hit his head. I called his doctor..."

"I remember your telling me about that," I say. "There is nothing different that you can do. You can stop bleeding on the outside, but not when someone taking an anticoagulant bleeds inside their head."

Lena shrugged her shoulders and closed her eyes. "Well, you can't stop thinking how empty things are without that person who was so much a part of your life, even after all these years."

"Yes," I hear myself say while I withdraw for a few long moments into the memory of how it was with Lezlie. I remember how I could come into the empty house at the end of a work day. I would walk up the cold stone steps and fumble at the front door while balancing something, perhaps a half gallon of skin milk that I had stopped and picked up at the twenty-four-hour store. Then I'd flip on the light and raise my head and call upstairs as if there were someone there besides the dog. "LeH-zlee, Lezlie," I would call out into the emptiness. Then I would pause and hear the echo of her voice in my mind. "Hi! O..." she would call back.

But all of that was later. In the beginning, after Lezlie's death, Craig and Kate were still there, and Rick stayed on for a week until the funeral was over. On the first morning, November 6, I awakened at 7:30 and telephoned friends and colleagues to tell them about Lezlie's death. I was surprisingly uplifted in my thoughts by the spirit of her passing that had seemed to rise out of her and penetrate my consciousness. Colleagues had sometimes spoken of the "good death." As a family, we had achieved that for Lezlie.

Phone calls, remembrances, hours on the telephone...the repetitive telling of the events that accompanied her dying...all were part of the grieving.

I was cautious at first in the way that I shared the events of Lezlie's death with my parents. I felt guilty about the pain they had experienced when Lezlie excluded them in those final days, and I questioned my own actions. Should I have pressed Lezlie to see them? *Probably not.* Did I take some odd unseemly pleasure in the exclusivity of her choice? *Perhaps.* I wondered again if I had been annoyed with them for being old yet outliving my wife. *Possibly so.* As we talked together on the phone, I could feel those tensions dissipate. When the children and I visited the grandparents for dinner that first night after Lezlie's death, I was grateful for the comfort that their support provided. I was also characteristically dismissive about the concerns they expressed that seemed overdone. There was that time-worn request that I call them when we arrived home after an evening in Milton, so that my parents could be assured that all were safe. I had invariably complained and poked fun at that. Now Craig and Kate and I rediscovered the silliness of those homeward bound journeys. "I think you should call them and report that only 25% of us are dead." We laughed together, irreverently, at the gallows humor.

Our mourning was punctuated with sardonic humor. Kate called her brother "master of the inappropriate." "When Mom was dying, he said, 'This is like a scene from The Godfather,'" Kate recalled. None of us could explain the comment. Craig had never seen the movie.

I cried in the mornings as I remembered Lezlie's suffering and I pretended to embrace her when I drifted into sleep at night.

Friends continued to call. The children and Rick and I worked together on the memorial service. When we received her ashes from the funeral director, I remembered how it had been years earlier when her father, Bruce, had died. Rick's family, our family, and our close Victoria friends, the Macombers, had spread his ashes by the track at the new stadium at the University of Victoria. I remembered how the ashes were really not ashes but bone chips, and how the dust from them blew in the gusts of wind.

Lezlie's ashes were contained in two urns. Rick and the children and I decided to bury the larger of the two urns at the Pine Hill Cemetery in Sherborn. We would take the other one to Victoria at Christmas time. We would join the Macombers at their private lake in the Victoria Highlands and we would spread the ashes out over the lake where our families had summered together every year for as long as Lezlie and I were partners.

In the week after her death, I visited the local travel agent and ordered December airline tickets for the children and me. I felt sad—*how forlorn you must look*—as I concluded arrangements for the trip. I walked slowly, in a desolate way toward the door. Then I noticed the carnival-colored rack of travel brochures in the entry and exit way. I paused and surveyed the folders. There was a longing that began to awaken in me and I was embarrassed by it. I saw the young couples, the tanned and smiling women tastefully attired in bikini beachwear. There had been that time—I remembered it now—in Acapulco with Lezlie the year before we married and the other time at Christmas in my internship year when the two of us made last-minute plans for a Caribbean trip and all the flights were full except one to Antigua. I remembered how we had been the only white couple in St. Johns, and how I tricked the adolescents who surrounded our rented Volkswagen, how they dispersed when I rebuked them in a feigned West Indian accent. "We needa' tourist to come und visitus an' you gonnal be'ave lie-diss! Shay-mun-yoo." Then there was the other time, not in the subtropics but at the ski slopes in Waterville Valley when one of the innkeepers had taken photos of Lezlie and me at dinner as part of a ski-weekend promotion. *I wonder where I put those pictures. Or was it a dream? No, it really happened.*

I had those thoughts then as I stood blankly in front of the rack of advertisements like the one the two of us really had appeared in for Waterville Valley...only it was the bikini-clad women that I gazed at longingly...knowing at the same time how silly that was because I felt so damned old—was old. Then I saw a Club Med brochure and secreted it away among my other papers as if it were a Playboy. I confessed about it later to Rick. I told him that I wanted to visit the South Pacific in the following April. It would be a birthday gift to myself. As I talked to him about it, I was appalled at my selfishness, because Rick was grieving, too, and because it seemed bizarre to plan anything for April, the anniversary month of Lezlie's diagnosis...the "cruelest month."

We met with the minister that week, separately and together. I told Ashley how much Lezlie had helped me with my sense of self. I talked about her attachment to family, how her father's full-length political poster had ended up in my closet after Lezlie and I began our courtship in Montreal. I told•Ashley about Lezlie's devotion to her brother, how so many people she liked seemed to her to look like Rick, even when there was no such resemblance.

There were sad things and funny things and sometimes an air of the mystical, like the time I bragged to my mother-in-law about a professional citation in the Marquis series. As I spoke to her, I recalled that Lezlie had forbid me to say anything about it. "If anybody says anything, it will be me," she had instructed. Now that she was dead I could boast if I wanted to and so I did...But just as I got into the telling, the doorbell began to ring. It rang insistently and for no apparent reason. There was no one at either of the front doors. We searched for the origin of the ringing. The sound seemed to come from the master bedroom closet. I picked up the telephone and dialed the number to the alarm company. "They don't have a clue," I told everyone...mystified...laughing. Then the ringing stopped and I vowed to be more humble.

Later I shared that story with my patient, Susan Canby, when she called with her condolences. "Techies often report odd things happening on their computer screens when loved ones die. She really is with you."

I am thinking about these things now while gazing silently at my patient, Lena Frye. There is an irony about it that I am considering almost without guilt. I am open with my patients, especially those like Lena whom I have known for so many years and who are like family...but my openness is selective. What of those things I choose not to tell about?

How shocked Lena would be...or maybe she wouldn't be shocked at all. There is little that has escaped her in her professional life as well as in retirement when she works for a suicide hot line and sometimes masturbators have called to relieve themselves in the midst of a fabricated tale. So she might not be shocked, perhaps only disappointed—maybe not even that, at least not terribly disappointed—to know how I acted and the choices I made later after Lezlie had died and the children and my brother-in-law and his family left and the house was empty. What would Lena think if she knew that on November 12, 1994, nine days after Lezlie's death, I began looking through the personal ads in the *Boston Globe*?

I began to read the personals, somewhat casually at first, then obsessively so that the phone bills would be a thousand dollars at month's end. That's what the eminent psychiatrist was doing...I shake my head and gently admonish, then forgive myself as I recall the pain that enveloped me like a dark November wind. I know now what I was doing then. I was looking for Lezlie. I would come home and the house was empty and I would call out to her and I would feel the memory of the sound of how she responded to me, and then, after a time, I would open the personal section from the Thursday edition of the *Boston Globe*...I would save it every week and reflect on it as I now do with the *New York Times* Sunday crossword puzzle. I was searching then for a different kind of answer to the enigma of the aloneness, and the search would take me back in time in my marriage to when I met her when we were twenty-two in Montreal and the snow was fresh and crisp underfoot.

That image is so strong. I wrote about it in a poem before she died. I called it "Lezlie and I." At the funeral I read it for a eulogy:

> *In the evenings*
> *We walked along*
> *Snow-covered Canadian streets*

it began…

Crisp footsteps
Hands swinging…

I kept thinking about that image after she died. I still do. Some moments in life give rise to a permanent trail of neurons deep in the jungle of living brain connections. That image of us two is like that.

Eight days after Lezlie's death, there was the funeral…the burying of the larger of the two urns with her ashes…the grave-side prayers.

Friends and colleagues and townspeople and relatives filled the white colonial church at the fork in the road in Sherborn where Main Street and Route 16 diverge. It is a small, warm, unadorned Unitarian Church that comfortably seats three hundred. Lezlie was such a private person but she wanted everybody to come who had been important in her life, so I borrowed one of the classrooms upstairs, where the two of us sometimes taught Sunday School together, and I installed a television screen so that an overflow of those who were special to her and to us both could watch.

The church pianist played *Jesu, Joy of Man's Desire* and Ashley gave the opening words from Philippians:

> *Whatsoever things are true…*
> *whatsoever things are just…*
> *whatsoever things are lovely…*
> *think on these things.*

We all read the Twenty-third *Psalm* and sang a hymn that Lezlie especially liked. Called "Leisure," it began: "What is this life if, full of care/We have no time to stand and stare…."

"Now that she is gone," the minister said, "no longer can we touch her, but she remains a presence to us. For all our loss, yet we are grateful that Lezlie lived. She entered our lives. She left. She blessed our days."

As Ashley spoke, I recalled how Lezlie had endeavored to micromanage her own memorial service, how I had petitioned my dying wife on the minister's behalf so that she might have time to speak. Ashley talked about Lezlie's role in the church, in the religious education program. "I am not wearing my ministerial robe," she continued. "Lezlie asked me not wear it. She said she wanted me to look friendly today…Are you watching, Lezlie?"

"You know what I like about worship?" Lezlie had mused when Ashley visited her in the hospital. "I love sitting in the sanctuary, watching the light come in, looking out at the trees as they change year round."

Ashley recalled that discussion for the congregation. "This place with its simple lines and white walls was a place of solace for Lezlie. Over the years, whatever was preached or said or done, she returned for its comfort."

Then Craig and Kate and Rick spoke. Craig told of how Lezlie dealt with her father's death, how she would look for her father in a star in the night sky. "What star will you be in?" he had asked her.

"All of them," she had said.

Kate hoped people would do things in memory of her mother that would make Lezlie smile.

I do not remember what Rick said. I only recall his surprise and admiration at the great outpouring of feeling on his sister's behalf and how different that was from the Lezlie he grew up with in Victoria where she had been so much less of a presence.

Then I read my poem:

> …*A Man and a Woman*
> *was our song,*

it continues…

> *Our love was eager,*
> *deep with passion*
> *respectful*
> *evolving.*

> *We married on moon-landing day*
> *in 1969.*
> *Friends gave their home*
> *for our honeymoon…*

> *The private highlands lake*
> *the gardens*
> *Rose petals on our sheets…*

As I spoke, I looked about at the people who filled the pews and I felt their deep genuine affection for this lovely lady who was my wife. There was a comfort in that, more powerful than I had ever expected.

> *…I loved her legs;*
> *She valued my wit*
> *I loved her intuition;*
> *She celebrated my creativity.*
> *I loved her subtle acts of valor;*
> *She tolerated my indecision,*
> *I loved her aristocracy;*
> *She treasured my candor.*
> *Her smile overwhelmed me!*

My gaze stopped at the sixth row on the right where an old friend, Ed Billings sat with his wife. When I had spoken to him on the previous night he had asked about the location and time of the service—questions that seemed irrelevant since he lives with his family in Princeton where he teaches at the University. I learned later that he had begun the drive to Boston at 4 am.

> *I loved her companionship.*
> *She was ever at my side.*
>
> *Our first date was magic,*
> *Her kiss, mystical.*
> *Beauty became our home,*
> *On Mount Royal*
> *At Waikiki*
> *In Sherborn*
> *With the children…*
>
> *Motherhood was Lezlie's calling;*
> *And when Craig and Katie achieved independence,*
> *Cancer visited us*

Where the ova formed
That gave them life.

Only then was Lezlie's work complete,
And so she died.

But what is Death after all?
Does the soul not hear or speak?
In Japanese tradition,
The starts and stops of life
Are not so clearly delineated.
I like that way
And so will think of Lezlie
With me for a time
That stretches out in sweeping possibility,
With options abundant
And limits indistinct.

And then there was the procession to Pine Hill and the finger sandwiches that Persnickety Caterers (Lezlie's name) had provided for those who returned to the church.

I left that occasion in a tragic but heroic vein, her death having been a beautiful story as well as catastrophic...so odd that both are often associated. And that was that. But it wasn't what I had expected, a quiet time of reflective mourning and what people refer to nauseatingly as closure. It didn't take long for me to know that my family role as Moses was past and that the promised land was a dark and empty place without guideposts. I knew then that I was lost and being lost, began to go about in circles all the time looking for someone circling in a parallel or even opposite arc, someone with a hand to grasp. It would not matter whether I or the other had the firmer grip.

26

MOVIE PEOPLE

○ ○

Deye mon, gen mon.
(After the mountains, more mountains.)

—*Haitian saying*

Guillermo Jones arrives at the office, breathing hard. His face is gaunt, dusky. He looks weary and sits speechless for a time, collecting oxygen. He's been waiting for a lung transplant at University Hospital. We do not have that program at our center, but Gil, as I call him, receives his primary medical care at Boston Hospital. Gil's lungs have failed because of an inherited condition called *alpha one antitrypsin* deficiency. His pulmonologist, Grover Wind, is a world expert on the disorder and has helped him through numerous hospital admissions. Gil's doctor has the perfect name.

Now I sit quietly with Gil as he tells me in short bursts of speech that he wanted to get to our appointment on time.

"Why did you rush?" I ask him. "You know I'm always ten minutes late."

"I like to be on time," He says, still working hard at his breathing, but it is getting easier.

"Your lips are blue."

Gil shrugs his shoulders as I turn to my desk and telephone Dr. Wind's office. His nurse answers. "Gil Jones is in my office," I say. "He looks cyanotic."

"I saw Gil an hour ago and he looked pretty good," she says.

"I'd like him seen now," I reply, insistently. "Shall I bring him down to you?"

"Sure," she agrees.

I've changed so much since Lezlie died. It is not a new insight, but I continue to surprise myself. I have a gentle nature but have become uncharacteristically assertive, especially when one of my patients is in distress.

A week passes. Guillermo and I meet again. Now he comes to my office with portable oxygen. He must still work at his breathing but his color is good now and he is no longer in distress. This time he is late…by about ten minutes.

"Thanks for last time," he says. "I'm glad you know what you're doing."

"You're welcome," I respond. I have a boyish pride in my medical judgment, so the praise is welcome. "How are you?"

"Good," Gil says. "Very good."

"I was concerned when I looked for you a few minutes ago," I confess. "I guess you were visiting your friend."

Gil laughs. In two years of helping him with the stressful wait for transplantation, I have seen him smile, but never laugh. The wait is indescribably arduous. I think of it sometimes while swimming a pool length under water, trying to get to the end of a lap before my air runs out. Now it is easier for Gil. He has met someone.

Like me, Gil is a widower, but with a different story. He and his late wife were estranged at the time of her death. Now, catastrophically ill, Gil has met the love of his life. She is a sweet Brazilian lady who has spent weeks in Boston Hospital with complications of juvenile-onset diabetes mellitus.

"It's strange," Gil says. "I've never felt happier in my life. If this disease weren't going to keep degenerating, if things could stay just exactly as they are, I would like to freeze this moment and hold it forever."

"Wow!" I say it aloud then sit silently in thought. The stories I hear now are so much more real since Lezlie's death. The intensity of my own emotions has burned away the barrier that doctors erect with exposure to repeated human tragedy. I remember the tender moments with Lezlie when she was ill and we lay in bed together at night and held hands while she drifted into sleep. Then in the weeks after she died, I would fleetingly feel her presence—a ghost's embrace. I think, too, of the yearning that I had then, that adolescent longing for love. It was an unseemly romantic quest for a bereaved man in middle age. It embarrassed me. I invented a sociobiological excuse: I wasn't an unfaithful husband of an only recently dead wife. This awkward drive was simply part of nature's plan to preserve the species. It was an inventive idea, if nothing more.

"You're thinking about something," Gil says.

"Yeah," I say. "When I was coming of age I had a special romantic fantasy. It was war time. I was with a young beautiful French woman. We were in the burned out shell of a building, holding each other."

"It's funny you should mention France," Gil says. "I've never felt so comfortable talking to a woman. Sometimes we just sit in her room and hold hands. We don't know what happens next. Does she get a kidney before I get lungs? And after that…? But we were joking together and I said, 'We'll always have Paris.'"

"Casablanca," I say. "You wore blue and the Germans wore gray."

"Yeah," Gil says.

It was memory of the suffering that pursued me after Lezlie's passing. On rare occasion, I would even look back at a photograph Craig had taken of his mother in front of the house and see the inescapable reality of her wasted body and the incongruity of her irresistible smile and I would sob aloud in a rush of tears. Then I needed, even more, to hold and be held and to have the love of a woman.

My exploits with the personal ads were odd as I look back now, but strangely adaptive. Within two weeks of Lezlie's passing, I had become a post-pubertal schoolboy again.

It was true that I sometimes had noticed if not read the personal ads. I am not a baby boomer and regretted as some others have that I missed the sexual revolution. I remember one time at Pizza Plus in Natick when I was tired and bored and the family seemed transiently like an encumbrance. I saw a listing of personal ads that set off the kind of fantasies that married men will confess to only at gun point. But that was fantasy.

This was real and real is not the same or even somewhat the same. The ads ran on like apartments to let. I still remember one that was written by "a Nordic beauty" in search of a "classy 50-year-old." I responded to the ad but never heard back (I couldn't have sounded very classy). There was also a 32-year-old named Bridgette. She had a delightful voice, full of life.

I was drawn particularly to the ads of younger women. It didn't matter that my contemporaries might be horrified by this. In fact, I told those who inquired that I did not want to meet anyone over age forty. It was not just youth and beauty that appealed to me but the wish to find my wife again at a younger time before the perimenopause and all its troubles that seemingly culminated in cancer and death.

My good friend, Max, seemed to understand it in a way. I had been disconcerted that first night after Lezlie's debulking cancer surgery, when he and Alice met me in the room on Trowbridge 9 and Natalie was there looking so beautiful. I imagined a gentle rebuke in Max's demeanor. Then, within days after the funeral, I was on the telephone with him astounded by his advice. "Owen," he said, with characteristic directness, "you need to fuck your *brains out.*"

I don't know how, I had thought as he said that. *How do you do that…just go to a bar somewhere? Find some woman and stand beside her and say, 'excuse me, but…'*

Is that what I want to do? No...that's not it. It can't be just anybody and even if it was...I couldn't...

Certainly part of what I was feeling was sexual. How had he known that? Why was I shocked at his observation? *No,* I had thought when we were on the telephone together. *That's not it...then what is it?* It was basic, if bizarre. I wanted to be in love again.

Unpredictably, after Lezlie's death, I began to look at women colleagues, nurses, administrators...those who had been attractive to me. Some—very few—had been a source of extramarital fantasy; all, now—at least theoretically—attainable as partners. "I've always admired you," I confessed to a thoughtful junior colleague who had been supportive in my grief. "I like your smile, the sound of your voice..." She had a boyfriend. Then there was the gorgeous nurse on Fullbrook 3, the one with the pale blue liquid eyes, seemingly seductive with every visual encounter. She was engaged, she said. One day I saw a beautiful young businesswoman, perhaps a lawyer, sitting with a nondescript man over coffee in the hospital cafeteria. She sat at an angle and I could see her exposed, shapely legs, like Lezlie's. My heart quickened and I retreated to the elevators as she began to turn in my direction. No doubt she could feel the intensity of my gaze. I always wonder about that: how it is that we know when we are scrutinized by another out of sight.

The Personals Section of the *Boston Globe* protected me, if not completely, from making a public fool of myself. Those pages were like a treasure hunt. Sometimes they were fantasy-provoking..."Nordic beauty," "Asian beauty." Sometimes they were cruel..."No chrome domes, please." Sometimes self-conscious..."loving, professional, Rubenesque, seeks..."

So I would study the list as if culling medical references for a research project and I would call and leave voice mail messages about being a widower, and so forth. I felt silly sometimes or self-conscious, but also there was a bit of adventure, something titillating and offbeat. It was a wonderful diversion.

Many of the people I met or spoke with looked like someone famous, or said they did. I would announce to my son or daughter that I was meeting Gina Lollobrigida for lunch (they didn't know who she was). One woman looked like Sophia Loren, she said, and possessed the same eternal youth; another was a dead ringer for Sigourney Weaver. Actually, that was my observation. "Has anyone ever told you that you look just like..."

Most of my outings with the personal ad women were on the weekends. Typically it was a midday, Saturday afternoon event over a light lunch at some prearranged public meeting place. Some of the people I met were interesting, some deadly, like the journalist with foul breath who complained nonstop about the noise from a Beacon Hill supermarket that maintained some sort of roof top machinery. There was the author who had never written, the divinity school lady who planned to adopt the five young children of a deceased friend…and the lady with the dead eyes.

The dead-eyed lady was one among my series of secondary prevention sallies. If someone had a concerning psychiatric disorder, I could not keep it to myself or didn't care to.

She was late meeting me in front of Biba's restaurant across the street from Boston Common, near the Four Seasons Hotel. I had waited a half hour when I saw her pull up in a red Jaguar. She was a big-busted, middle-aged woman with platinum blond hair and big lips with cosmetic adornment that matched her automobile.

"Well," she said over lunch, "whaddya think?"

Big mistake. "I think you're depressed," I said, clinically.

She was startled. "Why do you say that?" she asked.

"Because your smile is forced, and your eyes are dead," I told her. They were flat, like a no-gloss photographic finish. "You need to see someone about it," I instructed.

"Really?" she asked.

"Yes." I produced one of my printed cards and jotted down the names of two colleagues.

The dead-eyed lady drove me back to Boston Hospital. She moved near to me in the front seat. "Sometimes it can start quickly…" she said.

I felt so alone. Sometimes after I met someone, I would drive toward home and cry for Lezlie. "Where are you?" I would ask her, despairingly striking the steering wheel with a closed hand fist.

I'm here, she would tell me. Lezlie spoke to me that way sometimes…not out loud, but in a kind of memory voice. She would be there and I would feel a kind of tingling like I did at the ball park as a kid when they played *The Star Spangled Banner.*

I wrote a poem about it. I called it "Snow Flurries."

> *Your spirit envelops me*
> *With a touch of snow flurries.*
>
> *Your love is everywhere,*
> *Affirming*

Soothing

Uplifting

Like the hand of God...

It started like that...And what exactly was the hand of God, some permanence, some life force, some comfort, maybe a delusion?

So recently you left me
In your other, earthly way.

Now in this new form,
You visit me at intimate places.

I am surprised by this at times
When deep in other thought,

I wonder how You choose such
To appear.

And will you always come to me
Like this
As decades test the memory
Of our former world?

I was still in love with her—even more so because the memory of love that lingers after death has such intensity—as if death were a commencement for a life more vital.

Then I met Elisabeta. I met her in a Friendly's restaurant at the corner of Route 27 and 109 in Medfield. It was an odd place for a rendezvous, because I lived about a mile and a half away, across the Sherborn border. The Sherborn people that I knew rarely seemed to frequent the restaurant or did so at other times, so I did not expect to be sighted. A widower is like an Audubon Society sighting. Mostly, I didn't care who saw me. *Fuck 'em. They can think whatever they want. Let them see what it's like.*

Elisabeta had a musical telephone voice, gentle and endearing. She was wonderfully kind and unexpectedly beautiful. It was late in the fall of 1994, but it felt like winter. The wind was biting, blustery. She was seated in a booth to the right of the entrance, across from the ice cream take-out counter, closed for the season.

She was delicate, in a simple cotton dress with a muted floral pattern. I could see her arms, long and thin, hands gently folded on a plain gray wool coat draped for warmth across her lap. Her hair was long, waist-length and very light blond. She looked like someone one might see in a movie. Her blue eyes were moist, welcoming. She had flawless skin, but pale and with a light flush to her cheeks. Is she ill? I wondered. She seemed a lost soul, like me, and I was drawn to her immediately.

She was slightly guarded when we began to talk, but strangers can be surprisingly revealing if one asks in a gentle way and takes good time to listen. She had a trauma history. I was not surprised, but the cruelty of it evoked a protective, almost paternal feeling. Her father was Norwegian...the last name was Knudson. He was a binge drinker, recurrently depressed...hit a tree in his car and died. It could have been a suicide—probably was—when Elisabeta was four. Her mother was psychotic, paranoid, caustic, and terrifyingly unpredictable. The worst of it was with her son from another marriage. One day he sneaked some prepared food from the kitchen and she held his hand to the hot stovetop. The burns were third degree. She said it would teach him not to steal.

Elisabeta wasn't at all waif-like. She was poor, but with a certain dignity, and she was very lovely. She said she was working as a waitress at Marconi's family Italian restaurant in Ashland. She had completed college courses at Framingham State and was saving for graduate school. The owners were very encouraging. She wanted to be a social worker. No wonder.

This was not the woman of my dreams, not Jane Fonda—in her movies that I saw as an undergraduate in Montreal—not Lezlie with her more simple, unselfconscious beauty...the endless smile. Elisabeta's beauty was almost childlike. She was tall with a tiny waist and schoolgirl figure. She spoke well despite her difficult background; she was clearly very bright. She was not a siren; she was needy and wonderfully warm.

In the parking lot of the Friendly's restaurant, I said goodbye to her. She nodded almost sadly as if knowing that we would not see each other again. I thought that but didn't know. She was so much younger...thirty-two...twenty years my junior. But I know of colleagues in their middle years who had remarried much younger women. Elisabeta was not a child, just childlike...lovable, vulnerable, wounded. I was wounded, too. Then, impulsively, with no particular forethought or expectation, I wrapped my arms all around her thin but shapely form and hugged her.

"Oh," she said.

"I'd like to call you again," I said.

"All right."

I drove home, not two miles distant from that meeting place. For the first time since Lezlie's death—only a month, but seemingly an eternity away—I felt that I was no longer alone in the world.

27

IN THE HIGHLANDS

o o o o o o o o o o o o o o o o o o o o o o o o o o o o o o o o o o o

Of dusty glances fallen to the ground
or of soundless leaves burying themselves.
Of metals without light, with the emptiness,
With the absence of the suddenly dead day.
At the tip of the hands the dazzlement of butterflies
the upflight of butterflies whose light has no end...

—Residence on Earth
Pablo Neruda

It is June 22, 2000—Craig's birthday. I will join him later for dinner. Craig is twenty-eight now. *Imagine.* I think of him now as I speak to a young man, Ken Givers, who has come to my hospital office to talk about donating his kidney. His wife is with him. I met them two days ago with Alice Witherspoon. Dr. Witherspoon runs the surgical program for kidney transplantation as she did in April, 1994, when she showed me the report of Lezlie's abdominal CT scan. Craig was twenty-two that year.

Ken Givers wants to donate a kidney to a friend, a young woman who has lost her kidney function to diabetes mellitus. Diabetics seem to have the hardest time on hemodialysis. Her family hopes she can avoid that, but all of the relatives have incompatible blood groups or are medically unsuited for organ donation.

Ken is perfectly healthy and has proven to be a good match—an excellent donor. His wife Esther sat in stony silence two days ago at the family meeting while Alice Witherspoon discussed the risks and benefits of the planned operation. No donor has ever died at Boston Hospital, but there is a risk, Alice said, about the same as the risk of driving sixteen miles daily to work.

Now Esther Givers sits with her husband in my office. They are Craig's age and only recently married.

"You don't want him to do this," I say to her. It is my first comment after I greet them and we walk together from the clinic registration desk to my office.

Esther cries. I gesture towards tissues that are well within her reach. *That's pretty direct,* I tell myself. *It's okay.* I want her spontaneous response.

"Have you lost someone?" I ask her. "A family member, a friend? Has someone died in the past who is close to you?"

"A friend," Esther says, "in college, but I don't think that's what it is." *She is talking now. Good. That's better than it was at the family meeting.*

"Now, just a minute," I say, joking in an avuncular way, "I am the psychiatrist. I'll decide what is important."

Esther laughs weakly. I face her as we talk. Ken sits near her, outside of my range of vision. I wonder what his face is doing, but I will not look—not just now. "What happened to your friend?" I ask.

"It was horrible. She was my best friend." Esther tells me about losing her teenage friend in a motor vehicle accident. I listen and at the same time think of Lezlie and Sandra—their friendship—and what it was like when Sandra died of pancreatic cancer. I think again of the photograph of the two of them the summer before that when Sandra was well and led Lezlie by the hand into the water at the Saanich Inlet on Vancouver Island. In the photograph, Lezlie wades into the water cautiously, her right hand resting lightly on Sandra's left shoulder. Sandra's head inclines toward her friend. Perhaps they are conversing. What would they have been talking about? Sandra's right hand sweeps the surface of the sea. There is a symmetry to this. Lezlie's hand touches her friend. Sandra's hand reaches into eternity.

"What are you afraid of now?" I ask Esther.

"That something could happen to him. He could die. I know it's not really going to happen." She pauses, then adds, "I thought this is the kind of thing he would do for me. I feel a little bit alone at this time."

I turn to Ken. His face is impassive. "I thought the odds were so far off," he says. "One of my friends is a nurse. She said it was very unlikely that I would be a match, so I went forward with the testing before discussing it with Esther. It was the one thing I did wrong."

"Let me ask you a question," I say. It occurs to me that my father always posed questions that same way. *How long has it been since he died? Two years? Three? The anniversary of his death is coming up—July 3. I keep finding him in me.* "I want you to respond as spontaneously as you can, without editing. Just tell me what comes to mind. Okay?"

"Okay."

"Okay. Now imagine the story is different. You know that the chances of testing positive for being a donor are over ninety per cent. Do you do it?"

"Absolutely!" Ken's response is immediate, convincing.

"Why?"

"It's an incredible gift to give somebody life. I'm her friend. It's also a message to the children…"

I turn back to Esther. Her face, still wet from crying, is relaxed now. She does not want to share her husband in such an intimate way but accepts his wish to donate a kidney. "That's the only thing she's getting," Esther says, and we laugh together.

I want Ken to acknowledge the power of friendship between two women and the significance of Esther's teenage loss. I find myself telling them about Lezlie and Sandra. Lezlie is alive in my practice.

Ken and his wife finish their session with me. Alone in the office now, I record some notes and reflect on the unheralded changes and dislocations in life. Ken's act of altruism has become an occasion for conflict and fear. Newton's third law of thermodynamics: "For every action there is an equal and opposite reaction." There is now a change in the history of this marriage, perhaps for the better.

There is no preprinted program for the ceremony of life. I think again of how I asked my father when he was dying what he had learned of life's meaning. "I was born. I lived. I died," he said. It reminds me now of a Gauguin painting I admire. *Ou viens nous? Que sommes nous? Ou allons nous?*…I come, I am, I go…three stages in the mystery of life. In May, three months ago, I showed the canvas to my Japanese colleagues when we visited the fine arts museum.

I told them of Gauguin as I imagine him from Somerset Maugham's fictional account (*The Moon and Sixpence*), the shifts in direction from stockbroker in London to impoverished leper in Tahiti and now eternal master in museums.

What of the directions my own journey has taken? I am the same person who feared Henry, the schoolyard bully in grade three at the Blue Hill Avenue Yeshiva. I kissed a classmate, Emily, at recess time…first kiss. Much later, I found love, married, became a psychiatrist. It was a parallel process. I married medicine and Lezlie at the same time. After we were together for twenty-five years, she died. The medicine that I learned and loved could not overcome her ovarian cancer. There was only the pain of helplessness—mine and hers. What beauty would come now like a butterfly?

Things went back to normal after the November of Lezlie's death in 1994, but it was not the same kind of normal that had been before she died. Nothing ever goes back, and what is normal? Normal is every way. All the ways that things happen in nature are part of the spectrum of life. Today in *The New York Times* there is an article about young rejected suitors in impoverished Bangladesh and their victims, the young women—one was thirteen—whom the boys douse with sulfuric acid to erase the beauty that has escaped them. That is normal. Cancer is normal. Starvation in the Sudan is normal. Miracles, too, are normal. It is all an expression of life...horrible, sad, wonderful.

In December of 1994, the month after Lezlie died, I took the family to Victoria to our friends' lake in the highlands. We had Christmas there. Our host Angus Macomber dressed in a Santa suit. There was a certain gaiety at dinner. Was it artificial? It is difficult to celebrate and mourn simultaneously.

After dinner, we formed a procession and trod along the smooth wooden walkway that wound its way to a pier. Rick was in front of me, within arm's reach. The path was slippery. Suddenly I was half airborne like a cartoon character launched from a banana peel. Reaching out frantically, I grabbed at Rick's jacket. I felt clumsy, incompetent. Would I take Rick down with me? Thoughtless! But it was all right. Rick was all right; that tug at his jacket was enough to break my fall. Rick turned. "Are you all right?" he asked, concerned.

It came to mind that of the two of us he is the more thoughtful. I felt like a jerk. Then I remembered the time that I had jumped fully clothed into the lake up island and pulled my nephew from the water. Actually, I pushed him up and out into Rick's hands. Graeme was about seven and could barely swim. Rick was reaching down in a pleading way from the boat dock as I sank beneath Graeme—below his feet and pushed up, kicking hard with my legs. It was my only act of heroism...ever. Maybe we were even, Rick and I. No. What he did for us, for Lezlie, was way ahead of even. I felt like a jerk because I was thinking like that. It was all in an instant.

"Yeah, I'm okay...it's okay...thanks," I mumbled. Nothing was broken, nothing dislocated, but there was a deep pain in my shoulder. *A rotator cuff tear,* I thought. *Will I need surgery? Damn it! They take forever to heal...*It took months.

Everything was on automatic pilot that Christmas day, 1994. Kate, Craig, Rick and his family, and our friends who own the lake, continued the procession to the pier. Then we floated lit candles onto the lake. I had brought the urn and we spread the remainder of Lezlie's ashes. It was a deep sadness, like the ache in my shoulder. There was, nonetheless, a certain comfort in the injury, as if I had performed an act of penance, an apology for my survival after Lezlie's death.

Some who are bereaved do not survive. "The world breaks everyone, and some are strong in the broken places. The ones that do not break, it kills."

When we returned to Boston, Craig readied himself for the second semester of medical school and Kate prepared for her return to Haverford. I can't remember our talking much together, but we were busy together like preschoolers at parallel play.

Perhaps the greatest surprise was that of the three of us—Craig, Kate, and me—Craig did best. He was the most open about his anger before Lezlie died and about the grief that followed her death. He did well with his medical studies and visited often on the weekends. One Saturday evening at dinner, he said, "I want to sleep over and go to the cemetery with you tomorrow. We'll stay there for a while and talk about Mom."

The next day we went to Pine Hill with Shadow and sat on the great rocks that Bill Williams had taken to Lezlie's grave site. I had been collecting memorabilia from the basement of our Sherborn home and brought slides of a trip our family had made to the petting zoo in Menden when Craig was five and Kate was two.

"Did you see this picture of Lezlie feeding the giraffe?" Craig asked. He held the slide up to catch the morning light.

"Oh!" I said. "She's a blond in this picture." I was embarrassed because I had wanted to fall in love with someone who was blond. Lezlie had dyed her hair for me. *Silly.* "I don't think that worked."

"No," Craig said. "It really didn't. Tell me a story about her."

I shared the old stories about the early days Lezlie and I had in Montreal, our walks through the city snow, the convenience store dinners of barbecued chicken and potato salad, that I can still taste in memory. I was a young medical student then, like Craig is now, as I reminisced with him while gazing at the ground and the shifting light patterns that swept over it from clouds drifting under the sun. "It's time to go," I said.

"Wait," Craig said. "I want you to see that cloud go past first."

I waited impatiently for the cloud.

"It changed direction," Craig said.

I began to walk, absently, toward the car.

"Watch."

I watched the ground darken and then lighten again.

"Shadow is watching the shadows," Craig said about the dog. "Lezlie would have liked that."

"I love you," I said, hugging my son.

28

FLIGHTLESS BIRDS

o o o o o o o o o o o o o o o o o o o o o o o o o o o o o o

To love at all is to be vulnerable. Love anything and your heart will certainly be wrung and possibly be broken. If you want to be sure of keeping it intact, you must give your heart to no one, not even to an animal. Wrap it carefully round with hobbies and little luxuries; avoid all entanglements; lock it up safe in the casket or coffin of your selfishness... The alternative to tragedy, or at least to the risk of tragedy, is damnation.

—*The Four Loves*
C. S. Lewis

One time in that first year after Lezlie's dying, Alice Witherspoon asked how I was doing. "I felt like I was eviscerated." I said it in the past tense as if I had in some way been put back together again with my insides neatly in place. It was pure denial.

Today, one of my patients compliments me on a red tie I often wear these days. It is a Hermes tie with ostriches. Their heads are buried in the sand. I purchased the tie inflight on last October's return trip from Hirosaki, Japan. It is a good denial tie.

My patient, Buff Redman, is a retired journalist who sees me for an anxiety disorder. Buff is afraid of heights, but improving. I see him weekly for medical hypnosis. We work with guided imagery then ride the Boston Hospital elevators to their highest point and peer out over the city landscape. Buff is a cynic, so I am not sure what is coming next, but I enjoy the compliment. "Thanks," I tell him. "I thought it was a good psychiatrist's tie."

"Too bad about the farmer in Australia who was disemboweled by one," the erstwhile newspaperman says.

"By an ostrich?" I ask in disbelief.

"Oh, ye-e-e-s-s," he replies.

I am sorry for the farmer and wear a trace of guilt about the ostrich motif. "It would be a pretty bad kick."

I was a practiced expert on denial in the months after Lezlie's death. I reassured everyone—friends, colleagues—that I was all right. It was nonsense. I was anything but all right. Had I been in a bereavement group, I would have shared my grief with others who were also grieving.

One morning in the first weeks after Lezlie died, I was in my clinic, taking a break at the coffee urn where the bagels accumulate, gifts of pharmaceutical representatives. One of the psychiatry residents, a young woman, was conversing with a fellow student. "Sometimes I wish the family weren't around so that I could really get some writing done," I hear her say.

I have an undisciplined way of entering conversations that I overhear. It is really quite rude, but I always feel there is some compelling observation that I must share…a mitigating circumstance. "The problem is…" I said sardonically, "that when you really are alone and the family isn't there and you finally have time to do the writing you want to do, you can't get anything done because you're too alone." It's true.

The aloneness was dreadful, but the suffering was also my own hidden treasure. I could share the secret of it—as if it were secret—with a single person, then another, but not with many at once. It seemed to me that being in a support group would make it almost ordinary, as if my loss were not unique. There was the Sherborn church, of course, where the impact of Lezlie's death was considerable, but that was too threatening. The grief of my co-parishioners was like a magnifying glass—too much for me to bear.

I called Elisabeta in January of 1995 after coming back from Victoria. Would she see me? She was so much younger. *It's stupid*, I thought. *You're stupid*, I told myself.

"Yes," she answered. Her voice was musical. *She's just being nice*, I thought…*a sweet person. You're old…and ugly.* My inner dialogue was caustic. I chided myself about it. *You counsel your patients to be aware of this kind of negative self-talk. You show them how to counter it. Why, then, don't you do it for yourself? You're not only old and ugly…You're a hypocrite.*

Elisabeta's beauty and youth were a balm. She was long and graceful and her natural white blond hair was so supple, delicate, sensual. She was like those T.S.

Eliot seawomen riding on the waves. I called her my mermaid. "I met a mermaid," I told my colleagues at the hospital. It was why I was all right..."A real mermaid," I told them.

The first time I saw Elisabeta after returning from Victoria, I took her to the Framingham Cinema. Jody Foster was in the lead role as a wild woman, Nell. The occasion was electric, overpowering. I felt as if I were on the forward arc of a giant ferris wheel. It had been so many months—at least ten—since I had been to a movie. In the intervening period, they had redone the entire cinema complex. It was so grand, resplendent.

I collected the movie tickets from the window cashier and smiled at Elisabeta as if we were discovering a new land together. We walked past a thicket of video games to an endless food service counter, then entered the screening room.

We sat four rows from the front. Elisabeta was on the aisle to my left. As the movie played, I repeatedly turned toward her, pausing to gaze at her in profile. She had such fresh, simple beauty. I felt graced, thought the woman beside me could as well have stepped into the audience from the screen. It was that wonderful to look at her.

Elisabeta responded each time, turned to me, smiled, liked the way I looked at her, thought I was silly, liked it anyway. And then I imagined the most remarkable thing. I imagined that Lezlie was there, in the aisle, at eye level, looking at me with Elisabeta and smiling at us. She was young and vital again, smiling that wonderful Lezlie-smile that I cherished so much. She was so happy for me and radiant with love. It was like the way it was when I was with her three decades earlier, when we were twenty-two in Montreal and the world was fresh and white and new.

I saw Elisabeta in the evenings after work and on the weekends. Sometimes she joined me in Sherborn. My role there was little more than property manager. I shunned the emptiness of my house, although once in it I had a sense of Lezlie at my side. At night, at home, alone in our queen-sized bed—big as an ocean—I would wrap my arms around myself and pretend that she was there with me.

One evening I brought Elisabeta to see my office at the hospital. It was late. No one was there but the maintenance people. I knew them, if not always by name. In the years before Lezlie's illness, I was often in the hospital until ten o'clock and would return briefly to my office, weary from the after-hours consultation. Now I wondered, *What do they think about my being with a woman so much younger? She could be a patient...No...It is obviously more personal than that...Maybe they will think she is a patient, that I am having an affair...God! a horrible thought! Anyway, it's not like that with us yet even though she is not a patient...I won't stay long.* I felt like an intruder.

"Ohhh" Elisabeta said as I showed her about almost furtively. *This is stupid,* I thought. *You're a fool. Why are you doing this? Obviously you want to impress her. I don't have to impress her. Then what are you doing here and why at night, why the secrecy?*

"Well, this is it," I said, gesturing inclusively. I stood with her in the empty waiting room and turned awkwardly back toward the corridor door. *Owen, it's your office. There is nothing wrong with this...Her hair is so long.*

As we walked along the corridor to the bank of elevators, I saw two of my senior colleagues. *Why are they here this late?* I felt my face become warm. I was perspiring. *You're being ridiculous...We'll just walk by them,* I told myself. *She is so much younger, isn't dressed like a doctor, or a nurse, or anyone you should be dating, if you should be dating anyone so soon after Lezlie isn't here anymore...Maybe they will think she is a family member...Who?...She's young, but not that young. She's not your daughter, for God's sake. She is thirty-two years old; could be a cousin. Any family member will be okay. God. How do you get yourself into these things? They'll think you're a lost soul. No. You think that way...Well, if the shoe fits, wear it.*

I tried to pick up speed as we walked, became aware of Elisabeta trailing behind me for a step or two. We were almost past them. *They won't even notice. They are having a discussion, something clinical...could be hospital politics. They are definitely not thinking about you. Anyway, you can wave or nod your head. No one expects you to stop. Why can't she walk faster?*

"Aren't you going to introduce us to your friend?" The one who spoke wore a short white hospital jacket. A stethoscope filled his pocket. They were both cardiologists. The other wore a suit. It looked expensive, or at least grown up. I felt shabby in contrast, and what was I doing with this mermaid?

"Hi," I said weakly, walking more slowly now. I could have been speaking to them from the window of a commuter train grinding its way slowly from the station. I glanced fleetingly at Elisabeta. *She is so incredibly sensitive.* I knew that my timidity was offending her. I interrogated myself like Rasputin. *Are you ashamed of her?*

My colleagues smiled supportively.

"This is a friend," I muttered, "Elisabeta." I repeated their names for her, was aware that my voice had faded. I was walking very slowly now, could feel my companion's disappointment, saw my colleagues look back at me quizzically. My face was damp with the heat of the moment. I wondered if they had seen that. I reminded myself that they liked me, respected me, knew that I was bereaved.

They'll think you're crazy. Of course I'm crazy...And what of her? I was not sure which was worse, having been so thoughtless about Elisabeta or maladroit among my fellow physicians. The first of these was worse. Guilt, shame, sorrow encased me like a wet suit. I thought of Lezlie, groped for her in my mind. *Where are you?* I asked her.

Elisabeta forgave me. She forgave everything. She was so fabulously loving and gentle. Often when I drove to meet her I would call ahead on my cell phone. "Let down your hair, Rapunsel," I would tell her. Elisabeta's apartment was a garret—small, cramped, with cerulean blue wallpaper and a fading fleur-de-lis motif. I felt physically big there and out of place like a refugee—escaping from myself.

"Do you ever think," she asked me once, "that I am a person in your own play and that you are a person in my play and that the two plays are entirely different?" Perhaps she was right about that. For me, there was a fairy tale glamour to her surroundings. It was not glamorous to her—too poor for that. *How,* I wondered, *did she picture me? Was I a rich doctor or a wounded soul, or both? Did she know...(I did not know)...that there was no permanence to our being together?*

There would only be the things left over like an evening dress I bought for her so she could join me at the Massachusetts Medical Society banquet. There were matching shoes. "Are you engaged?" a salesman asked while we waited for assistance with the purchase.

"No," I replied. "Not yet."

Elisabeta blushed when I said it. "That's not what he meant by 'engaged,'" she said.

Sometimes when I was with her and we held each other, I imagined to myself that Lezlie had sent her to me. I remembered that I had felt that same way when Lezlie had her last of the four hospital admissions, and her private duty nurse, Natalie, accompanied me to the conference in Richmond.

This was my fantasy world after Lezlie's cancer death.

The children were surprisingly accepting of Elisabeta, especially Kate, who became fond of her. I knew that Kate worried about my well being, fearing that she could lose me, too. I don't think that Kate and Craig worried about my dying; more that their father would simply fall apart, as if a father could be made from loosely assembled playing cards, and a light breeze would blow, and that would be that.

Kate was involved in her own work, having returned to Haverford in January of 1995. She was relieved that I would not be left alone. College, however, was a kind of excommunication from her once-comfortable world of Sherborn and Concord Academy. I arranged for her to fly up to Boston, monthly at first. Kate often visited her Mountain School friends. Sometimes we two would see a movie or she and Elisabeta and I would dine out. There was a special Wellesley restaurant that our family had frequented and that seemed especially comfortable for the three of us. Kate was a vegetarian and Bel Canto had great salads. I would be playful with Elisabeta there and she would take great joy in teasing me with Kate's help.

"It's just like when you and Mom were together," Kate said one time. I was stunned.

"I was never threatened by her," Kate told me much later. "I knew she was too young for you and that it wouldn't last."

It was really quite curious being with a mature 18-year-old daughter who insisted she was taller than me (she is not), and also in the company of my model-tall mermaid friend. Sometimes I felt like they were both my children, but mostly it was rejuvenating for me.

I spoke frequently to Kate by telephone when she was in Pennsylvania, though she was never one for lengthy discourse. Kate rarely shared her deeper feelings. That had been Lezlie's only complaint about our daughter. "She won't talk!" Lezlie would say.

Kate's silence was now worth an oral dissertation. She gave no sound of joy in our discussions. Her voice was expressive and clear, but softer in tone, never playful, never silly in the way that had always contrasted appealingly with her intellect and poise. She did not say she was happy…she spoke of friends but seemed isolated in the friendship. Her manner of speech was loving, pleasant, but with a certain remoteness. Most powerful in her communication was the absent expression of grief. She was going about the loss we each had experienced with tears shed but never shared. I was sure she felt alone—like me—but I could not help that any more than I could arrest her mother's cancer.

I shared these worries with Elisabeta. We talked endlessly together, so much so that I told friends that my mermaid was also my bereavement counselor. It was an intimate though not an erotic love (*You can't have intercourse with a mermaid*, I would remind myself). Elisabeta needed safety. I needed affection. There was a warm closeness to how we were together. She was nurturing and I, protective.

I knew when I met Elisabeta that her health was a problem. Life, the maker of ironies, had done it again. Old as I felt in bereavement, I had considerable more stamina than my two-decades younger friend. Elisabeta had rheumatoid arthritis. Her insurance coverage was adequate for the most part, but the company, for some reason, refused to pay when she developed carpal tunnel syndrome and needed an elective operation to relieve pressure on the nerves in her wrist.

Elisabeta had saved almost enough money from her waitressing so that she could return to graduate school in the fall. She could pay for the carpal tunnel repair or study social work. She could not do both. I wanted to take care of the cost for her.

She declined. "I don't want you to do that," she said. "It's too expensive."

"I have a small inheritance from Lezlie," I replied, "a life insurance policy—nothing extraordinary—but there will be more than enough left after I fund your carpal tunnel operation.

"Besides, Lezlie was a pediatric nurse. She worked a lot with children from homes like yours. She wants me to do this for you! She would be furious at me if I did not."

She refused again. I persevered. Helping Elisabeta in this way was for me the most vital part of our friendship. My desperate struggle to help Lezlie, to vanquish or even arrest the spread of her cancer, had failed. I was Don Quixote in the attempt.

There would be no windmills to slay for Elisabeta—only dragons.

29

FLAMING ARROWS

o o o o o o o o o o o o o o o o o o o o o o o o o o o o o o o o o

You left in the morning. Tonight my heart is in a thousand pieces.
Why are you so far away?
By the image of Amida I light no candle
and offer no flowers. I sit here alone,
my heart heavy, full of gratitude.

—*Mourning for Hokuju Rosen*
Yosa Buson

Today is July 12, 2000. Lezlie and I married on July 19 thirty-one years ago plus one week. It was 1969. Three Americans landed on the moon then.

The past is always in the present. I tell that to one of my patients who is on the inpatient psychiatry service. He is withdrawing from anti-anxiety medication which he takes excessively—to escape. I admitted Morris Grant four days ago. Now he wants to leave. Four days are not enough. If he leaves, he will relapse and the process will begin anew. He can choose to leave and is determined to do so. He is a practiced victim and will victimize himself as trauma patients often do. My job is to help him overcome this "repetition compulsion"—Freud's term.

I am in Morris' room, at bedside, observing. He appears defeated, self-conscious, angry. He too is observing. "Nice suit," he says, as if building a verbal bridge. "Looks like a new one."

Without warning—I use this element of surprise—I abjectly bow my head, contort my face. "I am a little boy ten years old, bundled in fear." I tell him this as I begin to act out this one-character play. Its script is from my memory of Morris' childhood past as he has described it to me in our therapy sessions.

"…My father has a gun at my mother's head! It is terrible…even to think about. I hide my face in my arms. 'Oh, please,…please, please!' I say silently to

171

myself alone. I'm too afraid to speak out loud. 'Please, please, please!' I feel so helpless…so completely helpless."

Now I look up from where I sit bent over with my chest against my knees—at my patient's bedside. I uncover my face. There are no tears…there would be tears if I allowed it. With a play about someone else's life I am in control.

"Is that the way it was?" I ask.

My patient, at first astonished, now nods affirmatively. Then he says, "I don't remember." This is a contradiction. He verifies the facts but cannot imagine it.

"You were helpless!" I tell him insistently. "Absolutely helpless. There is nothing…nothing…you could do. That will never go away. It will always be there—a path of neurons deep in your brain. Whenever you are challenged, really stressed, you will tend to go back to that helplessness. The only power—the only power—is the partial power of a victim. 'Look what you are doing to me,' you can tell them, the people who seem to be assailing you. The only power is to create guilt. Do you understand that?"

"Yes," he says. He is focused intently, full of emotion, but understands what I am telling him, that he is practiced in a useless defense of filling himself with tranquilizers and hiding under the covers. He is bright, insightful, knows that he is hurting himself. Leaving the hospital now would be another self-inflicted trauma.

The tragedy is that I understand this, I think, as I talk with Mr. Grant. "I know you…how you think…I wish I didn't," I tell him. I know it because it is something I have experienced, not the same but similar.

Morris nods his head. He knows about Lezlie's death. In our sessions, I have told him only that I made mistakes after Lezlie died and that they were costly. I left the rest to his imagination.

"We cannot make that go away," I tell him. "The only choice is to strengthen other pathways, develop other ways of adapting. That is the work we have to do together."

Mr. Grant concedes that he will stay in the hospital until there is a good plan to continue his outpatient care.

As I leave the psychiatry unit, it occurs to me that I am discharging myself. It is not the only time I have felt that way. I know, especially since losing Lezlie, that I am no different from any other. Fate's dice roll the numbers.

Okay, Owen, you can go now, I say as if I am my own patient. The treatment for Morris Grant is the same as the treatment for Owen Surman. *What's good for the goose is good for the gander—what a trite old adage.* I too need a plan to go forward with my life. I feel it slowly taking shape now. I have stopped being self-flagellant.

Flaming arrows. I think of how I have often told Morris, "If you were in the Wild West and under attack by flaming arrows, you'd pick up a rifle and begin shooting at yourself." It is insight from my own past actions.

Tony Bellavia was the first to point it out to me. "You are punishing yourself," he told me. It was late in the summer of 1995, the first summer after Lezlie's death. We were sitting in Charley's at Chestnut Hill Mall. I was sipping the first of two bloody mary's and eating the boiled scrod.

The dinners with Tony became a monthly ritual. I do not recall how it began, only that Tony was like an AA sponsor. He has not forgotten the wife he lost to malignant melanoma, but he is remarried now, with grown children applying to college.

"It's not your fault she died," he said. "You did what you could. I did what I could. That's all you can do."

I wanted to believe Tony in 1995 when my guilt was still fresh. *You should have been able to prevent it, should have insisted she have her ovaries out when the ultrasounds began for her benign cyst. It was a shot across the bow,* I told myself. *But Lezlie was adamant about keeping you out of her gynecologic care…There was, after all, a conflict of interest. Our sexual intimacy had declined. It was easy for you to blame her uterus and want it out—like a wisdom tooth extraction.*

But wasn't there more? The kids, the applications to college and medical school. It was an inconvenient time for her to have surgery. Didn't you tell yourself that? How you were going to talk more with her about a hysterectomy when it was just the two of you…

No, she did not want to have her womb removed—give up her 'bits and pieces' was how she said it. You would have felt the same way—you didn't even want a vasectomy. She kept asking. You joked with her; said it was like cutting your nuts off, said you didn't want to give up your ability to have children. She asked why. You couldn't tell her…that you knew she would die before you? How would I know? No one knows. Then why do you feel so damned guilty about it?

I talked to Tony about these thoughts, about how I had thoughts of other women…even when Lezlie was terminally ill…about Natalie Ralston and later, after the funeral, about the personals. *How long did it take you to get into the personals?* I would torment myself with that question. *Ten minutes? You were crazy. You're still crazy…Don't be an asshole! Everybody has fantasies, Owen. You know that. You're a fucking psychiatrist, for God sakes.*

"You're punishing yourself," Tony reminded me. Soon I was telling myself the same thing, could hear the memory of his admonition. The dinners with Tony were a help, even though I was not yet ready to act on his counsel. He gently questioned my relationship with Elisabeta.

On Labor Day weekend, Elisabeta and I walked together along the path that circles Farm Pond, a mile from my house in Sherborn. Shadow ran alongside, darting in and out of the trees, stepping into the lake, then back to us. I like taking her to the lake. It pleased me in an adolescent way that the lifeguards noticed her. *Stupid. What's the point? Grow up!* It was increasingly frustrating. Elisabeta would always be a mermaid, with mermaid limitations, and I would always be two decades older.

We were about to complete the circle, approaching the beach from the east side of the lake. A copse of trees obscured the path. "The plot thickens," I said.

"That night," I confessed to Tony, "it was Saturday. I could no more sleep than climb the Matterhorn. It was driving me nuts. Elisabeta is there in the bed where Lezlie and I were together for twenty-five years, and I'm horny as hell in the family room…In the morning, we argued. I said I couldn't take it any more. She was upset. 'Why didn't you tell me?' she wanted to know…"

"Owen," Tony said, "you deserve to be with someone who can love you like a grownup. You are not cheating on Lezlie. She's gone…and you didn't make that happen."

"I want to help her," I said.

"Of course, you do," Tony said, "but who exactly are you trying to save, Elisabeta or Lezlie?"

30

A SUFI TALE

The lion calls a meeting to help the wolf, the bear, and the fox. They have come from the hunt with a rabbit, a chicken, and a lamb. "How should we divide it?" the lion asks the bear.

"You are mightiest," the bear replies. "So naturally you should have the lamb. I'll take the chicken...and our friend the wolf should be happy with the rabbit."

"What?" roars the lion—a terrible roar. He strikes the bear who runs into the woods. Next, the lion turns to the fox. "Do you have some ideas?"

The fox considers the options. "You are a big fellow," he cautiously answers. "You can't beat rabbit for breakfast. For lunch, there's the chicken...And lamb is ideal for dinner."

The lion nods agreeably.

"Later, if you want a snack," says the fox, "there's always the bear."

It is August 1, 2000. The pace slows in summer, as if people were taking a vacation from illness. I am sitting in the office with Newton Winslow. I love the name.

"I worry most about what to say when they ask what I do," Newton says. We are talking about his meeting a woman. Newton suffers from severe depression. He is reclusive, but recently more active.

"What **do** you do?" I ask.

"Nothing," he says, candidly. "I am trying to get well."

"That's what you do!" I tell him enthusiastically, then I speak for him in the first person. "I have a disabling condition, and I am working very hard every day to get a handle on it. It is slow, but I am making progress. I am hopeful about it. As time goes on, there will be things to be involved in." My regard for Newton is unmistakably positive. He is a good person...Also, he reminds me of Kate because at age eighteen he lost a mother to a tragic accident. She was on cross-country skis and was struck by a commuter train. Some thought it was suicide.

"You said that well," Newton smiles. "I should take you with me. Some people take a lawyer. I'll go with my psychiatrist."

"Fine idea," I laugh. "We'll doubledate." My mood reflects his progress. Today he has made it to our appointment despite having to deal with a flat tire...and without being overwhelmed with worry about being late.

"I figured I would find you somewhere around the hospital," he sanguinely explains, then adds, "I don't seem to be as blocked by things as much as I was. Still, it's not that big a thing to be worried about."

"Nothing that we routinely worry about is that big a thing," I say, recalling the morning news of an airline tragedy. "You are in the lobby of an airport hotel. Suddenly, a plane falls out of the sky at take off and kills you and ten others. Do we worry about that sort of thing?...No...We worry about being late while in traffic...Suddenly, for no reason, your life can end without warning. That's the kind of thing we should worry about! We don't. The big things are beyond our recognition. It is the inconsequential events that torment us."

Newton nods, pensively, perhaps with thoughts about his mother's death. How often does Kate think of Lezlie's death? "Every day," she says.

After the funeral and the trip to Victoria, we returned to Sherborn and I helped Kate pack for the winter term, her first complete semester at Haverford College. I missed her terribly and worried about her when she returned to school. At first, she did not want to leave me alone. She had become the woman of the house.

Often after Kate left, I thought of Haverford College, its arboreal campus, the duck pond, the bluegreen grass with gentle blades like soft bristles in a brush. Then I could see Lezlie in memory and how she looked when we accompanied Kate to her initial school orientation. Soon after that, she returned to care for her mother.

I remember Lezlie at that Haverford visit, pictured the kerchief that fit loosely on her scalp, parched like a desert by chemotherapy. Her skin was sallow, her eyes intense but in retreat deep within the bony structure of her face like a cadaver. I remembered the sounds of Lezlie's deep wrenching sobs. She had struggled against that part of her that wanted so much to let Kate go, but knew that she would never return to visit her daughter at that beautiful place.

"Do you picture Mom there?" I asked our daughter.

"No," she said. "I don't want to talk about it."

I visited the campus often and arranged for Kate to fly home at frequent intervals. Money was tight. I had purchased insurance to cover lost fees if my daughter left school because of illness. After Lezlie died, the insurance company would not pay…It was not Kate's illness that had interrupted her semester, they rationalized, but her mother's. The Haverford administration thought otherwise and absorbed most of the cost.

On one of Kate's home visits, she accompanied me to the hospital and visited Trowbridge 15 and the nurses who treated Lezlie in each of her four admissions.

"I kind of expected to see Mom there," Kate reported. We were driving back to Sherborn in the Volvo that Lezlie referred to as "the yellow helicopter."

"Oh," I said. I was glad when she could tell me about that sort of thing. She did so infrequently.

"I saw one of your friends there," she continued. "A thin man with dark hair."

"Tall?" I asked.

"Sort of," Kate said. "His hair was dark."

"He wore a suit?"

"I think so," she said.

"That's Amos Archer. Amos is a good friend. Lezlie liked him a great deal. He operated on her melanoma. That was a long time before the ovarian cancer. When she was so ill with that, he used to visit with her and hold her hand. He was very soft spoken and warm to her."

"Yes," Kate recalled.

"Did you speak with him?"

"I hid," Kate said girlishly.

"He's quite an interesting man," I told her. "Sometimes he flies off for a weekend to consult for royalty in a North African country or for a billionaire in Greece."

"Hmmm," Kate exclaimed. "It's nice when someone who is soft spoken and low-keyed like that gets the recognition they deserve."

I was moved by this conversation with my daughter, by her sensitivity. "You're not at all like an undergraduate student," I said. "Talking with you is more like speaking with a Ph.D. candidate."

"Thanks."

It was also a joy to share my professional life with her, especially now because her mother was gone. There was a respectful intimacy that we had as father and daughter. We were each at loose ends, able to recognize it in the other and to be encouraging. In one of her trips, I shared a paper I had helped write about viral illness and depression in transplant patients. "I like your paper," Kate said. "Who thought of it first?"

I told her about how one of the infectious disease specialists and I had observed that transplant patients were often depressed when they had cytomegalovirus (CMV) infection. "How do you decide the order of authors?" Kate wanted to know.

Her interest surprised me. One never knew with Kate. She was often silently reflective, but there was little that she missed.

She said little about her life at college. I had helped her organize her curriculum and she was comfortable about sharing the content of her coursework. Beyond that, I knew only that she studied sixteen hours a day. She was not socializing, although classmates often asked her to join them. At first it seemed all right, but her brother was outspoken about it and family friends began to notice. "She's so thin. I worry about her," Lezlie's friend Alice, Max's wife, had said.

I worried terribly about my daughter, but felt powerless as her parent. Parenting was a joint venture of Lezlie's and mine. Lezlie had said that. Sometimes I sought her advice from the recording of her interview with Craig on Trowbridge 15. "Do you have any advice for me as a father or as a husband?" he had asked her.

"Yeah, yeah, I do," Lezlie said. "I have lots...I would like you to be as much like Daddy, as much like Owen as you can be as a father, okay? Because what...what a wife needs in a husband and what a husband needs a wife to be back...is two people working in the same direction for children and there's no time for any—you know—private grandstanding. It's got to be...you don't have to agree with what you want done for the children, but it can't be...it can't be about you when it comes to the kids. It has to be about the kids..."

Now there was only one of us. I felt so inadequate and preoccupied in my struggle to shake off the grief.

I tried to nurture Kate, but could not tell if that was at all successful. I listened, even when she had nothing to share. I told her repeatedly that I loved her.

Craig would become more graphic as his sister's weight loss progressed. "She's starting to look like Mom did." It was a shocking observation. Kate's facial structure had the bony prominence of a high fashion model. It might have been attractive had her eyes not been in retreat, like her mother's.

Months later, Kate would confess, "It hurt when I sat down."

In many ways, Kate and I were alike. There was even reference to it in Craig's interview with Lezlie. "It's been kind of hard to watch her grow up sometimes," Lezlie said, "because we always thought she'd be a little girl. I mean you and I did. I don't think we really thought...I think Katie took a big jump and got more grown up and you and I said, 'What happened here?'"

"She's a lot different than we are," Craig responded. "I've never really understood quite where she came from. I think it had something to do with Dad."

"Katie's a lot different from you and me," Lezlie said. "Katie is like Owen and you and I are a lot alike. Right?" Then she added, "But you're a lot like Daddy…so you have both of us in you."

There was a lot of Lezlie in Kate as well. She was competitive and self-determined like me, but also intuitive and goal-directed like her mother. Like Lezlie, Kate was even tempered and she was less emotionally demonstrative than either of her parents. It was inevitable that she would internalize her grief. The two of us were very different in that way. For me, grief hung out like a loose shirt at the waistline. For Kate, it was neatly tucked in, but potentially lethal to her. Craig saw that. When he said she was starting to look like her mother, he was afraid his sister would die from her anorexia.

"I keep telling her she has to talk with someone," I told Craig. "She won't do it. She won't have anything to do with it!" How could I blame her, when I too needed professional counseling and steadfastly refused to acknowledge it. The cost was even covered by our catastrophic healthcare plan. Kate and I could each have all the professional support that we needed. I sensed that Craig was annoyed with me about this. I had always been an anchor for him. Now his sister needed me, but the anchor was on deck and the ship afloat in the current.

One weekend when I visited her in Pennsylvania, we stopped for lunch at International House of Pancakes. We sat together in an ample booth. Kate ordered a salad without dressing. I looked at the waitress blankly then sat in dismay as my wonderful, take-charge daughter forced down the dry salad greens.

"If Lezlie were here," I said, trying to diffuse the tension with humor, "I know exactly what she would be doing."

Kate smiled back at me without enthusiasm.

"She would say, 'Owen, look! She's not eating!'" I imitated Kate's mother with a strained stage whisper.

Kate was impassive.

"She would say, 'Owen, do something!'" I smiled at Kate lovingly, as if soothing the wound of a child who had fallen at play and scraped a knee. She was thin, but her color was good. Her expression was all right. She did not look pained or depressed, nor was she suffering from anorexia nervosa. Kate was not complaining about being overweight. She just had no appetite. But it would get better, I reasoned, as if a father's affection were a match for the devastating loss of a teenage girl's mother. It was no match, not even close.

I encouraged her to take care of herself. I also paid the bills. They were oppressive. Money became a symbol of control, not only for current needs, but for some future life that I might discover for myself. The more vulnerable I felt, the more I monetized the vulnerability. I daydreamed about scoring big and ineptly threw money at foolhardy ventures, as if some liberating windfall would free me from fear of a future without the most important and stabilizing person in my life.

My work wasn't suffering, but my finances were in chaos. I became obsessed by the stock market. One of my patients had lost two million dollars shorting it. *He will leave the market just as it collapses,* I thought. When I told my broker, he cautioned, "Don't stand in front of a speeding train." I did. Not only would I short sell the market, but also I would invest all available pension funds in gold mining shares.

My friend Max tried to help. "I was reading in this weekend's *New York Times* about speculation," he instructed. "It hadn't occurred to me that it could become addictive." Pretty subtle for Max.

The irony was that I had been considerably more outspoken with a colleague, a surgeon who liked to take risks when he was not in surgery. He too had something to hate himself for...the patients' deaths he could not prevent. His sister died from a ruptured aortic aneurysm that could have been detected before it became life-threatening. "All my funds are in Fletcher, Inc.," Dr. Thorncroft had confided. It was his brother-in-law's company.

"That's stupid!" I told him. "You treat all these people in the financial district. Ask one of them to send you to a good solid investment advisor." He did.

Before Lezlie's death, my anger had settled on the cancer surgeon, Millard Watkins. Now it was more diffuse, surfaced unexpectedly like a U-boat. One time while driving Kate to Logan Airport for her return to Philadelphia, we were stopped by a state trooper on the Mass Pike. "I'm taking my daughter back to school," I told the policeman. "Her mother is dead."

It was a shameful way to avoid a speeding ticket. Anger has no decorum, knows no pride. At times it would surface at work as it did early in Newton Winslow's treatment. I had admitted him to the psychiatry service and requested a series of consultations. His illness was complex and highly treatment-resistant. A week passed. None of the consultants appeared. Newton's family became restive. I called the inpatient doctor in charge of the case. "Where are the consults?"

"I didn't order them," he said unapologetically, "I didn't think they were necessary."

I was livid. "If you screw this up," I glowered, "I'm going after your job!"

I think of these things when talking to Newton and think of them now as our August 1 session comes to an end. Newton is like Kate. Also, I think of him…have told him…that he is like gold. "You have basic value," I've said to him, "solid, dependable, basic worth…It's been a long bear market…but your worth will be discovered. You can count on it."

"This is a qualitative change," I tell him. "This business of your not being blocked by the flat tire is not just a quantitative thing. It doesn't have to do with amount of anxiety…but its relative absence." Ever the thespian, I paused. "I see a rally for gold next week."

"Really?" asked Newton.

"Really!"

I opened the door to the office. He stepped into the corridor, turned momentarily. "Thank you," he said.

31

TOUR GUIDES

o o o o o o o o o o o o o o o o o o o o o o o o o o o o o o

...Maybe
it's time for me to practice
growing old. The way I look
at it, I am passing through a phase:
gradually I'm changing to a work.
Whatever you choose to claim
of me is always yours;
nothing is truly mine
except my name. I only
borrowed this dust.

—*Stanley Kunitz*
Passing Through

It is Saturday, the first day of the first August weekend, 2000. The summer has been rainy, but the weather is perfect today. I arrive at Farm Pond and walk from the parking lot along the asphalt path that ascends then drops to the beach. A four-year-old blond-haired boy is hurrying up the hill in a bid for independence. He has had his day's swim. "I'm going away from my dad...and...my mom," he chants, "going away from my dad...and...my mom." I nod to the boy's father who smiles in return. The mother is just beginning her ascent. She carries her baby tucked neatly in a shoulder harness and holds a beach chair in hand.

"Your son is making a bid for independence," I tell her.

"Yes," she says, pleasantly enough, but too fatigued for a lengthy rejoinder.

"It will take him another fourteen years," I say as we pass. I am thinking of Craig, who was also aged four that first summer in Sherborn after our family

182

returned to Boston from Hawaii. I delight in the winter memory of Craig clutching his sand pail and hurrying outdoors to collect the white dazzling flakes of his first New England snowfall.

Young parents are beginning where Lezlie and I began in 1975. I think of her now as I plunge in and begin to circle the lake with a slow, steady crawl stroke. The water, clean and translucent, was once a reservoir for the state hospital in an adjacent town.

Always, when I swim out at Farm Pond, I picture Lezlie in her beach chair, working on her knitting under a broad-brimmed sun hat. I think now, also, of the times when the children were young and I swam off on my own while Katie and Craig dove in repeatedly from the U-shaped dock.

I like to pretend that Lezlie is still watching me as she did in Sherborn and before that in Oahu when I waded into the ocean with my red and black striped surfboard and paddled out through breaking waves.

Sometimes, I talk to her as I swim, tell her something about the kids, or a hospital case, or just about the changing times.

Now, six years after her death, there is not the desperate sadness of losing her that I had then. It is a calmer feeling, an after-image of that acute grief that I recognize in the office when a patient tells of recent loss. There is Karen Goldman, for example, whose son died in a nearby teaching hospital after an attempt to replace his heart. Karen sees me weekly now.

"Nothing makes sense anymore," she said in our visit last week. "I can't focus on anything...even driving. I want to look up in the sky for a sign—to see some shape. I think of Jake roller blading through the sky."

Karen knows about Lezlie's death. It has made it easier for her to talk about the devastation of losing a son. Jake had a viral heart disease. It occurred when he was applying to college. He was an athletic youngster, wanted to become a physical therapist.

"The summer kills you," Karen said. "Every place you turn there are kids his age...He missed so much!" She paused and wiped her tears. "Everything reminds me of him. My sister Martha and I were at the lake the other day. I saw a black and yellow butterfly...It was showing the Bruins' colors, so I knew that it was him. I told Martha. She looked at me like I was crazy. Later we talked about it. 'I never thought of that black and yellow butterfly being Jake,' she told me."

"...Sometimes I really think I'm losing it...This is a funny question to ask you. You're the psychiatrist. You should be asking the questions. You don't have to answer, but did you ever think when your wife died that you didn't want to live anymore?"

"No," I responded. "I'm glad that you can be frank with me. Life seems meaningless when you lose someone so close."

"Exactly," she said. "That's what I mean. There's no meaning anymore—no reason for being here."

"You'll find a purpose," I said. "You can't look for it like a set of keys. It will find you."

I think about this advice to Karen. It was like the way poems happen—words falling in succession as if airlifted from flights of experience. *Is what I said true,* I wonder. *Yes, we are all surrounded by possibilities. They bump against us gently, like dolphins, playing.*

There were bottle-nosed dolphins in Elat when I visited Israel in 1995. It seems like a September dream, but I have a videotape from the Dolphin Reef. A diver, Betty, a lovely blue-eyed woman in her twenties, photographed the encounter as I reached out to them and listened to their mystical music. It was a kind of deliverance. After the swim, I said that she had a lovely voice.

"It's *choribble,*" she replied with gutteral emphasis. She hated her accent, part Brazilian, part Israeli. It was beautiful to me. She called me "Asher," my Hebrew name. It was easier than "Owen," which was for her an unknown sound cluster. I invited her to come to Boston—wrote about it in my journal. Now I can see the words from the journal and the pictures from the videotape. My face was bathed in grief, but the dolphin pool felt healing in a way that also made me smile.

Before Lezlie became ill, I had accepted the invitation of a South Korean colleague, Professor Koh, to present a paper for a September, 1995, psychiatric conference in Jerusalem. We were all very excited about it at the time. Friends told me that the visit to Jerusalem would change me in some way. Pilgrims expect this. Some who arrive at Ben Gurion Airport have been suddenly overwhelmed with messianic delusions.

Before I left Boston, ten months after his mother's death, Craig said that it would be a spiritual journey. Leave it to Craig. He is the Greek chorus of my life play.

En route from New York, I read a Berlitz primer on conversational Hebrew. It recalled my early grade school experience with Jewish orthodoxy at the Maimonides Yeshiva. ("Ya shiver at Yeshiva" was the standard grade school joke.) I was a little older than the little boy who would sing fifty-one years later on the Farm Pond path.

As I reacquainted myself with the once-familiar Hebrew alphabet, I felt uncomfortable—even sacrilegious—about my Unitarian conversion. I reassured myself that this abandonment of faith was not the cause of Lezlie's death.

In Jerusalem, I found the room I had reserved at the Holiday Inn with the help of a bellman named Dror, who instructed me that all Hebrew names have meaning. "Dror is freedom," he told me. My Hebrew name, Asher, means "loyalty."

After a seven-hour sleep, I returned to the hotel desk to cash some travelers checks and queued up behind a European doctor who was nervously trying to communicate with the desk clerk. "Not *three* rooms," she was saying, "*free* rooms. Do you have any *free* rooms?" The clerk, a thin, angular dark complexioned man, had an earnest but puzzled demeanor.

"Dror," I said to the clerk. He smiled, then responded to the lady's question.

How did I end up in Jerusalem, I wondered, fatalistically, surveying the landscape of my life. I was in Israel, revisiting my Jewish heritage in living color. My wife was dead. Craig was reeling from his mother's death. Kate had lost more weight over the summer, after she "dumped" her boyfriend Dana Marsh…Elisabeta and I also had decided to be just friends, as if we, too, were resolving a high school romance.

The conference on psychosomatic medicine opened with an address by Shmuel Pinchus, Director General of the Hadassah Medical Organization. I heard the speaker refer to his mentor, a European-Israeli psychosomaticist, Dr. Hruen…Hruen…The name rumbled from Dr. Pinchus' throat. *I know it…from where?* Elsa Froehman. I pictured my elegant patient who had escaped from Germany in the Holocaust years. Once free, she had become ill…it was stress-induced. Hruen was the one who saved her from unnecessary surgery.

Israel. Jerusalem. Yaru-show-lie-him. Now what? What's the message. I listened intently to the next speaker. Dr. Levy quoted Victor Frankyl, the concentration camp survivor who later wrote *Man's Search for Meaning.* There were three challenges in life, he said: "To create…to experience…to cope."

Next day, I presented my paper about psychological effects on the immune system, then scheduled the Elat excursion and a Saturday tour.

On Saturday morning, I looked about doubtfully in the hotel lobby. It was the Jewish sabbath. There was no commerce in the city and the tour bus had not come. In front of the hotel, I found a lone taxi with an Arab driver and apologetically woke him from a light sleep. He suggested a drive to Bethlehem. "One hundred fifty sheckles." *Are you supposed to bargain?* My cash was running short.

"One hundred sheckles," the driver said with finality. "That is the lowest I can do it for." I would need to stop in Bethlehem to cash a traveler's check. "No problem," he assured me.

The roads were empty as we drove out of the city to a check point where a uniformed soldier passed us through. Now the streets were busy with Arab trade. *Are you being kidnapped?* I wondered, then pictured myself in a solitary clandestine cell. *Is this another one of your impulsive decisions? Ever since Lezlie died, you've had both feet planted firmly in the air! You should have checked at the hotel. How do you know this is all right?...Well, if it isn't, the joke's on them...there's no money, just the traveler's checks. You think so? Guess again. If it's not all right, the joke's on you...Some joke! You're being paranoid; besides which, he thinks you're Christian. They don't kidnap Christians, only Jews. You're a Unitarian...Big deal!*

The taxi stopped across the street from a jewelry shop. The driver was orderly, businesslike, not overly friendly, drove a Mercedes, seemed straightforward. *That's the sort of thing you have to watch out for. It's better if they look like thieves. Those are the ones you can trust...Don't be a jerk!*

A second Arab appeared, entered the front passenger seat of the Mercedes. "This is your tour guide," the driver said.

We stopped next at the site of the Nativity. "We will enter illegally," the tour guide said. "It takes too much time the other way."

He exchanged some words with a priest who nodded agreeably. We passed the queue of visitors and descended to the shrine. The Gospels are in conflict about the site of Jesus' birth. No matter. This was the way Lezlie believed it. *Look*, I said, speaking to her in my mind. *Can you believe this?* Then I knelt on the ground. *What microorganisms are...? Who cares? Maybe you'll die of something exotic.* I kissed the shrine. *You're showing off...Who for? You are doing this for her. It means so much to her.* I was crying a little. *Best to control it here*, I thought.

On the way back to Jerusalem, I talked politics with the driver. It was safe to identify with him now. "Shalom Aliechem," I said as we approached the gates of the old city.

"You're Jewish," the driver said.

"Yes," I said, surprised at his observation. "How did you know?"

"You said 'Shalom Aleichem,'" he explained.

"I thought it was the same in Arabic," I said defensively.

The driver laughed. "Saalam Alychem," he said. "It is a different meaning."

"Oh," I replied, repeated it the Arab way. It sounded like "sail 'em I like 'em."

At the old city, I found Abraham, a seventy-ish fellow, another tour guide. We bargained about his charge for a walking tour. *Heretical*, I thought. *His name is Abraham and he's working on Shabbus.* Then I told myself, *This is the pot calling the kettle black.*

He talked nonstop as we walked the Jewish section then parted at the Arab Quarter. "Tell them you're there for prayer," Abraham counseled. "They won't bother you."

As I wove through the throng in the Arab section of Jerusalem, it occurred to me that I really was there for prayer. Craig was right again. It was a spiritual journey.

In the Christian Quarter, on the Via Dolorosa, I met a German internist from the conference. He was dressed in Bermuda shorts and carried a camera case. "You made several talks and gave a paper of your own," he said.

"Yes," I said, self-consciously. It was good to see a familiar face.

"There was a lot of information," he said.

I nodded, respectfully, asked about his itinerary.

"It's hard to visit here as a German," he said, then continued on his way. I felt sad for him, burdened by his country's war history. Only the good have guilt. The evil know no shame.

At the Church of the Holy Sepulchre, I sat on a stone step and watched the monks in prayerful procession. Inside the church, I found my way to Station 12 of the Cross. The crucifix…a replica of Mary…both in candlelight, were awe-inspiring. A gentle Greek Orthodox priest in black dispensed tapers to some among the groups of visitors. I approached him hesitantly, felt solitary, inconsequential, was aware of my own body heat enveloping me as if I were being baptized in Lezlie's spirit. "Father," I said, "I want to pray for my wife. Can you tell me how to do that?"

"I don't know," he said, appearing perplexed by the request.

"May I take a candle?" I asked. I groped for coins but recovered only five sheckles. Was it okay? The priest nodded. I took the taper from him and lit it and placed it at the shrine with the many other candles brightly glowing. Then I said aloud, "Lezlie, this is for you."

The tears were warm and soothing like the movement of the bottle-nosed dolphins at the reef. I retreated to a vacant alcove. Long, deep sobs came like waves in a set. Then I returned to the priest, retrieved more coins for his collection, saw him looking at me inquiringly. "Are you Catholic?"

What am I, indeed, I wondered, as I made my way back to the Jewish section and the Western Wall. I found some paper, wrote the words, "I love you," then folded it deliberately and placed it between some stones in the Wall. Now I stood with my forehead resting against them. As I cried there, I heard the Rabbi chanting the Kaddush, the Hebrew prayer for the dead. Then he asked if I would like to help make a minion, one of the essential ten to start "Mincha" and "Maariiv," the evening prayers. I felt proud when he asked me. I respectfully declined. It was time to go home.

Weeks later, I saw Reverend Kenneth Powell, the Congregational minister in Sherborn. He inquired in depth about my recovery from Lezlie's death. She had always held him in high regard. "Are you dating?" he asked.

"Yes," I replied. "You are the first to ask in such a straightforward way." Then I told him about the experience at the Church of the Holy Sepulchre. It felt somehow that he was Lezlie's representative, linked to her by a bond of Christianity.

"You were a Jew, isn't that right?" he said. It was the same directness with which he had asked about my dating. *Were you a Jew?* I repeated this to myself. It was such a telling question. *What are you? No…what do you want to be? You're not a Christian…No…but…you don't believe in the divinity of Jesus Christ. But there is transcendence in his passing.* It had given me such solace. How unexpected! The suffering of this rabbi on the cross was Lezlie's…as was the redemption.

"Yes," I said. "I'm still a Jew, even though I am a Unitarian…The priest wanted to know if I were Catholic."

"What did you tell him?" Ken asked.

"Unitarian," I told him.

Ken smiled broadly. "They don't know about that in the Holy Land," he said.

32

A MYSTIC

○ ○

Senses and mind are tools and toys;
Behind them lies the self.

—Thus Spoke Zarathustra
Friedrich Nietzsche

I removed my shoes and entered her apartment as if I were disrobing my curiosity. It was a Saturday morning in October, 1995. I had always wanted to meet a psychic and learned of this remarkable lady from my patient, Susan Canby.

Sydney was a Creole woman from Haiti but schooled in Boston. She had brown eyes and arresting beauty. Some time after coming to American, Sydney drowned and was revived. This was when she saw the light and turned to mysticism. She said she was a mystic.

Sydney had a particular routine. She gestured toward a wing back chair and sat opposite me with a tape recorder nestled in her lap. She would record the session and give me the tape. It would cost seventy-five dollars. A check would be fine. Two cats loitered in the apartment, which was replete with wall hangings, deep red fabrics, and antique angels that reminded me of Thomas Wolfe. I am allergic to cats but made a decision to ignore the dander.

She was very gentle, obviously insightful, and somewhat tense. "I don't remember what I tell people," she said, after ushering the cats into another room. "I have people take a tape of the session if they want to have it."

"Are there things you want to know about me?" I respectfully asked.

"No," Sydney replied. "That isn't necessary."

This feels like it did when I was a first year psychiatry resident in therapy, I thought.

She inquired spontaneously about my father (he would die in the following summer). "What were you thinking about as you drove here?" she asked unintrusively.

"My daughter," I said. "I was thinking of my daughter. My wife died."

Sydney winced.

"It has been very hard for Katie—Kate. She prefers Kate. She is in college, at Haverford. It's a beautiful school, but she isn't happy there." Sydney nodded affirmatively. "It's a fine school. They are extremely supportive and understanding, but she is unhappy. I suppose it would be like that whatever school she was at."

The mystic gazed at me with deep concern. "You have a fire in your house," she said. She spoke softly but distinctly. Her eyes were kind, engaging, deep, loving. "You have a fire at your house," she repeated.

I smiled back, affectionately, then felt the smile fade. *What would your colleagues think of this?* I asked myself. *Not to mention your patients. They'd think you were nuts...Maybe...There's something special about her...She's incredibly intuitive.*

"She studies all the time," I said, "doesn't socialize. I told her, 'What you really need to do is pass breakfast, lunch, and dinner.'"

"She needs you," Sydney said. "Katie needs to be with you." She closed her eyes as if calling forth some pictorial memory. "I picture her in a nineteenth century setting. I picture her seated in a ballroom where everybody is dancing, and she is waiting to be asked."

"Her school is very nineteenth century," I responded. I thought of young men I had seen there playing cricket in whites on a well-manicured expanse of blue green lawn.

"She's strong," Sydney continued. "She will be all right, but right now she is in crisis and needs your support. You need to listen to her. She knows what she needs."

At home that night, I shared this experience with Kate. We sat together in the family room as she listened to the recording. "She's just repeating what you told her about," she said. Then we came to the part about the nineteenth century. "I like her voice," Kate finally said.

It was such a simple thing for Kate to say, but hopeful. There was magic in the encounter I had with Sydney. Sources of good fortune vary like patterns for a snow flake.

I recall the warmth of Sydney's gaze when I told her how alone I felt.

"There are thousands of women who will want to be with you," she said.

"Where are they now?" I replied almost whimsically. It was not entirely capricious. I knew that I would ultimately find myself and that others would also find me. Nothing, however, can compare with the companionship one finds while in pain.

Sydney did not answer but smiled affectionately.

I drove Kate to Logan on Sunday, while she supervised my driving. "Pick a lane…any lane," she said. Her teasing was welcome. This was my daughter. "I've decided to talk with somebody at school," she said.

At Haverford, Kate met with the Dean. She would complete her second freshman semester and transfer to Harvard. "It will be easier to spell," I told her.

Kate sounded better in our telephone discussions. She had found someone to counsel with. "My person" was how she referred to the psychologist. By the twenty-first of the month, she had completed her transfer application. We spoke by telephone that morning. I wanted to know how she was doing.

"All right," she replied. Her voice still sounded a bit uneasy. "I am writing a paper about India," she said. "I'm writing about Gandhi. I like learning about him, but it's boring to write about."

"Why do you suppose he garnered so much attention?"

"Because he starved himself."

"You starved yourself," I replied, "but it didn't create a revolution."

"I didn't starve myself," Kate said, unoffended by my attempt at humor.

"Stopped eating," I said, "same thing."

"Well, he made people—the untouchables—feel good about themselves. There are a lot of people there."

As we talked, I recalled part of a dinner conversation from the prior evening. I had met somebody new—Amy *(good name for a companion)*. It was Amy who had introduced me to Sydney the mystic. Before dinner, we were at an Edward Albee play, "Three Tall Women," at the Colonial. Amy had spoken of a friend who had visited India and described the smell of decay, the people dying. "It makes sense," I told Amy, "that where there is a lot of death, there is also a lot of life." Now I repeated this to Kate.

"You found someone," Kate said, "that you don't feel you have to rescue. What is that like for you?"

"A relief," I admitted. "I told Amy that she is an eagle." *Not a mermaid*, I thought, then remembered Sydney's brilliant characterization: "a woman on a trapeze."

Kate laughed. It was good to hear her laugh. "She's very warm," I said about Amy. Sydney called her a soul mate.

"Eagles don't seem warm," said Kate.

Animal metaphors have their limits, I thought, feeling inadequate about my choice of words.

"Well, she's a warm eagle," I explained.

33

THANKSGIVING

o o o o o o o o o o o o o o o o o o o o o o o o o o o o o o o o o o o o

Non Sub Homine Sed Sub Deo et Lege
(Not under man but under God and law)

—Inscription
Harvard Law School Library

Life is unpredictable. Today, August 16, 2000, Mark Lever rolls into my office in his motorized wheelchair. Samantha Harris follows in hers. They come like two horseless chariot drivers to the coliseum. Mark is smiling broadly. His eyes bob about in an undisciplined way and every facial muscle seems intent on individual competition.

"We need to get blood tests for our marriage license," Mark says in the faltering speech that multiple sclerosis allows him. "Can you order them for us?" Mark's right arm launches upward as if signaling the start of a race. This too is a part of his illness.

Samantha listens and nods supportively. She is older and, unlike Mark, retains full use of her arms and her vision is intact. She looks part wife-to-be, part older sister, as if two roles could merge like traffic.

They met on the Ride and were engaged two weeks later. It began as a game. Mark saw me for depression. Nothing helped. He had a quick mind, a subtle sense of humor, and no prior depression despite his medical ordeal. The multiple sclerosis was relentless. His personal care attendant was overzealously controlling. That was something to work on. Mark and I conspired together while his caretaker sat dutifully in the office waiting room. We would devise some doctor's orders.

Mark's first assignment was to circle the block solo in his chair. His mother held her breath, she later told me. His second assignment was to take the Ride, a public transportation van designed for wheelchair access. This is how Mark met Samantha. They fell in love.

Sometimes there is no way out, but Life finds a way.

There seemed little to be thankful for in November, 1995, a year after her mother's death, but Kate came home from Haverford to join her brother and me for Thanksgiving weekend.

Kate had been meeting with the psychologist, her "person," twice weekly. She was regaining weight. "I guess I was starting to look like Mom did," she admitted. Dressed warmly in sweats and running shoes, she would take a jog before we visited Max and Alice for a turkey dinner. "I really looked pretty awful."

What a relief to see her looking better. Craig, too, seemed to be having an easier time. I remembered a comment Amos Archer had recently made. "You are lucky to have those kids," he said. It's true.

"Do you have a copy of last week's *Suburban Press?*" Craig asked after Kate left in a rush of cool fall air. I had not yet seen the newspaper.

"My picture is on the front page," he said while putting two slices of whole wheat bread in the toaster. There was a piece with a photo of Mike Kickham, the scoutmaster, and the Eagle Scouts from Sherborn Troop 1 who had come to honor him at Pilgrim Church. "'I recognized all the boys,' Mike told me at the farewell party. 'But I wondered who the one with the beard was. Craig has really changed and grown.'"

Now Craig rummaged through the tired old avocado-colored refrigerator. "You don't have any jam?"

I confessed that I didn't. "We leave for Thanksgiving dinner with Max and Alice at one o'clock," I said after he finished his breakfast. "The dress is casual."

Craig left for his room. I changed into a warm pair of khakis and a loden green shirt and returned to the kitchen for another cup of coffee. I looked about me and thought of the work it would take to modernize. Lezlie had always wanted to do that. "If we wait long enough, it will be back in style," I often told her.

Kate was back from her run. I heard her in the family room. She was crying. "I ran to the cemetery," she said.

"There and back?" I asked, stroking her back and patting her head. "Lovings" was the word Lezlie used for this.

"Yes," Kate said.

"That's four miles." I was surprised at her stamina.

Now Craig reappeared. "I was on the front page of the *Dover-Sherborn Suburban Press,*" he told his sister.

"Oh, really? That's good."

"And Dad threw it out," Craig said sardonically.

"Oh, no!" Kate replied in mock horror.

Craig told his sister about the farewell party for Mike Kickham. His wife had been there. "I can't believe someone that small had seven kids," Craig commented.

Kate laughed.

At noon we were on the road to Max and Alice's house. "Pick a lane, any lane," said Kate, the self-appointed navigator.

"Pick a lane and not your nose," said the medical student. This was Craig's family car persona, all nonsense and regression, the reason for Lezlie's mandate that one of the children sit in the front passenger seat and the other in the back. They could alternate with one another. I see no reason to change the rules—ever, even when they're in their fifties!

Craig now turned to his sister in the back seat. Why had she not chosen medicine as a career? He spoke as if she were a Tory at the Boston Tea Party. Then he answered for her. "I think you avoided it because you followed me in so many other things."

"I followed you in everything," Kate replied lovingly.

"Let me know when we get to the Burlington Mall," I said. "I hope we haven't passed it." It was like the old family times, driving with the children like this. Lezlie was not there. We did not discuss that.

"No," Craig reassured me, "we've still a ways to go."

After dinner we played a dictionary game with Max and Alice and their two children. The point of the game was to invent meanings for obscure words and challenge the players to choose the best definition. Kate declined to play. I reminded our hosts that she is dyslexic.

"How did you do on your verbal SATs?" Max wanted to know.

"Fabulously well," Kate said dramatically. "People came from everywhere to find out. Crowds gathered."

It felt good to be with our family friends. It felt safe in a way, as if we were on vacation from tragedy. I doodled and drew sketches of everyone, then shared the sketches.

On the way back to Sherborn, Kate mentioned that she had to work on a college assignment. "I thought you got an extension," Craig said. "I'd like to spend more time together."

Kate began to cry. "I'm doing the best I can," she said. "I don't want to be guilt-tripped."

"I'm not trying to make you feel guilty," Craig said apologetically. "I just want us to be together as a family."

"It's good that one of us thinks that way," I interjected. "Kate needs to do whatever works best for her." She was crying volubly.

"I didn't know that this evening was that hard for you," her brother said.

"Every day is hard for Katie," I said. She was in the front seat now. I reached over and stroked her head. Kate leaned against my shoulder. "Lezlie's death has been hard for us all," I said. "It's just different for Kate. I think of what it was like when I went off to Montreal to first-year college, of what it would have been like if my mother died then, or what it might have been like for you, Craig, that first year at Oberlin, if Lezlie or I had died."

"I guess I'm just angry," Craig said candidly.

We were silent for a time. Then I explained to the children that Max was a trustee to my estate and would work with our lawyer at Hale and Dorr if something happened to me. "I expect to outlive them both," I added.

We were in Sherborn now. Craig began to complain that I was driving too fast. This was something Lezlie used to do, even when I wasn't driving at all fast. At other times, she said I was driving too slow.

"I'm doing forty," I told Craig.

"But it's a thirty mile-an-hour zone," Kate interjected. I laughed to myself. ("Another country heard from" is what my mother would have said.)

We were passing through the center of town. "Beautiful downtown Sherborn," I called it. There isn't a lot there; a fast food place, a bank, apothecary, fire station across the street next to a used car lot, then the railroad tracks crossing Main Street, and after that the distinctive fork in the road with our classic white New England church in the middle.

"They say to beware of people who drive Volvos," Craig said. "They buy them for a reason." I wondered what he thought the reason was but decided not to ask.

"The police just wait here to give people tickets," Kate said in an official sounding way.

"This sounds just like Lezlie," I objected. "Look, I've been driving in Sherborn for seventeen years and I haven't gotten a ticket yet."

"You were stopped by Officer Charles," Craig countered.

"But he didn't give me a ticket," I said, emphatically.

"You probably treat him," Craig said. *He never gives in.*

"I don't treat Officer Charles," I said.

We were back at Stoney Brook Road now. As we walked to the house, Craig said, "Let the dog out so she doesn't pee on the floor."

We were home again. Shadow was greeting us. We were together.

EPILOGUE

✦

EPIPHANY

o o o o o o o o o o o o o o o o o o o o o o o o o o o o o o o o o o o o

Love a friend, a wife, something, whatever you like,
but one must love with a lofty and serious intimate sympathy,
with strength, with intelligence, and one must always try to
know deeper, better and more.

—Vincent Van Gogh

It is the last chapter of summer—Sunday, August 20, 2000. I am once again at the museum, at the end—and also at the beginning—of a circle. Once again there are portraits. The artist is Vincent Van Gogh. The first canvases show desolate faces of impoverished pensioners. I have often seen faces of "orphan men," as Van Gogh referred to them. *You were an orphan when Lezlie died,* I think. My ego was broken then. It was not the same, though. These faces are full of surrender.

I stop next at a portrait of the bearded postman, Joseph Roulin. It is a kind face, honest, generous, virtuous. Did Vincent entrust his correspondence to this friend? Did the artist await some specific message?…Might there be some answer to the meaning of it all?

A self-portrait of the artist now captures my attention. Unique among the self-portraits, this face is seeing, reverential, persevering, calm. The artist has painted an inscription in French: "A *mon ami* Paul Gauguin." Beneath the painting, borrowed from the Fogg Museum is Van Gogh's narrative: "I've a portrait of myself, all ash gray…not wishing to inflate my own personality, however, I aimed rather for the character of a bonze (Japanese monk), a simple worshipper of the eternal Buddha." It is a moment of discovery for the ever-searching artist. What did Van Gogh know then?

Perhaps he had learned the Buddha's four noble truths: life is sorrowful; sorrow comes from craving; sorrow can be stopped with an end to craving; craving ends with moral conduct, discipline, and meditation.

In this last chapter of summer, six years after Lezlie's death, my sorrow remains. It is no longer a burden, only a reality and a memory.

I am growing in my life, have come to where I am by choices that vary like the surface of the sea. Love is greatest among the calming choices, and professional dedication which is also a kind of love. It has also helped to believe in a spiritual way, even though the way I believe is in a constant state of change.

Lezlie had encouraged me to exercise and overcome my physical stiffness. "You should take yoga," she said. Wouldn't it surprise her to know that I did? There is an aerobic yoga, Ashtanga, which also helps relieve stiffness of the mind. There is one meditation time that I re-experience now.

I am very old in this dream. My hair, long and white, drapes like a shroud across a balding scalp. I am in Hawaii on the north of Oahu. (I lived near this place once in a cottage at Sunset Beach in the summer after my first year at medical school. I said I was a writer. At night my neighbors and I chased crabs across the sand. It was wonderful, liberating, until my money ran out, gone like the crabs that buried themselves in the mile long beach. I ate canned squid and sold my motorcycle for the price of airfare to Boston.)

Standing in moist sand that captures my footprints, I am awestruck by the beauty of a rising surf. I am agile with age and yogic practice. I find equanimity here before the vastness and strength of nature; but also, I grieve for my youth. The days of my physical being are coming to an end.

Tourists on the road are busy taking photos of the great waves. To them, I am very odd in appearance, an aging solitary figure with a surfboard tucked incongruously under my right arm. The wind lifts my hair. The moist salt air embraces me. I stride resolutely to the sea and am aware of a sinewy strength that my muscles retain from decades of training. My skin, however, tells time...has a looseness like oversized clothing. My skin is white but sun resistant. It is marked by blemishes and spots of aging, as if life has branded me.

There are very few surfers here today. Some of the swells exceed twenty feet, big enough in perspective to dwarf the telephone poles that form a wide-flung gate for the tourists with their telephoto lenses and adaptors. The sea is my home. I welcome its embrace as I glide forward into the receding current. Now I tip my board over, careful to keep it firmly in the grasp of my arms and legs. Lying securely beneath the board, I greet the roaring white water that rages over then welcomes me as if I had spoken a secret code for passage.

Well beyond the tumult of white water rushing for the beach, I flip the resilient board upright—an effortless action—and catch the rip tide that sweeps beyond more distant giant breakers. I am free. The beach is very far away. I ride up smoothly, quickly, on a mountain of ocean. I am Moses before the tabernacles.

Now an outside swell approaches. It is smooth and blue and looms behind me as it builds in height. Carefully I grip the board then pull forward with my arms like oars. I am in the steep high wall of this wave. It is enormous. My heart quickens. The descent begins.

Balancing with unexpected agility, I bend forward with my left knee and ride across the cresting wave. I am facing a blue green cliff wall that will release an avalanche of incredible grace and power. I turn the nose of my board in a counterclockwise arc and rocket down the wave as in a luge on ice. The speed is exhilarating. I have no fear.

The wave is breaking aft now in a white watery turbulence. I escape with bowed head through a giant tube of water. For the one time in my life, I am "tubed," a surfer's dream. I smile as a joyous feeling surges upward through my body.

I am like a caterpillar surfing its cocoon. In this metamorphosis, my legs are strengthening. My skin, too, is becoming youthful and my upper body is like a gymnast's. A wave of rejuvenating energy restores the face of my early twenties. My hair is thick and brown.

I peer ahead through this canopy of ocean and see a brilliant light that glistens in the surf. There are human forms there. Now I see Lezlie as she was when we lived in Waikiki. She is young and lovely. Her smile is like an inverted rainbow. Beside her are the children. I see them clearly as they were when they were much younger. They are waving to me. Through the light, I now see their legs and Lezlie's legs are diaphanous. This disappearance of form spreads slowly upward through each of them like a soul rising. Now I find myself in the same becoming. Soon there are no visible human figures, but spirits linked in an inclusive hug. In the distance, my father and Lezlie's father approach us in this mystical embrace.

The yoga teacher continues his meditation. My eyes fill with tears and my chest heaves in a silent cry. Water and salt bathe my face as if a wave of emotion rises in my body and breaks across my face…like the tide.

Dr. Owen Surman
168 Warren Street
Newton, MA 02459

978-0-595-35917-2
0-595-35917-5

362.196 S
Surman, Owen Stanley.
Aftter Eden

1/12/06

5c/7-06   (oct 2014)

Printed in the United States
40410LVS00005B/215